Designing end-user interfaces

Designing end-user interfaces

State of the Art Report 15:8

Pergamon Infotech Limited   A member of the Pergamon Group   Oxford   Toronto   Sydney   Beijing   Frankfurt

Published by
Pergamon Infotech Limited
Berkshire House Queen Street
Maidenhead Berkshire
England SL6 1NF.

Telephone: 0628 39101
International +44 628 39101
Telex: 847319
(Answerback INFO G)

Printed by
A Wheaton & Company Limited
Exeter Devonshire
England.

UDC   681.3
Dewey   658.505
ISBN   0 08 034120 9

© Pergamon Infotech Limited, 1988

All rights reserved. No part of this publication may be reproduced, stored in a retrieval system, or transmitted in any form or by any means, electronic, mechanical, photographic, or otherwise, without the prior permission of the copyright owner.

It should be noted that the copyright for the Report as a whole belongs to Pergamon Infotech Ltd. The copyright for individual contributions belongs to the authors themselves.

Contents

Editors' foreword	N Heaton and M Sinclair	vii
Publisher's note		ix

Invited Papers

1	ISSUE – a case study in expert system interfaces	D M Cleal	3
2	Human/Computer Interaction Engineering (HCIE)	J Dowell and J B Long	17
3	The user in a sociotechnical system	K D Eason	25
4	Methodologies for designing User/Computer Interfaces (UCIs)	A Gardner	37
5	Developments in Human/Computer Interaction (HCI) hardware	M Maguire	51
6	Guidelines and principles of interface design	J McKenzie	73
7	Developments in computing and the user interface – emerging issues in end-user interface design	M A Norman	85
8	Introduction to the design of end-user interfaces	B Shackel	97
9	Integrating human factors with system development	P Walsh, K Y Lim, J B Long and M K Carver	111
10	Communicating with the user	P Wright	121
Invited Paper references			131

Analysis

1	Definition of the problem	149
2	Psychological and social factors	157
3	Principles of interface design	167

4	Computer intelligence and interface design	179
5	Systems aspects of the human/computer interface	193
8	Conclusion	207

Analysis references 217

Bibliography

An annotated bibliography of end-user interface design *N Heaton and M Sinclair* 225

Index

Subject and contributor index 245

Foreword

The discipline discussed in this Report has many names — human/computer interaction, user/system interaction, user/computer interaction — to name but three, but only one theme — the need to consider the user as an integral part of the design process. Previously systems have been dominated by the hardware or software limitations. The QWERTY keyboard was designed to prevent key clashes when being used by skilled (that is fast) typists. The first software error messages were enigmatic and cryptic because it was cheaper to store them in memory that way. However, technology has changed, as has the user population. Computers used to be the exclusive domain of the expert and the enthusiast, now they are used by all. The implications of these changes, in the technology and in the user population, are that computers must now be designed for all.

To achieve this, designers must be knowledgeable about users, their characteristics, abilities and limitations, the organisations in which they work, their goals and motivations, and how the computer will be used to solve specific problems and meet specific needs.

All too often users have design solutions imposed on them. This causes many problems — simple ones, related to decreased productivity, more serious ones, related to rejection, and catastrophic ones, epitomised by the failure at Three Mile Island.

The aim of this Report is to detail the work undertaken in the field of Human/Computer Interaction (HCI), which is seeking to redress the balance between the computer and the user by adopting a more user-centred approach. The Report outlines work which is seeking to understand the user, to improve the software and its associated interface, and to design hardware which is suitable for use.

The Analysis is in six sections. Section 1 outlines the problems and makes the case for a user-centred approach. Section 2 looks at the psychological and social factors which influence the design of end-user computing. It considers sociotechnical approaches to the problem of interface design and how factors such as resistance to change can undermine even the best systems. Section 3 looks at the design of the interface. A related Invited Paper details specific hardware recommendations. This Section provides an overview of both the hardware and the software requirements. It considers dialogue design and how to improve it, and details some of the key issues associated with specific interfaces. Section 4 looks at the role of computer intelligence in the design of end-user interfaces. It looks specifically at the design of Intelligent Front End processors (IFEs) and the implications for interface design, as well as the problems associated with knowledge acquisition and the design of help and explanation systems. Section 5 looks at the systems aspects of the human/computer interface. It considers the need to look at the organisation and work teams, together with the methodologies available for interface design, and discusses the role of guidelines in end-user interfaces. Section 6 examines how end-user interfaces have changed — the effect of technology, the importance of human factors in the design process, the importance of national and international initiatives and the need for standards.

The Invited Papers examine specific aspects of the problem and detail some of the latest research which is going on, aimed at improving our understanding of the problem. These range from basic definitions of the problem, and the need to evaluate how we look at the problem domain, to fundamental work aimed at introducing human factors into all aspects of the design cycle.

The Bibliography details some of the key works in the field over the last 10 years. It provides useful references for both the expert and for those with an interest or responsibility to ensure that the interface is well designed.

N Heaton and M Sinclair: Editors

Publisher's note

This Report is divided into three parts:

1 Invited Papers.
2 Analysis.
3 Bibliography.

The Invited Papers in this State of the Art Report examine various aspects of designing end-user interfaces. If a paper cites references they are given at the end of the Invited Papers section, numbered in the range 1-99 but prefixed with the first three letters of the Invited Paper author's name.

The Analysis has the following functions:

1 Assesses the major advances in designing end-user interfaces.
2 Provides a balanced analysis of the state of the art in designing end-user interfaces.

The Analysis is constructed by the editor of the Report to provide a balanced and comprehensive view of the latest developments in designing end-user interfaces. The editor's personal analysis of the subject is supplemented by quotations from the Invited Papers, written by leading authorities on the subject.

The following editorial conventions are used throughout the Analysis:

1 Material in Times Roman (this typeface) is written by the editor.

2 Material in Times Italic (*this typeface*) is contributed by the person or publication whose name precedes it. Numbers in parentheses in the ranges 001-099 or 100-199 following the name refer to the original source as specified in the Analysis references or the Bibliography, respectively, which both follow the Analysis. References within the text are numbered in the same way. A contributor's name without a reference refers to an Invited Paper published in this Report.

3 The quotations in the Analysis are arranged at the discretion of the editor to bring out key issues. Three or four dots within a single quotation indicate that a portion of the original text has been removed by the editor to improve clarity.

The Bibliography is a specially selected compilation of the most important published material on the subject of designing end-user interfaces. Each key item in the literature is reviewed and annotated to assist in selecting the required information.

Invited Papers

1: ISSUE — a case study in expert system interfaces

D M Cleal

PA Consulting Group
London
UK

The first half of this paper identifies some shortcomings of current small-scale expert systems which arise from the particular difficulties that exist in providing interfaces to expert systems. The second half describes ISSUE, a system which was developed in an attempt to resolve some of these difficulties.

© D M Cleal 1988

D M Cleal
Dave Cleal graduated from the University of Bristol in 1982, with a BSc in Physics. He first became involved in the Artificial Intelligence (AI) field in 1983, working for the government's Future Concepts in IT Department, where he was involved in the investigation of various novel IT technologies, including early optical disk systems, document scanning, archival and retrieval, and various applications of AI. Since 1986 he has been working as a consultant within the PA Consulting Group's Intelligent Systems Centre, primarily concerned with the design and implementation of large-scale knowledge-based systems. A particular area of interest has been the development of interfaces to very large knowledge bases, and this has resulted in the development of novel interfaces to systems such as ESCORT, PA's real-time process control expert system. He is a joint author of 'Knowledge-based systems — implications for human/computer interfaces', published by Ellis Horwood in 1988.

ISSUE — a case study in expert system interfaces

Introduction

Knowledge-based systems pose particular problems for the interface designer. The first part of this paper will attempt to indicate why this is so; the second half describes ISSUE, a decision support tool which uses some expert system techniques and addresses some of the interface issues previously identified.

Problems with expert system interfaces

Multiplicity of actors

Most computer systems require only one interface, which is designed by the system builder for the use of the system user. Many well-documented cases exist which amply serve to illustrate the confusion which the differences in experience, understanding and objectives between these two can lead to. Typically, the upshot of this confusion is a system which does not do the things the user wanted it to, but does do some other things exceedingly well.

Expert system developments add two or three more variables into the equation, causing a correspondingly greater degree of confusion. An 'expert' is required, as is an interface to the knowledge contained within the computer system. More sources of difficulty arise and things go from bad to worse when a 'knowledge engineer' is added. Now, as well as disparities between what the user wants and what the system designer gives the user, we get differences between what the expert knows, what the knowledge engineer thinks the expert knows and what knowledge the user actually wanted access to. The interface to the knowledge may end up being an interface to any one of these three bodies of knowledge, varying in both content and overall form.

Knowledge interfaces and representation

A knowledge engineer is an oft-recurring figure in expert system literature. The precise role assigned to this individual varies slightly from one source to another, but essentially the knowledge engineer is faced with the task of taking knowledge from an expert and feeding that knowledge into a computer. There are perhaps four reasons why a knowledge engineer might be required:

1 Psychological difficulties — a knowledge engineer is required to help the expert express himself adequately.

2 Unavailability of the expert — the expert is too busy exercising his valuable knowledge to learn to operate the expert system or to input the knowledge in person.

3 Sheer complexity of the knowledge representation — the knowledge representation used within the

expert system is so complex (and often counter-intuitive) that an expert system specialist is required to 'translate' knowledge from human form to a form acceptable to the computer.

4 The interface used for inputting knowledge to the expert system is not usable by the expert (for example it requires the writing of a computer program).

Both points 3 and 4 are oft-occurring problems in the development of expert systems using the tools available today. Even the simplest of rule-based expert system shells use astonishingly obscure control strategies, whereas the more advanced tools encourage the development of complex knowledge representations.

One of the commonest shortcomings of the tools available is a failure to reflect the overall structure of the knowledge base. Consider a simple rule-based expert system shell, containing perhaps a few hundred if-then rules. Any ordering, sorting or grouping of those rules must be performed by the user. Furthermore, the user is denied any understanding of the network implied by those rules. In a consultation, the question 'why' typically invokes the chain of rules which link data and conclusion. This chain is just one path through a much larger network, in which each node is an assertion about the problem at hand and each link is a rule. The key to understanding the wider ramifications of any change to the knowledge in the system is to understand the network, which unfortunately remains implicit in most of the systems available today. Figure 1 attempts to illustrate the point, but the significance becomes redoubled as the number of rules increases beyond about 70.

These problems should ring alarm bells whenever they occur. Expert systems require far more regular maintenance than conventional systems. For an expert system to remain useful throughout its lifetime, or to reach its full potential as gaps in the initially engineered knowledge are revealed, the knowledge base must be regularly updated. If this requires the presence of an expert system specialist (or even worse, the particular specialist who designed the system's internal workings) then we are catapulted back into the bad old days of change requests and computer department mystique, and one of the biggest advantages of expert systems is lost.

Use and knowledge

A prime shortcoming of most current expert system shells is the disparity between the user interface's reflection (and thus the user's understanding) of the knowledge within the system and the knowledge itself. There are three major reasons for this:

1 Much of the knowledge within many expert systems is not explicitly represented at all. For example, many rule-based systems, faced with the choice of which rule to use first (and hence of the order in which questions are posed to the user) rely upon some strategy such as 'try the rules closest to the top of the knowledge base listing'. Thus in, for example, a PROLOG program, the problem-solving strategy is implicit in the ordering of clauses within the program listing, and not available for inspection by the user.

2 The frequency of systems which possess two quite distinct interfaces — one for inputting, modifying and maintaining knowledge bases, and a separate one for actually using the system. This kind of approach permits the growth of 'cognitive dissonance', whereby the user's internalised model of the system's operation is at odds with the reality.

3 This dissonance at best means that the expert knowledge used by the system is unlikely to rub off on users. At the worst, it may cause the user to make invalid analogies, misinterpret conclusions and ultimately carry quite erroneous beliefs away from a consultation with the expert system.

Problems with knowledge elicitation

Earlier, the author attempted to indicate some of the reasons why a knowledge engineer might be required. In particular, he mentioned the role of the knowledge engineer in extracting knowledge from the expert.

This can be a highly skilled job, particularly in cases where an expert is either inarticulate or (almost worse) highly articulate but in a totally unstructured fashion. Indeed, the requirement to take knowledge

If petrol gauge reading is ok then there is some petrol
If the sky is blue then the weather is fine
If the weather is fine and it is a school holiday then take the kids to the beach
If the weather is fine and it is not a school holiday then go and sit in the garden
If you want to go to the beach and the car is available then drive to the beach
If there is no petrol available then the car is not available

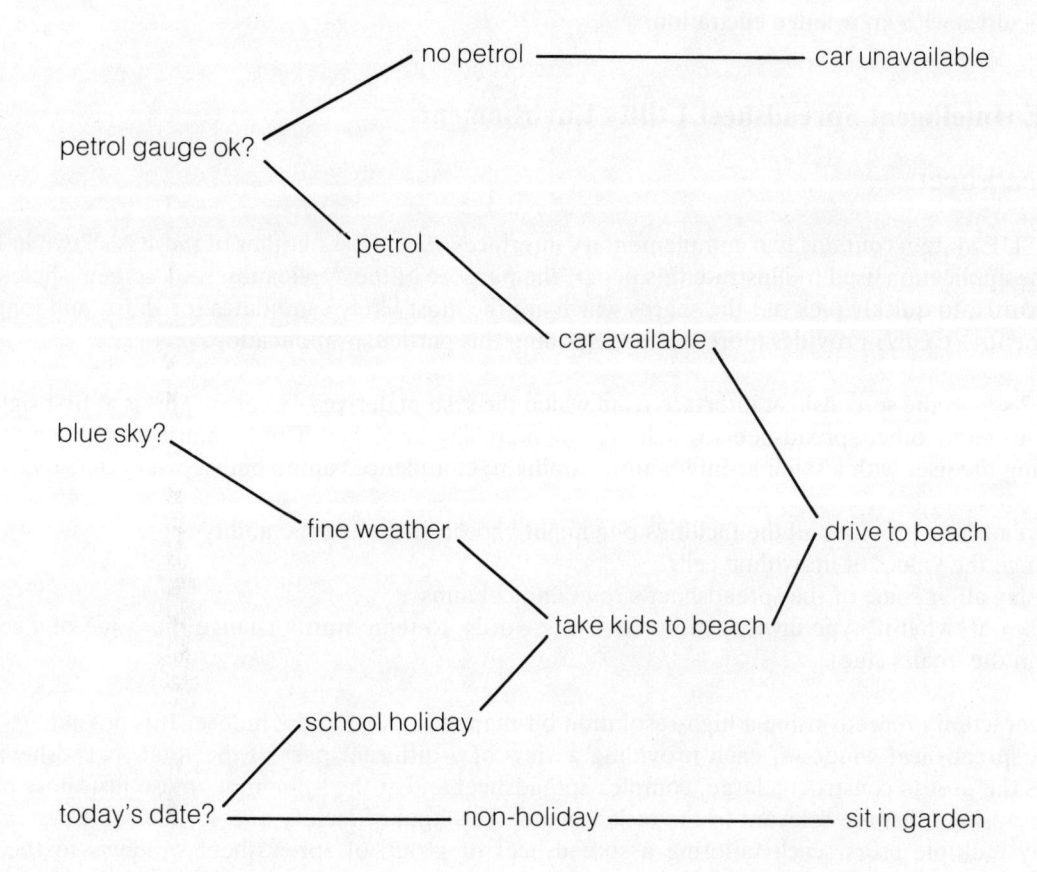

```
                              no petrol ──────────────── car unavailable
                             ╱
          petrol gauge ok? ──
                             ╲
                              petrol
                                    ╲
                                     car available
                                                 ╲
   blue sky? ──╮                                  ╲
               ╲                                   ╲
                fine weather                        ╲
                           ╲                         drive to beach
                            take kids to beach ─────╱
                           ╱
              school holiday
             ╱
  today's date? ──────── non-holiday ──────── sit in garden
```

Most people find the second, graphical representation makes it much easier to grasp the whole knowledge base and understand the wider implications of changes to the knowledge base

Figure 1: Rule-based networks

and structure it into one edifice of the form required by the computer is a problem which has attracted the attention of many workers. Methodologies proliferate — in some cases, computer-based tools have been designed specifically for this task. Some such tools have produced some worthwhile results. Unfortunately, there is a cost — we now have *three* separate computer interfaces within one project. In some cases, for example where user and expert are the same person, this unfortunate and highly confused individual will have been exposed to all three during the project.

In an ideal world, one interface would cater for the needs of all the different tasks that go towards the production of an expert system. To do this, and cater for computer-based support for the elicitation task, it is necessary to design the knowledge interface accordingly.

Summary of the difficulties

- Multiplicity of actors
- Complexity of knowledge representation and system operation
- Hiding the full structure of the knowledge from users
- Multiplicity of interfaces
- Difficulties with knowledge elicitation.

ISSUE (Intelligent Spreadsheet Utility Environment)

A spreadsheet

The ISSUE system contains two complementary interfaces. The most familiar of these is shown in Figure 2. In the application used to illustrate this paper, the purpose of the application is to 'screen' shares, or in other words, to quickly pick out the shares which are the most likely candidates for short- and long-term investments. *(CLE1)* provides more details regarding this particular application.

Figure 2 shows the spreadsheet interface from which the system derives its name. This is at first sight very similar to many other spreadsheets which are commercially available. This similarity is deliberate — by providing the user with a familiar interaction paradigm, confidence can be built up very quickly.

The spreadsheet provides all the facilities one might expect, including the ability to:
- Change the values of individual cells
- Display all or some of the spreadsheet's rows and columns
- Carry out 'what-if'-type investigations (in other words, to temporarily change the value of a cell, but retain the 'real' value).

The interaction proceeds using a high-resolution bit-mapped screen and a mouse. It is possible to create several spreadsheet windows, each providing a view of a different part of the total spreadsheet. This permits the user to construct a large, complex spreadsheet and at the same time to use just those parts of the spreadsheet that are relevant to the task at hand. This kind of facility enables the same system to be used by multiple users, each tailoring a spreadsheet or group of spreadsheet windows to their own particular tasks and modes of operations.

Calculating values

The description so far is of a reasonably straightforward spreadsheet, adapted to take advantage of some of the benefits offered by large screens and windowing software. However, closer inspection of Figure 2 reveals that some cells contain linguistic values (words) rather than numeric values. Where a cell contains a linguistic value, this will typically have been deduced from a number of other linguistic cells. The precise relationship between the various values is described by a rule-set, an example of which is shown in Figure 3a. The example shown is used to derive the value of the leftmost factor (in this case, 'long-term prospects') from three other factors (relative growth rate, future growth and current market). Also shown in Figure 3b is an example of the presentation of the numeric calculation required to derive a numeric value from a number of other numeric inputs.

It can be seen that the 'rules' used to derive a linguistic value from other linguistic values form little more than a decision table. The derivation of the consequent value is certainly something that could easily be

	SHARES						
	Rel.Price/NAV	Management	Share.Price	Fin.Pos	Short.Term.Rec	Long.Term.Rec	Add column
Company 1	−22.97	Good	220	Bad	Buy	Buy	Add row
Company 2	24.17	Good	118	Adequate	Hold	Sell	Create column
Company 3	.01	Average	152	Good	Buy	Buy	Create row
Company 4	7.09	Poor	146	Adequate	Sell	Sell	Refresh
Company 5	13.6	Poor	146	Bad	Sell	Sell	Clear
Company 6	−43.4	Bad	84	Bad	Buy	Sell	
Market.Ave	0.0	-	-	-	Hold	Hold	

Figure 2: ISSUE spreadsheet

performed by any one of the rule-based expert system shells currently available. The resolution of conflict (occurring when two rules fire simultaneously) is made by specificity (thus the rule containing the fewest wild cards is selected). However, a number of factors combine to make this style of interface easier to use.

Firstly, equations are represented as equations. The second line of Figure 3a is:

Good Average Good Good

which converts in typical rule-based shell syntax to something like:

if Rel.Growth.Rate is Average and Future.Growth is Good and Current.Market is Good
then Long.Term.Prosp is Good

which is by no means unreasonable. However, the equation shown in Figure 3b:

[Basic.Value] = (66 * (((Rel.Earnings.Growth + 100)/(Rel.P.E.Ratio + 100)) − 1))

might typically be represented as something like:

if $Rel.Earnings.Growth = Rel.Earnings.Growth
and $Rel.P.E.Ratio = Rel.P.E.Ratio
then Basic.Value = (66 * ((($Rel.Earnings.Growth + 100)/($Rel.P.E.Ratio + 100)) − 1))

The somewhat tortuous and certainly counter-intuitive preamble to the equation proper stems from the attempt to impose one uniform representation (rules) on all knowledge. Thus the ISSUE system improves upon the traditional spreadsheet (because it recognises that not all the factors that humans consider in the making of simple decisions can be reduced to numeric quantities related by algorithms) and upon the rule-based shells (because equations are represented as equations).

Long.Term.Prosp.	Rel.Growth.Rate	Future.Growth	Current.Market
Average	Average	—	—
Good	Average	Good	Good
Good	High	Average	Good
Poor	Low	Average	Poor
Bad	Low	Bad	Poor
Bad	Low	—	Bad
Average	Low	Good	Average
Poor	Average	Average	Poor
Poor	Average	Bad	Excellent
Very Good	High	Good	Average
Poor	High	Bad	Good
Average	High	Average	Poor
Good	High	Good	Good
Poor	Average	Bad	Bad
Poor	—	Poor	—
Good	High	Good	Poor
Poor	Low	Poor	Poor

a)

Edit Function For Basic.Value

(66 * (((Rel.Earnings.Growth + 100) / (Rel.P.E.Ratio + 100)) - 1))

b)

Figure 3a: ISSUE rule-table
Figure 3b: ISSUE numeric calculation
Figure 3: Calculating values with ISSUE

ISSUE also needs to allow for the translation between numeric and linguistic factors. This task could be accomplished in many ways, but in keeping with the philosophy behind much of the rest of the system, the simplest route was chosen. Cells may be defined as possessing a dual status, appearing as both numbers and linguistic values simultaneously. Thus a numeric value may be calculated for a cell, and then mapped onto a linguistic value to be passed onto a consequent cell, whose value is to be derived using a rule table. The mapping process simply associates a linguistic value with a numeric range.

The representation of the rules used to derive the value of one linguistic factor as a table (see Figure 3) provides two further advantages over the typical expert system shell.

1 The grouping together of all the rules whose consequents relate to a given factor helps provide some degree of structure for the rules in the system.

2 The sheer compactness of the representation is a bonus in that more of the rules can be seen simultaneously.

Making knowledge accessible

Understanding the structure of the decision embodied in an expert system shell is, as we have seen, rendered difficult by the fact that the rules in the shell provide the links in a complex network hidden from the user. Much of the same criticism can justifiably be made of spreadsheets. A number of cells have values which are input by the user. A number of other cells have values which are calculated from the other cells in the spreadsheet, using formulae which do not appear on the spreadsheet. Furthermore, consider a cell whose value is calculated from a cell whose value is calculated from a cell whose ... etc. Once again, we have a network of cell values, but a network which is hidden from the user.

In a nutshell, the spreadsheet provides a fine interface to the system's data, but not to all the knowledge in the system. Indeed, one might well compare a spreadsheet with an expert system shell. Figure 4 makes the comparison, and also includes ISSUE for completeness.

	Rule-based shell	Conventional spreadsheet	ISSUE
Inferencing	Typically backwards, but some data driven	Data driven	Data driven
Knowledge representation	Rules	Equations	Equations, rule tables
Dialogue style	Computer driven	User driven	User driven
Data types	Mainly linguistic, with poor numeric facilities	Numeric	Both

Figure 4: Comparison of decision aids

The mention of inferencing is of particular interest. The advantage of the backward chaining, goal-driven approach, favoured by most of the popular shells, is that such an approach enables a solution (most commonly to some classification problem, such as fault diagnosis) to be reached with only the minimum of information being required from the user. The style of the interaction tends to be heavily computer driven, with the computer asking questions of the user almost as side-effects of its attempts to satisfy its predetermined goals. This is fine if the predetermined goals match those of the user. This may be the case if the user wants to make a single decision, but is less likely if the user's objectives are less clearly defined. For example, consider the spreadsheet shown in Figure 2. If the user approaches the system with the goal of deciding 'Should I buy shares in company X — yes or no?', then the backward chaining approach may well prove sufficient. If, on the other hand, the user's goal is more along the lines of 'I'd like some help in deciding what shares should make up a portfolio which balances risk and potential profit', then such a well-structured interaction is unlikely to prove satisfactory. In this case, the data-driven approach, typical of spreadsheets, comes into its own. The ability to shortcircuit the reasoning process, by for example overriding some value which is otherwise calculated in painful detail from 10 inputs, is useful. So is the ability to very easily carry out the 'what-if'-type investigations mentioned earlier.

These and many other user operations fall under the general banner of investigating the consequences of new hypotheses. These are all helped by an understanding of the structure underlying either the rules or the spreadsheets that we have alluded to earlier. This structure comes nearest to being visible in the case of the shell when the question 'Why?' is answered by a regurgitation of the chain of rules connecting data and conclusion. This facility is provided within the ISSUE system and, indeed, its effectiveness is slightly enhanced because the spreadsheet representation makes all conclusions (intermediate as well as terminal) available for investigation. However, more is clearly needed.

Figure 5 shows ISSUE's answer to this difficulty. This browser shows the dependencies between different items in the spreadsheet, be they rows, columns or cells. In the case of the application shown, that of evaluating the worth of shares in various companies, the decision being made is essentially repeated for each row in turn. Thus the majority of the factors shown in the browser are columns, and the browser describes the rules linking the contents of individual columns which are common across a number of rows. However, also necessary for the model is the appearance of a number of specific cells in the general calculation for each row. Thus, for example, at the bottom of Figure 5, the relative earnings growth for the individual company shown in the browser is calculated on the basis of both the earnings growth for that company and the market average earnings growth (drawn from the intersections of the earnings growth column with the row representing this specific company and the row representing the market averages, respectively). Similar browsers might be drawn if the general trend of decision making were down the spreadsheet, showing general relations between rows. A satisfactory approach to representing the situation where a number of general relationships exist between both rows and columns has yet to be devised — fortunately, this type of problem has also yet to be encountered!

This browser provides an alternative to the spreadsheet interface. While allowing the inspection of essentially only one row of the spreadsheet at any one time, it does make the investigation of the details of a decision simpler. By mousing the various nodes in the graph, the rule tables and equations underlying the values taken by the various factors can be inspected. Because the full network is available for inspection, the effect of a 'what-if'-type query can be investigated very easily. Other related query types become possible. For example, the 'why not?'-type query. Previous work *(CLE2)* has noted the frequency with which this query type is asked of human experts, and also the difficulty in allowing a rule-based shell to provide a response. Furthermore, overriding the value derived for an intermediate value becomes a much more tenable operation. The system allows the user to see at a glance what factors will be ignored and what effects such a course of action may have. For example, consider the area towards the top of Figure 5. If the user of the system has personal knowledge which makes it certain that long-term prospects are bad for a given company, this value can be entered directly. Lack of access to the full structure of the browser might mean that the user was forced to answer six questions in order to allow the system to draw this already known conclusion. In summary, if the user knows how the system is working, then the two can cooperate as a partnership, without repeating each other's work. The alternative is a system-driven dialogue, where the user of the expert system is assumed to be a fount of all *data*, but of no *knowledge*.

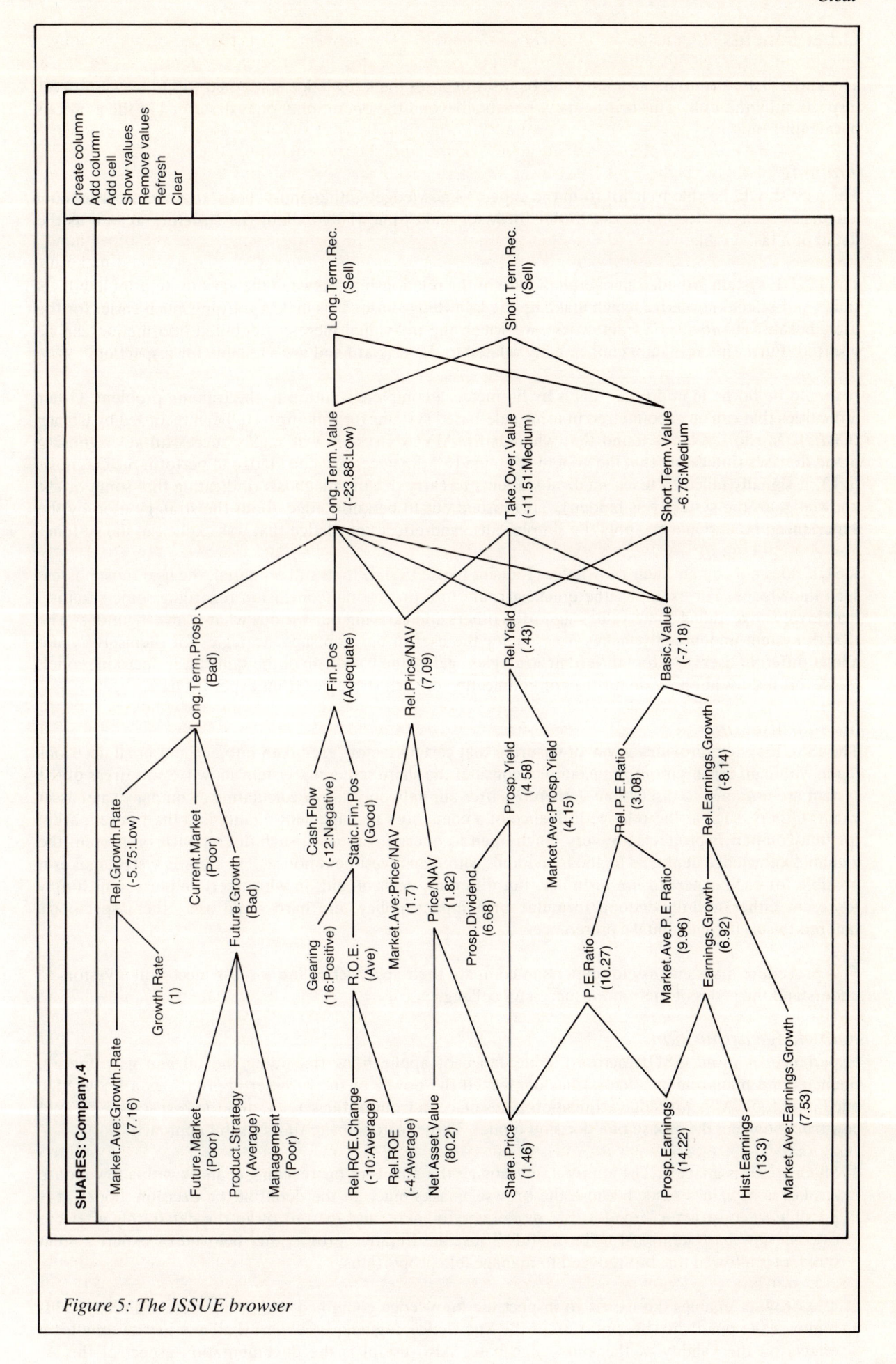

Figure 5: The ISSUE browser

Other benefits

The author has tried to indicate how the browser exposes the knowledge contained within the system for inspection by the user. This brings many benefits beyond the operational ones described in the previous paragraph.

Training

The user should be able to learn from the expert's knowledge. Unlike most shells, or logic programming languages such as PROLOG, the ISSUE browser makes knowledge about the structure as well as the detail of a task visible.

The ISSUE system provides an overall picture of the relationships between the various items of low-level cause-and-effect knowledge which make up the knowledge base. This makes learning much easier for the user, because it provides a framework into which the individual pieces of detailed information can be inserted. Furthermore, factors not directly related to the task at hand are available for inspection.

It should be borne in mind that this is by no means a complete solution to the training problem. Other difficulties that can be encountered in using rule-based systems for training have been recorded by Clancy *(CLE3)*. In short, Clancy found that whereas the MYCIN system was highly successful at diagnosing blood diseases (indicating that the system contained all the necessary knowledge to perform the diagnosis task), it signally failed to teach medical students to carry out the diagnosis (indicating that some of the knowledge in the system was hidden). This turned out to be knowledge about the strategy used by the experienced practitioner to apply the simple cause-and-effect knowledge that was explicit in the system.

ISSUE does not contain such knowledge. Indeed, to use ISSUE to its full potential, the user must possess such knowledge. For example, the quickest route to a provisional conclusion regarding some situation may involve overriding some values, ignoring others and carrying out various what-if investigations. The ISSUE system undoubtedly makes it easier for the user to develop such strategies for themselves, and allows different users to adopt differemt strategies against the backdrop of the same basic decision model. However, it does not provide for the communicating of such strategies from expert to user.

Standardisation

The ISSUE system provides a way of ensuring that certain factors are taken into account in all decisions made within an organisation. For example, consider the share screening system shown. Some areas of the system are not open to discussion — there is, after all, only one way of calculating a company's net asset value. Others, such as the relative influence of a company's management quality and the future market for that company's products are very much open to question. Indeed, such discrepancies represent the valuable knowledge deployed by the individuals within an investment house. The ISSUE system makes it possible for each expert to use a similar, but different, decision aid, in which certain parts, which may represent either well-understood formulae or company policy, are hard-wired and other aspects are tailored to suit the individual's preferences.

This procedure makes it easy for experts to compare their approaches and for less successful investors to understand the styles of their more successful colleagues.

Knowledge acquisition

Experience of using ISSUE across a wide range of applications (including the oil and gas, energy, financial and management sectors) has confirmed the power of the browser approach as a knowledge elicitation tool. All knowledge acquisition takes place in front of the screen, and the first stage is a rapid construction using the mouse of a decision model. Three factors make this a useful approach.

1 Sheer speed is a factor. The ability to investigate the effects of far-reaching changes with a few mouse strokes is of value. Also, because the browser masks much of the detail of the decision model, it is possible to construct a 'broad-brush' model very quickly, and then to fill in the detail only after the overall view has been seen to be useful. Thus, the iterative prototyping beloved of expert system builders is allowed for, but reduced to manageable proportions.

2 The browser enables the expert to inspect the knowledge contained within the system directly. This removes the possibility of confusion in the knowledge engineer — expert dialogue having long-term effects on the validity of the knowledge base. Also useful is the documentation aspect of this —

experience has shown that experts who take away laser printouts of the type shown in Figure 5 are more likely to come back to the next session with ideas about the expansion of the system than those provided with a list of rules.

3 The knowledge can be maintained by the expert. After continuous exposure to the system during the initial development of the system, most experts feel confident to take on the maintenance of the ensuing application. This useful state of affairs is also encouraged by the menu- and mouse-oriented nature of the system. Because the interaction essentially proceeds by pointing at some item and selecting from a menu, there is no need to remember command names and procedures. This makes the system much easier to relearn after some intervening period, so making maintenance as a part-time occupation a possibility.

This is not to say, however, that the need for a knowledge engineer has been completely removed. There is some skill in building browser graphs with reasonable nodes and interconnections, and particularly in the recognition of useful intermediate concepts. However, the role of the knowledge engineer can be reduced, perhaps taking the form of substantial effort in the early stages of the development of each model, reducing rapidly as the details are fleshed out.

Future work

The ISSUE system as it stands is just the first step along the road to a new kind of decision support. A number of areas are currently under consideration for possible enhancement. These include:
- Handling uncertainty
- Reversing the direction of inference
- Providing other representations for knowledge.

Handling uncertainty
ISSUE at present does not handle uncertain knowledge (incomplete knowledge can be handled by the careful placement of wild cards in rule tables and the strategy of conflict resolution by specificity described earlier ensures that such rules are not used when detailed information is available).

One aspect of ISSUE makes the uncertainty problem more tractable than is the case in other systems; this is the existence of the network shown in the browser prior to the apportioning of 'truth' or what have you. The kind of strategies currently under consideration revolve around the idea that it should be possible to apportion a value to each node in the network, and that these values should form a consistent whole (so that, for example, some constant relationship should exist between any given node and its consequents throughout the network). A particular difficulty is the investigation of alternative assumptions simultaneously, for example in the case where it is likely that a particular node may attain one of two values simultaneously. The use of multiple browser windows may be appropriate here. In this area, however, as indeed is the case with all the other enhancements being considered at present, the philosophy adopted is that a facility without a simple to use and understand interface is worse than no facility. This is in stark contrast to most of the expert system tools available today, where extra goodies are introduced with little regard to their presentation to the user.

Reversing the direction of inference
Rather than answering the question 'What are the conclusions to be drawn from the given data' it would be useful to ask 'What would the data need to be in order for some conclusion to be true'. Although this appears to involve reversing the direction of inference, this should not be confused with backward chaining. Rather, it is a form of automated what-if, where the system tries a large number of what-if enquiries and identifies one that has the desired impact upon the decisions of the model.

Providing other representations for knowledge
As it stands, ISSUE does allow the generalisation of a decision across a number of instances. However, the effectiveness of this is somewhat lessened because the system cannot easily take advantage of partial similarities between cases which are also different in some way. Two routes to extending the flexibility of ISSUE in this way are available:

1 Modularisation of the system, so that a number of modules are used to make some overall decision.
2 Incorporation of some kind of frame-based representation.

Conclusions

In conclusion it is useful to refer back to the list of difficulties identified at the end of the first section of this paper, and to consider how ISSUE addresses these, and what lessons can be drawn.

Multiplicity of actors

The same number of actors still exist. ISSUE has sought to reduce the problems that this causes in two ways:

1 By providing an interface (the browser) which can be used by all actors throughout the system's lifetime.

2 By reducing the reliance on a knowledge engineer. A logical long-term goal would be the total removal of the knowledge engineer from the equation.

Complexity of knowledge representation and system operation

The approach used in ISSUE has been to concentrate on extracting the full power from simple representations, rather than to use a more complex representation in a perhaps less thorough fashion. Ultimately other representations will be required for certain application types — however, it is critical that these do not become beyond the power of the user and expert to comprehend. A case in point is the use of numerical uncertainty factors — how many users really understand what it means when their expert system says 'Buy ICI (0.64)' and how often is their understanding mirrored by that of the expert?

Hiding the full structure of the knowledge from users

The browser is undoubtedly a powerful tool in combating this vice. However, as we have seen, ISSUE does not make available the details of the decision-making strategy employed by the expert.

Multiplicity of interfaces

ISSUE provides two interfaces (a spreadsheet and a browser). However, both interfaces are available (and necessary) to all the different users of the system. It is this shared view of the system which it is important to engender.

Difficulties with knowledge elicitation

The browser resolves many of these. It is not foolproof — in particular, an expert who functions almost entirely by heuristic knowledge, rather than through any understanding of the domain of knowledge being addressed, may have problems. However, in general, the system has been highly successful in this area.

2: Human/Computer Interaction Engineering (HCIE)

J Dowell

J B Long

Ergonomics Unit
University College London
London
UK

A conception of interactive user systems and their design is presented. Its intention is to support formalisation in the design and research of human/computer interaction and its emergence as an engineering discipline. In consequence, the paper provides a coherent definition of the concepts supporting the formulation of engineering principles for the domain. These are concepts associating work, human/computer systems performing work and the effectiveness of those systems. A conception of the design of computer-based user systems is correspondingly provided. Finally, a Computer-aided Design (CAD) research project is described, in which the conception enabled the formulation of its problem.

© J Dowell and J B Long 1988

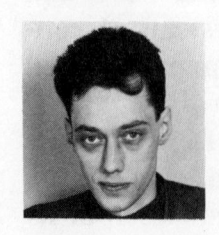

J Dowell
John Dowell is a Research Associate at the Ergonomics Unit, University College London. He is currently working on a project supported by SERC grant GR/D 57829, awarded as part of the Alvey initiative. The project, a three-year collaboration of academic and industrial parties, is concerned with developing methods of evaluating specifications for user-interactive systems. Mr Dowell graduated in engineering in 1982 and worked as a design engineer in industry for some years. He later took a postgraduate qualification in ergonomics and subsequently moved into human/computer interaction research.

J Long
John Long is Professor of Ergonomics and Director of the Ergonomics Unit, University College London. He worked initially as a manager for Shell International in Africa and the Far East. Subsequently, he became a senior scientist at the Medical Research Council's Applied Psychology Unit in Cambridge. His main research interests lie in the area of human/computer interaction, although he has also published papers on divided attention, typing, second-language use and interpreter training.

Human/Computer Interaction Engineering (HCIE)

Computer technology continues to give rise to concern about the effectiveness of its applications. It is no longer sufficient for systems simply to work — they must also contribute to the success of the organisations which exploit them. In particular, there is a need to optimise the interactions of users with the computers they operate in the course of their work — an interaction which determines fundamentally the effectiveness of these systems. The importance of this interaction has gone largely unrecognised and its design has been *ad hoc* and unprincipled. A formalisation of the design of human/computer interactions must necessarily occur if the effectiveness of computer-based systems is to be improved. It is a formalisation of both the methods of design practice and the principles that the practice employs. This formalisation currently supports the emergence of a new systems engineering discipline which is termed Human/Computer Interaction Engineering (HCIE).

HCIE is equivalent to the more traditional engineering disciplines (for example mechanical engineering); in contrast to them, however, it does not yet possess a corpus of formalised engineering principles. It is these principles which distinguish an engineering discipline from a craft in which knowledge is informally maintained and which may only exist in the practice of that craft. They may be principles of design methods for the discipline practice or they may be principles relating to properties of the artefacts which reliably exhibit desired properties and performance *(DOW1)* and, ultimately, a desired effectiveness; they therefore support the deterministic solution of the general design problem of that domain. Their formalisation is essential to the completeness and coherence of the corpus they constitute and so also to the formalisation of design.

The principles currently possessed by HCIE are fragmentary and lacking in formality. This is unsurprising when the novel and complex nature of the domain is considered. However, a basic obstacle to establishing coherent formal principles is the absence of a consensus understanding of the concepts which describe the domain. The lack of a shared view is particularly apparent within the research literature in which concepts are ambiguous and lacking in coherence. Those associating the interface (for example 'virtual objects', 'task semantics', 'user error', etc) are, unfortunately, good examples of this failure. It is inconceivable that a formalisation of principles might occur in the absence of a rigorous, explicit definition of the relevant concepts.

Van Gisch and Pipino *(DOW2)* have suggested the process by which concepts of a discipline achieve definition. They identify the most general level of activity as an epistemological enquiry in which discipline knowledge originates and from which a paradigm results. The paradigm may be considered to subsume all discipline activities *(DOW1)*; however, at the very least, it must subsume the way in which general concepts and methods are defined and both design and research problems specified (the position taken here). It provides, then, a unitary and shared conception of the domain; its power lies in the coherence and completeness that it provides in the definition of concepts and methods and in the conception of research and design problems.

HCIE does not currently possess a paradigm, even in the more limited sense — the available conceptions of human/computer interaction are fragmentary and ill-formed. This paper presents a conception intended to contribute to the epistemological enquiry of HCIE as a discipline. It is proposed that this conception represents the form of the paradigm which HCIE would ideally assume and which would precipitate its formalisation *(DOW3)*.

The conception of human/computer interaction is consistent with a proposition of the general design problem whose solution HCIE supports. An expression of the proposition which is held implicitly by most workers in the field and which would receive general agreement would be that the problem is one of: 'producing implementable specifications of human/computer interactions for a desired performance of work'.

The conception assumes the distinction embodied in this proposition between work; the entities which perform work, that is humans and computers; and performance, which relates the success with which those entities execute, or accomplish work. The following three sections present the conception as it addresses these distinctions. The conception is then extended to a description of HCIE design practice and to its application to research concerning graphical display in Computer-aided Design (CAD) systems.

Work

Work, as defined in the conception, occurs within, and is distributed by, organisations (for other features of work see *(DOW4)*). The world in which work is performed is conceived as discrete objects. These are physical or abstract and are composed respectively of matter/energy and information/knowledge. Objects are characterised by their attributes. The same attribute(s) identify classes of objects and so also a hierarchy of classes. Hence, letters which make up correspondence are a class (characterised by the physical attributes supporting the visual/verbal representation of information via language, the conceptual attributes supporting the communication of messages etc); income tax returns are a class of letter distinguishable from the class of personal letters by their attributes of content, intended correspondent, etc.

An attribute of an object is conceived as having a state which exhibits the potential for change. A *task* produces an intentional change in the attribute state of an object; its *product* is an object with some specific state of some attribute(s). For example, the task of completing a tax return and the task of writing to an acquaintance, of creating letters, changes the state of those objects' attributes (their content, format and status, for example) from zero. Further editing of those letters would produce additional state changes.

An *application domain* is a class of potential changes of attribute states of a class of objects and in principle may have any level of generality, for example writing letters or completing tax returns. However, application domains are principally determined by the technological and organisational contexts in which tasks occur, for example banking, process control, etc, and have immediate consequences for the organisational demarcation of work.

Organisations prescribe tasks within particular application domains by means of *task goals* which express specific desired states of objects. The desired state expressed by a task goal is the ideal product of the task. Task goals can express a complex of desired changes concerning objects in an application domain and this is significant for two reasons. First, tasks may be decomposed into subtasks at lower levels of description. Secondly, it implies that tasks producing state changes across many attributes of an object may produce different (compromise) products — different styles of letter, for example. *Quality* describes 'the actual product of a task with respect to the desired product (expressed by the task goals)'. Because it describes the product as a change effected by the task in the attribute state of an object (with respect to the desired change), quality enables all possible products of a task to be equated and evaluated.

Within this conception then, tasks produce changes in the objects constituting the world in which work occurs. The following section describes the entities of concern to HCIE which perform tasks, viz humans and computers.

Human/computer systems

Organisations assign work as tasks to the systems they maintain and control. Generally, a system is 'any identifiable set of mutually influential entities associated for the purpose of producing desired changes in the attribute state of objects'.

A system may therefore perform tasks and achieve task goals within its intended application domain. The *system* with which HCIE is concerned consists of two entities — the human and the computer. Such a system is the Personal Assistant Secretary (PAS) and Word Processor (WP) — the PAS/WP system. The entities of the human/computer system maintain representations of objects (within particular application domains) as symbols (physical or abstract) and concepts; their representations will be partial and may well be different.

The system performs tasks, producing changes in the attribute state of the associated objects. When the system is designed for a particular application domain, the human and computer are delegated subtasks. However, the human and computer are not equivalent entities of the system; the computer is conceived as a tool for the human to perform tasks. The human is therefore more descriptively termed the *user*.

Those tasks which users perform can be distinguished as being on-line and off-line — *on-line* tasks produce changes in objects represented by the human/computer system and *off-line* tasks produce changes in objects which are not so represented. The PAS/WP system, for example, is assigned the task of producing a paper-based copy of a dictated letter. The task then, is to change the attributes pertaining to the medium in which the letter is represented. The PAS has the off-line task of listening to, and transposing, the dictation; the PAS and the WP have the on-line task of representing the transposed content of the letter in a desired visual/verbal format of stored physical symbols.

The conception of the user as a system entity is consistent with systems theory *(DOW5)*. However, it should be noted that prevalent concepts of the system include only the computer and exclude the user *(DOW6)*. A particular incoherence in current concepts associating interaction and the interface may be similarly noted, for while it is accepted that the interface defines the extent of the interaction between the computer software and the user's mind, the interface is generally conceived as only extending from the central processor of the computer to the input/output devices *(DOW7)*.

The conception proposed here obviates such incoherence. According to systems theory, the behaviour of a system is not simply determined by the sum of the behaviours of its constituent entities; only when the interaction — the mutual influence of system entities — is known does the behaviour of the whole system become determinate or predictable *(DOW8)*. *Interaction* in the conception of the system is: 'the mutual influence of the user behaviour $\{U\}$, or part thereof, and of the computer behaviour $\{C\}$, or part thereof, and so crucially determines the behaviour of the system. Hence, the fundamental concern of HCIE is the optimisation of the interaction of the user and computer, rather than their individual behaviours *per se*.

The conception makes coherent concepts associating the *user interface* which now describe the extent of the interaction within the system entities; the user interface embodies all the functional aspects of both the user and computer concerned with the users' performance of their on-line tasks.

Performance

Tasks are conceived as intentional changes produced in the attribute state of objects in application domains. Systems constituting users and computers are able to perform tasks by effecting such changes to objects. The changes which systems are able to effect is determined by the nature and configuration of the user and computer; performance expresses the effectiveness of the system in accomplishing tasks.

The performance of a system expresses its accomplishment of a task in terms of quality. (As before, quality describes the actual product of a task with respect to the desired product.) However, in addition to the quality of the task 'product', performance must also express the resource cost of 'production', or *production cost*, incurred by the system. This is a cost in terms of the user's cognitive and affective resources, and of the computer's processing resources. *Performance*, then, is a two-factor concept expressing the effectiveness of systems as: 'the quality of task product and the incurred production cost'. We may assert that a most effective system would minimise the production cost in performing a specified task with a given quality of product.

Importantly then, in addition to distinguishing between tasks and the systems which perform them, the conception is also able to distinguish the quality of the task products from the effectiveness of the systems which produce them. This is clearly essential, as two systems performing the same task might be capable of producing the same quality of product, yet one might demand a greater production cost. Consequently, there would be a difference in the effectiveness of the two systems.

The performance of a system is determined by its behaviour, which in turn is determined by the interaction of the user and computer. *Behaviour* expresses the means by which it accomplishes its tasks. System behaviour then, is orthogonal to system performance and can be expressed in terms of the user's behaviour $\{U\}$, for example pressing keys, implementing heuristic strategies, making errors, etc and the computer's behaviour $\{C\}$, for example displaying screens, issuing prompts, etc. The user and the computer each have behavioural limits within which they necessarily operate in performing tasks. These are limits in terms of the current state of the user's knowledge, memory and patience, and the computer's processing power, screen size, etc. The behavioural limits of the user are not only difficult to define, they may also be variable.

This conception of performance is in contrast to others which describe performance, for instance, in terms of user error *(DOW9)*. (Errors according to the conception proposed here are specific behaviours of the human/computer system not contributing to achieving the task goals. They will therefore incur unnecessary resource costs with a consequent effect on performance.) However, the distinction between behaviour and performance is basic to systems theory *(DOW5)* and is implied by certain areas of psychological science *(DOW10)*. It is also implied by Carroll and Campbell *(DOW11)* who present a distinction between descriptive models of the user (consistent with performance) and explanatory models (consistent with behaviour).

If performance expresses the quality of task product related to the production cost of the task, system effectiveness can be characterised by differentiating the production costs incurred by the performance of the human/computer system.

Usability is a characteristic of effectiveness expressing the cognitive production cost of system performance to the user; for example it would relate the quality of the design produced by a designer and CAD system to the designer's retrieval of information from memory, the acquisition of new knowledge, etc.

Acceptability is a characteristic of effectiveness which includes the affective production cost of system performance to the user; for example, it would relate the quality of letter produced by a user and word processor to the user's frustration, etc.

Functionality is a characteristic of effectiveness expressing the production cost of system performance to the computer — a production cost in terms of operations, processing, response time, etc. Note that if the computer is unable to perform a task at all, the effectiveness of the system in that task is described as having a null functionality (that is production costs would be infinite). In the task of substituting all occurrences of a certain word in a text file for another word, for example, it has a null functionality in the search subtask if it is able to substitute but will not search. Alternatively, if the computer is only able to perform search tasks with a large number of operations, it has a low functionality (that is the production cost to the computer is excessive).

Engineering human/computer interactions — the design problem

The conception of HCIE proposed so far has defined the concepts necessary to describe human/computer systems, the work they perform and their effectiveness in performing that work. It therefore enables the formalisation of engineering principles by which the design activity might prescribe required properties of human/computer interactions and the effectiveness of human/computer systems. However, HCIE design practice is also subject to a formalisation of its methods. The conception is correspondingly extended to a conception of the practice of engineering human/computer interactions.

It was earlier proposed that the design of human/computer interactions sought solutions to a general design problem, expressed as one of 'producing implementable specifications of human/computer interactions for a desired performance of work'. This proposition is re-expressed in terms of system behaviour and performance to become the general HCIE design problem:

Specify and implement $\{C\}$ and $\{U\}$ such that $\{U \text{ interacting with } C\} = P_D$

where P_D is the desired performance of the system. P_D therefore expresses a desired quality of task product for a desired production cost.

The expression of the general HCIE design problem can be seen to concur with the general problem of interactive system design *(DOW12)*. Its significance for the design activity is that the many alternative interactions of user and computer may, in principle, produce the same product. However, a most effective system (that is, one which exhibits P_D) will necessarily require an optimal interaction if task goals are to be achieved at an economic cost to the system.

The expression of desired system performance for the purposes of design is in terms of criteria. These may be regarded as expressing critical instances of desired performance in the absence of a complete model of system performance. Hence, each criterion relates a critical instance of the desired quality of a task product and the production cost. Criteria, then, describe the required effectiveness of user systems for the purposes of design and may be classified as concerning the usability, acceptability and functionality of the system.

It must be emphasised that specific HCIE design problems are generally ill formed such that P_D is poorly expressed; furthermore, the performance of a system represented only as a specification is not accurately determinable (at least not currently). The result is that an implemented system may exhibit a less than desired performance — it may not be able to perform a task to a required level of quality or it may be too demanding in its production cost.

The expression of the general HCIE design problem asserts the objectives of HCIE design practice. It therefore supports the formulation of the engineering principles of HCIE design methods which are able to assure the achievement of that objective.

Application of the conception — the case of CAD displays

The exploitation of CAD by manufacturing industry is typical of the widespread adoption of computer technology within an application domain. The opportunities for exploiting computers in design has resulted in a steady expansion of CAD technology and, consequently, the possibilities for the interactions of designers and CAD computers. In particular, there are now many alternative ways in which CAD systems may graphically represent those artefacts which the design task produces (indeed, certain representations have only become feasible for utilisation in design with the evolution of CAD itself). However, there is a serious lack of understanding of the appropriateness of different forms of representation for the design task, and so also of their consequences for the effectiveness of CAD systems. Aspects of the conception proposed here were employed to formulate the problem of CAD representation as addressed in a piece of research *(DOW13)*. A description of that application will serve to exemplify the conception.

The aim of the research was to evaluate the usability for the mechanical engineering design task of commonly available forms of CAD graphical representation. The research identified three generic forms in which mechanical objects are represented — Generic Representation Forms (GRFs). These were the 2D orthographic, the 2½D wireframe and the solid model. The computers which support each class of GRF differ widely — the 2D orthographic is predominantly supported by microcomputers, whereas the solid model is necessarily supported by a more powerful workstation or mainframe. However, to a degree it is possible for each GRF to be employed for the same design task. The research intended to determine the relative usability of the three GRFs for the general mechanical engineering design task.

For the study, a carburettor was designed to satisfy a set of specified functions. It had, however, a number of design 'faults' — incorrect structural variables which meant that the design would fail to meet certain of its required functions. An example was the needle jet to piston skirt height, designed so that the carburettor could not achieve a specified characteristic of its mixing. The design was maintained in the database of GEOMOD, software which was able to represent the carburettor in each of the three GRFs. A number of mechanical design engineers, familiar with GEOMOD, were given the task of assessing the carburettor design against the listing of its required functions. Each designer was provided with the design (represented in just one of the three GRFs) and was observed as he performed the evaluation of the carburettor design.

The conception supported the rationalisation of the problem which the research addressed and hence its specification, with coherence and completeness. It therefore enabled the identification and control of variables in the research and the presentation of its proposed solution. The underlying theoretical difficulty in specifying this research problem concerned equating the performance of the different GRF systems so that their relative usability could be evaluated.

The application of the conception provided a categorical equation of the tasks, independent of the GRF. In terms of the conception, then, the *application domain* was mechanical engineering equipment design or, more specifically, the design of dynamic fluid mixing and metering equipment or, more specifically still, the evaluation of automotive carburettor designs. The *task goal* was to assess the carburettor design to ensure that it satisfied each of the functions required of it. Correspondingly, the *task* produced a change in the state of the attributes of the object — the representation of the carburettor. The attributes of the carburettor were those structural variables pertaining to its required functions. The change of state of those attributes occurred in their assessment, that is, their adequacy was made known. (As a part of the complete design task, the designer would subsequently have modified those structural variables.) The task *product*, then, was a representation of the carburettor whose functionality was evaluated; its *quality* was the total of identified, faulty, structural variables in the representation of the carburettor, with respect to the actual total present.

Each designer was required to interpret the functional specification in terms of the carburettor operation, identify the relevant variables of the carburettor design and indicate those variables which produced a failure to meet a specific requirement of the carburettor's function. The designers' *on-line* tasks were therefore interrogating the design to identify the variables which realised its operation and to identify the faulty variables. The research was only concerned with these on-line tasks.

The *system* in the terms of the conception comprised the two entities of the designer and the GEOMOD software. Both the designer and system maintained representations of the carburettor, though these would certainly have been different and partial. The congruency of these representations would, however, directly affect the cognitive compatibility of the computer and the designer — and therein the interaction optimality for interaction of the particular GRF.

The concept of performance was employed in evaluating the relative effectiveness of the three human/computer systems distinguished by the GRFs. The conception relates the quality of the task product to the production cost incurred. The quality of the task product was determined and aggregated for each GRF system. The aggregate production cost for each GRF system was also derived on the basis of the time to complete the task (time is a resource) and the errors committed (errors indicating an excessive cognitive effort). No affective production cost to the user, or processing cost to the computer, was assessed. Hence, a unitary value for the *performance* of each user system was derived and the relative effectiveness of the three systems established on the basis of the *usability* of the GRFs.

The concept of *behaviour* was used to explain the apparent effectiveness of the three systems. The designers' verbal protocol, recorded during the performance of the task, enabled an analysis of the knowledge use and computation required by the designers in the evaluation of the carburettor. It was a qualitative analysis of the differences between the GRF groups in design fault identification and in cognitive production cost. Hence, an explanation could be presented of the differences between the three GRFs which resulted in their apparent usability.

This concludes the illustration of the application of the conception. The conception enabled the rigorous formulation of the problem specification for the research; the coherence and completeness of its concepts was reflected in that specification.

Conclusion

A conception of HCIE has been described which, it is suggested, will support the formalisation of engineering principles of human/computer interaction. It is a conception of human/computer systems, the work they perform and their effectiveness in performing that work. It also provides a conception of the practice of designing human/computer interactions.

An application of the conception has been described, exemplifying its application to the formulation of research problems. It is suggested that the conception would similarly support the conception of problems in the design of human/computer interactions.

The conception is intended to contribute to the epistemological enquiry of HCIE as a discipline. It is proposed that the conception represents the form of a paradigm which HCIE should ideally seek to assume.

3: The user in a sociotechnical system

K D Eason

HUSAT Research Centre
University of Technology
Loughborough
Leicestershire
UK

Computer users in organisations rarely work alone; they contribute to shared work tasks. As a result they may cooperate or compete with fellow users through the medium of the system. This paper examines a number of ways in which systems may founder because they are designed without reference to the sociotechnical context in which users must operate. It examines the implications of this context for the systems analysis methods which are required and details the need for interfaces which are easy to use, secure, flexible and adaptable.

© K D Eason 1988

K D Eason
Ken Eason is Reader in Cognitive Ergonomics in the Department of Human Sciences at Loughborough University of Technology and Codirector of the HUSAT Research Centre. Over a 20-year period he has researched the impact of computer systems upon their users. His doctoral studies investigated the impact of systems upon managers. Latterly, he has researched the system design process in order to identify methods by which the characteristics of users and their organisations can be better recognised by design teams. Dr Eason has published two books 'Managing computer impact' and 'Information technology and organisational change', and will shortly publish another 'The application of information technology' with Mrs S D P Harker.

The user in a sociotechnical system

Introduction

Most of the work undertaken on human/computer interaction has so far concentrated on individual users. An implicit assumption has been that users have individual tasks which they can undertake with the support of computer systems and that successful human/computer interaction will result in the effective performance of these tasks. While this has led to significant advances in ease of use and ease of learning of computer systems, it leaves other critical issues out of the equation. There is considerable evidence to suggest that these other issues create major problems of implementation and acceptability, and they need to be more formally addressed if these problems are to be avoided.

These issues originate from the fact that most computer systems are used in an organisational setting where it is normal for people to share tasks, which means that the system has to support not individual users, but people who in some way divide activities between them. Division of labour is one of the basic principles of organisational practice; in order to get large, complex tasks undertaken they are decomposed into smaller subtasks, allocated to individual work roles and coordinated by some form of management or control system. This process produces a task performing structure which moves from role to role and may involve contributions from a considerable number of people. At present the consideration of human issues in systems development pays very little attention to these realities of organisational life. It is the purpose of this paper to make these issues explicit, show the dangers of not treating them formally and to suggest some of the implications for the design process.

There are many organisational theories that could be used to underpin an analysis of these issues. This paper will use the concept of sociotechnical systems *(EAS1)*, because it is a well-established theory which focuses upon the relationship between the social systems and the technical systems which co-exist in any organisation. Mumford *(EAS2)* and Pava *(EAS3)* have both developed this theory specifically for use with the design and implementation of IT systems. We therefore have a good basis for understanding the sociotechnical context in which a user works, and its implications for the design of a computer system. In the next section, a brief introduction to sociotechnical systems theory will be given and this will be followed by some examples of case studies where a lack of understanding of the sociotechnical context has caused technical systems to flounder. The final section proposes a number of ways in which these issues need to be incorporated into mainstream systems design and examines the implications for human/computer interaction.

Sociotechnical systems theory

Figure 1 presents a framework for sociotechnical analysis taken from *(EAS4)*. It depicts an organisation as an open system taking inputs from its environment (for example raw materials, orders, information, etc) and using them to produce valued outputs which are exported to the environment. The work process consists of taking input objects and undertaking a series of tasks which convert them to useful objects which achieve

Figure 1: A sociotechnical system

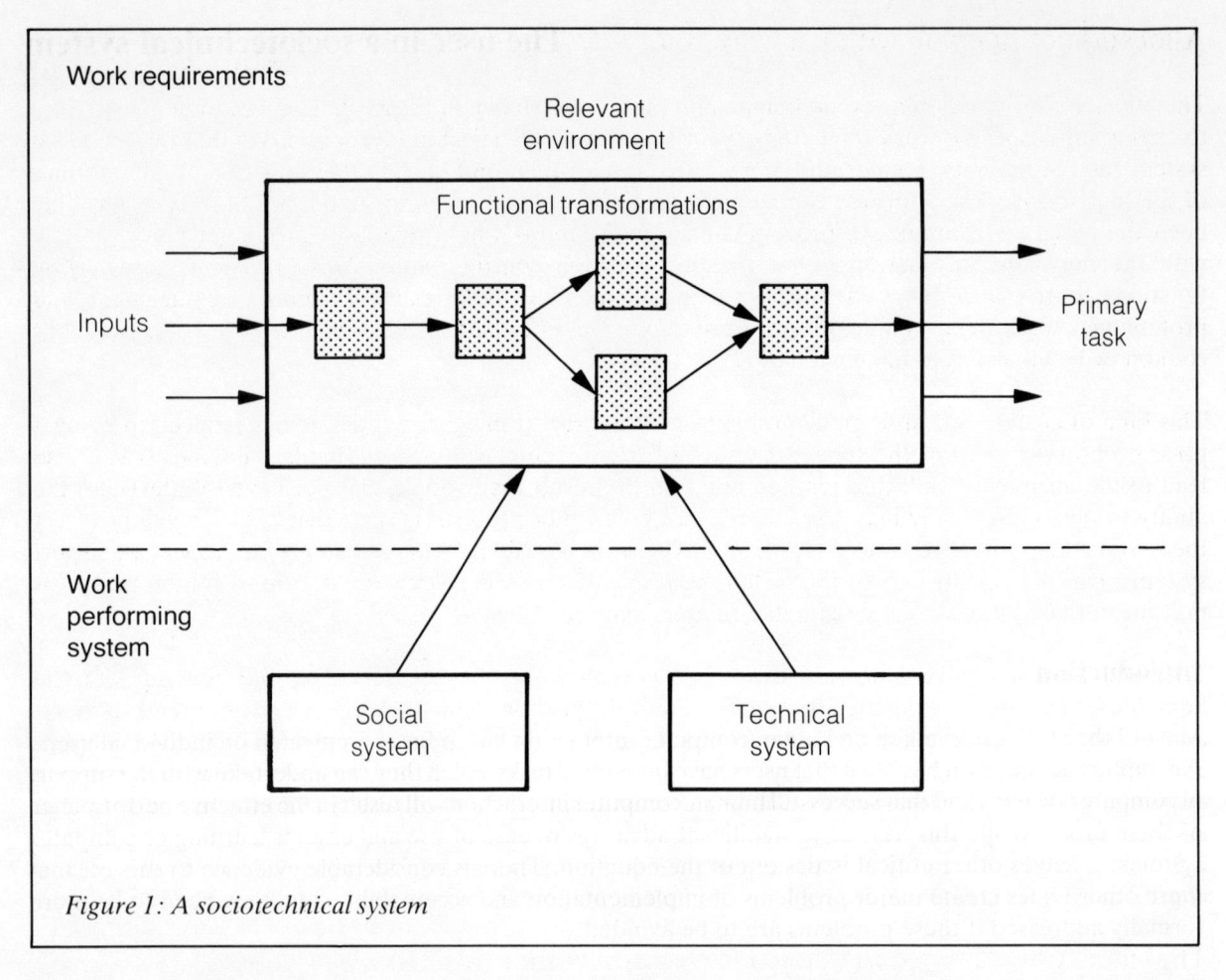

the 'primary' or overall task, for example turning bits of metal into motor cars or 'fresher' students into qualified graduates. An open systems analysis of this type indicates the major subtasks (and their interdependencies) which are necessary to achieve the primary task without specifying how these tasks are, or should be, undertaken. They constitute the task demand characteristics of the enterprise.

The vehicle that meets this task demand is the sociotechnical system which describes the resources which can be brought to bear to do the work. It consists of two kinds of resources. Human resources are organised into a network of work roles in which each person is allocated responsibility for some part of the total work programme. A typical organisational chart is an attempt to portray the structure of the social system, but is usually only a weak representation of a much more complex and changing reality. The second system is the set of technical tools and methods which are used to support work tasks. Some technical systems are a loose collection of separate general-purpose tools, for example telephones, pens, paper, photocopiers, paper clips, etc, which constitute a 'toolbox' for people in work roles to use as necessary in the pursuit of their task goals. Other technical systems are highly integrated, are directed at specific tasks and play a much more direct role in the task performing process, for example an oil refinery, a jet airliner or an assembly line in a factory. It will be apparent that there is a complex mapping of the social and technical system. Sociotechnical systems design has the foundation principle of 'joint optimisation', that is because of the complex interdependencies there is no point in optimising one of these subsystems without considering the implications for the other because, if it causes the other to perform suboptimally, the whole sociotechnical system will perform suboptimally. Evidence from early sociotechnical studies *(EAS5, EAS6)* demonstrates how attempts to optimise technical systems to perform task goals had negative effects upon the social system and caused overall failure. There is ample evidence that the same kind of process is underway with respect to IT systems. The next section will analyse a number of cases in sociotechnical terms before turning to how IT systems may be designed as sociotechnical systems.

IT systems in their social systems context

In order to explore the implications that IT systems can have for social systems, we shall examine four situations that often arise:

Allocation of function within a work role

The allocation of function between human and machine is shown in Figure 2. This situation is restricted to changes in a specific work role. It is often the case that technical innovation means that the technical system can play a much greater and more active role in relation to a task than hitherto; in effect more of the functions to be performed can be passed from the human operator to the machine. This has long been the case, for example, in process control installations where operators no longer work directly with the raw materials but supervise the process from control rooms. This process of transferring functions to the technology is now occurring in many work domains, including management and professional work. The coming of expert systems, for example, means that many decision functions could now be allocated to the technology.

This kind of change can raise many problems for the user. It may be that the user is reduced to being a passive observer most of the time, which is not usually perceived as a desirable outcome. It can also lead to the atrophy of skill through non-use with the result that, should the user have to intervene, the ability to do so effectively may have disappeared. Another problem may be that the user will not trust the system to perform the task effectively. This can be the case particularly with respect to expert systems; can the conclusions of the system be trusted as a basis for making decisions? These problems may mean that systems are unacceptable to users and are rejected.

To avoid these negative outcomes the broader implications for the functions that remain with the human user have to be examined before allocation of function to the technology is determined. It is not a question of allocating as much functionality as possible to the system but of allocating what is appropriate to the effective operation of the sociotechnical system. It may be that the most appropriate outcome is not for the designer to allocate the functionality but, as Singleton *(EAS7)* has suggested, to enable the user to 'delegate' functionality to the system when it is appropriate. Thus a user may control a process directly or hand it over to a system for automatic control for a period. This maintains overall control in the hands of the user.

The impact of a service to one work role on another work role

This situation is illustrated in Figure 3. It is common to examine the impact of a system upon the users who are to receive a service, but it is rare to look at the impact upon people who are not direct users. There are often people who work closely with direct users whose work is dramatically affected. A case in point occurred in a hospital study reported by Eason *et al (EAS8)*. Hospital doctors were given a system whereby they could make block bookings of tests to be undertaken on patients instead of writing a separate 'prescription' for each test. The result was that very soon the staff of the laboratories of the hospital were overloaded because each doctor ordered many more tests than hitherto. In another case reported by Björn-Anderson *et al (EAS9)* the planning staff of a factory were provided with a planning aid which made it possible to schedule factory production in great detail. The result was that the works manager of the factory found he had very little to manage. In both of these cases, and many more, the technical system introduced extra tensions within the social system which prevented optimal sociotechnical performance. Some support for the users in the uninvolved work role had to be provided to help them perform their legitimate work before the system was fully accepted and effectively harnessed.

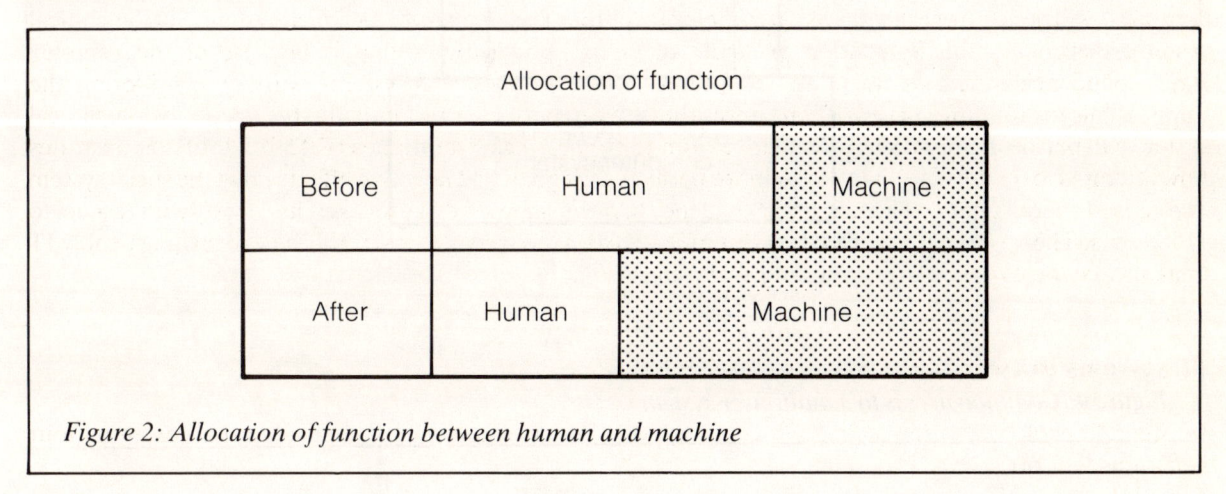

Figure 2: Allocation of function between human and machine

Figure 3: Impact from one role to another

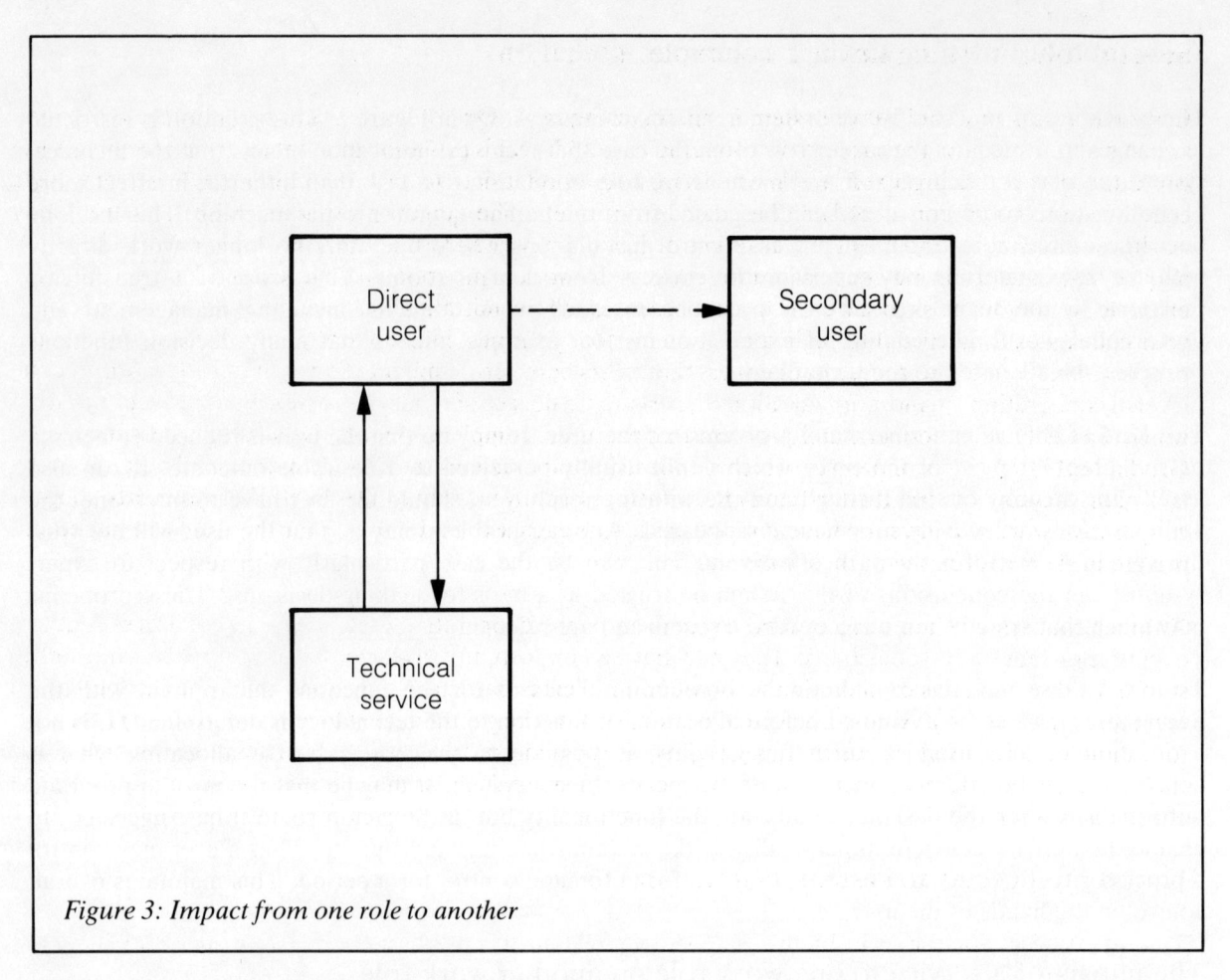

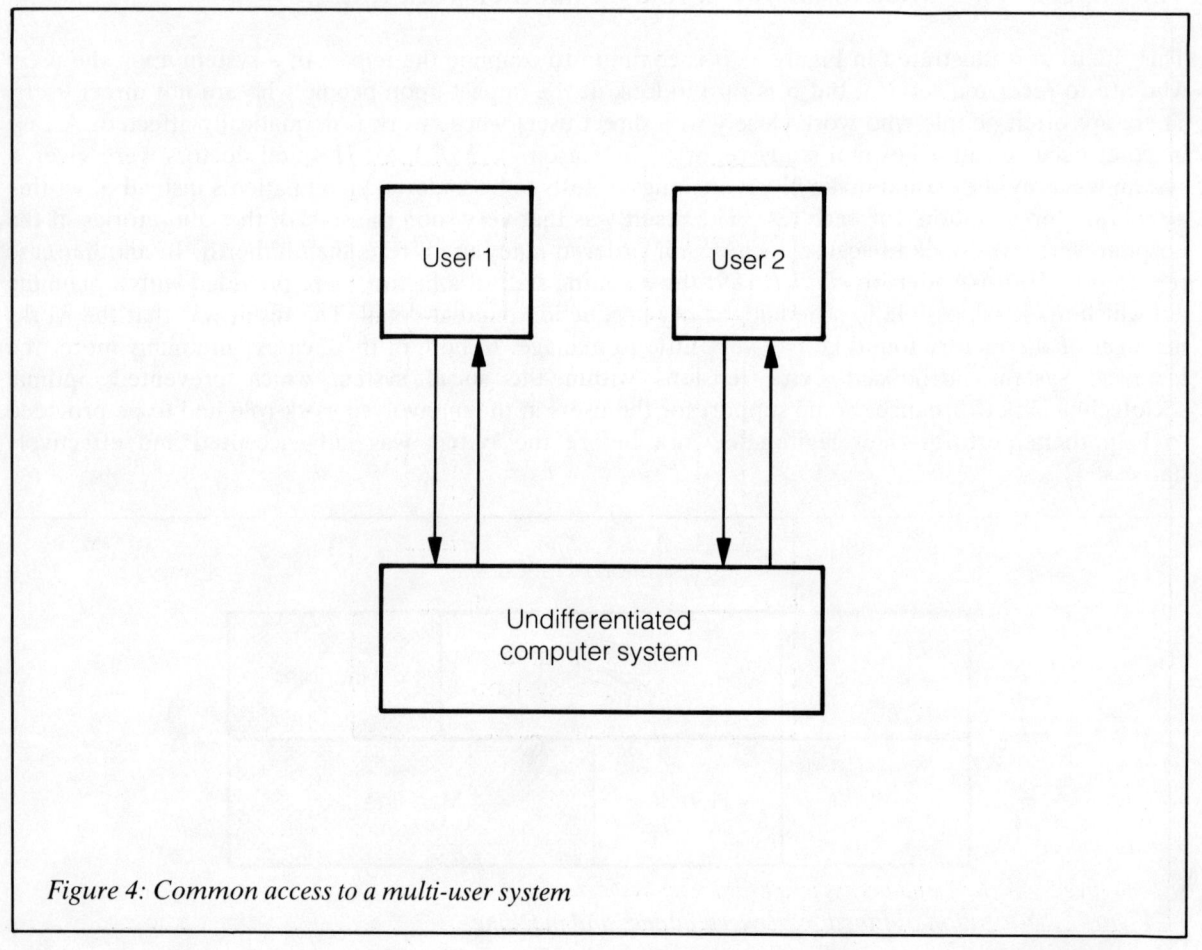

Figure 4: Common access to a multi-user system

Several roles working through computer mediation

Common access to a multi-user system is shown in Figure 4. One of the major targets for the integrated systems of tomorrow is the support of 'cooperative work', that is provision of a system which facilitates the working together of a group of people who share a common task objective. In this case each user may have equal access to a common set of functions, data, services, etc. The danger with this approach is that users may not have similar roles and may have different degrees of power and influence over one another. The result may be that some users may be hesitant to reveal their 'work in progress' to their fellows. You may not, for example, want your boss to see early drafts because of all the mistakes you have made. You may not want your colleagues (and rivals) to be in a position to steal your best ideas. Work groups function best when people can negotiate the degree of openness that exists between members and can therefore determine the level of cooperation. In most organisations there is also a degree of rivalry and assessment in every situation which can easily block cooperation. A system that presumes complete openness is unlikely to be widely used. Grudin *(EAS10)*, for example, reports that collective diary systems tend to be unsuccessful because of the lack of privacy and control it affords over the structure of daily work lives. It is likely that systems to support cooperative work will have to include opportunities for each user to determine the line between public and private in their dealings with their colleagues.

Another concern is when some potential members of the cooperating groups have equal access, but less expertise or sense of responsibility. They may have an opportunity to change existing work to which other staff have devoted considerable time and attention. This is particularly the case when the inexperienced members are senior staff whose access to the system cannot be gainsaid. Gower and Eason *(EAS11)* report, for example, a case in which secretaries using a sophisticated word processing system were very worried that their managers might access the system after work hours and, through ignorance, accidentally erase the entire day's work.

Differential access to system facilities and data

This situation is illustrated in Figure 5. If it is important to recognise the different needs of the work

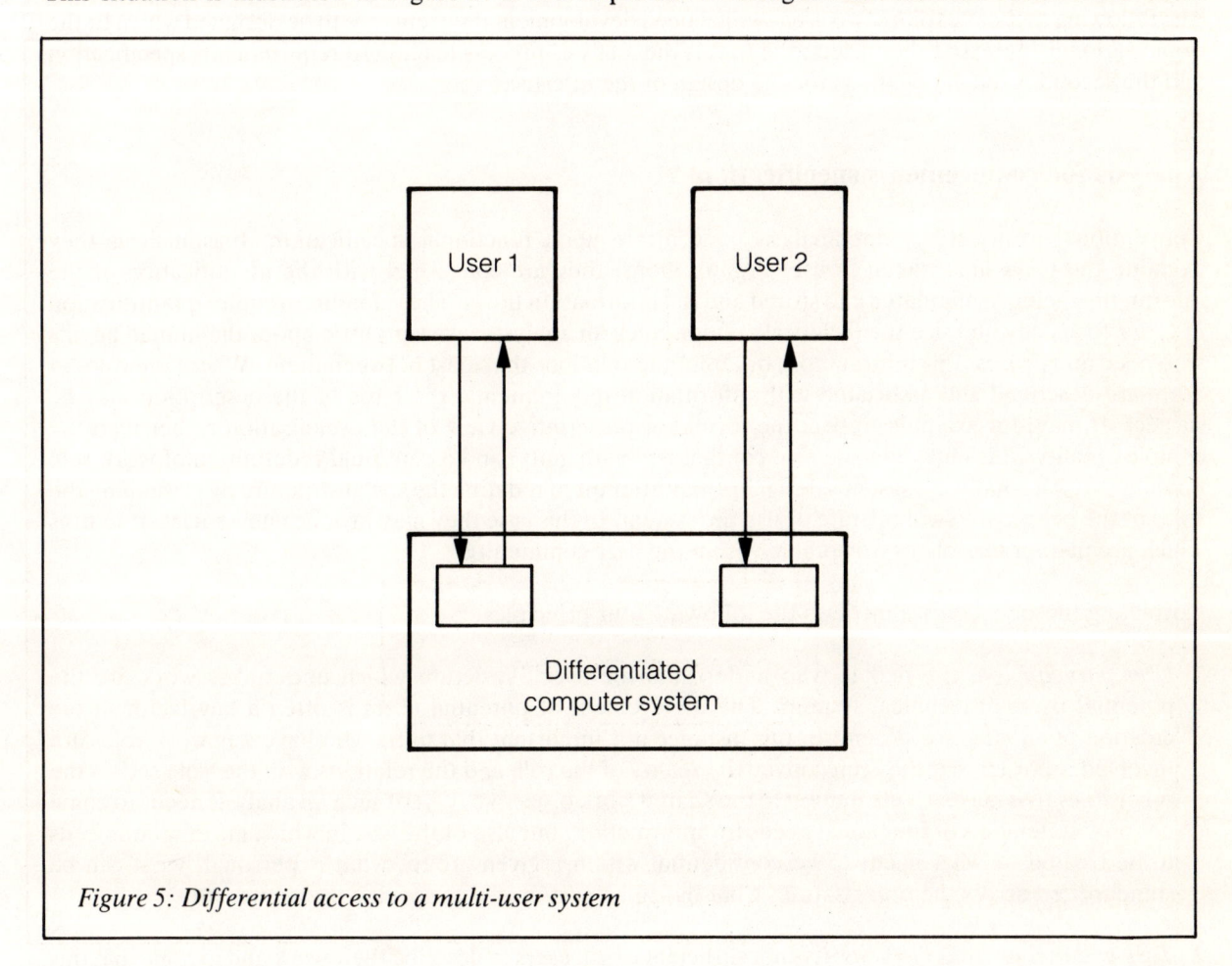

Figure 5: Differential access to a multi-user system

roles in a social system, it may be appropriate to allocate different rights of access to different work roles. Some may therefore be given access to all facilities, while others get only a few. Some may have access to some databases but not others, some may have 'read only' status while others may have 'write' status. If this approach is adopted it is essential that the division reflects the requirements of role holders for the proper execution of their responsibilities. Too often it becomes simply an expression of role stereotypes rather than reality or, worse, a new kind of status symbol to signal the power structure of the organisation. Hannigan and Kerswell (EAS12), for example, report the implementation of digital PABX telephone exchanges where users could be provided with up to 25 facilities for setting up, storing, diverting calls, etc. Differential access could be provided. In most organisations senior managers were given full access, while other grades received limited access. Since senior managers rarely had time to learn all the facilities, many of them went unused while the main communication managers of the enterprise (for example secretaries) went without facilities they would have learnt and could have used to advantage.

Matching information systems with the social system reality

These four examples of the impact of technical systems upon work roles and their relationships are illustrative rather than exhaustive. There are many more ways in which a mismatch between what the technology provides and what the social system reality necessitates can lead to dysfunctional consequences. It may, for example, lead to non-use or under-utilisation of the system because facilities are in the wrong hands or people fear the consequences of others being able to access the work they have done. It may lead to the unacceptability of the system because it does not support the work role responsibilities of its intended users. It may lead to strife between work roles as those in the best positions use it to extend their influence over their colleagues.

As we develop systems which integrate services for multi-user work structures so it is necessary to pay more explicit attention to the social structures that are to be served if effective support is to be given. These requirements are not well met by current forms of analysis or design.

The following sections explore two areas which need development if systems are to be designed which fit the organisational context of their users; the first is the analysis process leading to requirements specification and the second is the implications for the design of the interface.

Analysis for requirements specification

Conventional forms of systems analysis concentrate upon functional specification. Inasmuch as they examine the tasks undertaken in user organisations, they are concerned with the identification of the information being manipulated and stored and the information flows. These features require quantification in order to specify and size the technical system. Such an analysis says very little about the human agents who need and process this information, or about the relations that exist between them. Where the roles of users are described and associated with information requirements, the basis of the description may be suspect. It may, for example, reflect the formal or prescriptive view of the organisation rather than the complex reality which may include role conflict and ambiguity, and a continual redefinition of work role boundaries. Alternatively, systems designers may attempt to redefine the social structure by presuming the roles of the people who will operate or use the system. In this case they may produce new social structures which are neither feasible or acceptable within the user community.

Correcting these tendencies involves the following four principles:

1 *User participation:* the people who understand the social structure which undertakes work are the potential users of technical systems. The involvement of potential users is often a key factor in the creation of an effective system. In this instance it is important that users who have key work roles are involved, in order that they can convey the reality of the role and the relations with the 'role set' — the other roles that make a contribution to the shared work objective. Out of such an analysis needs to come not only statements of functional needs for information, but also of the way in which information needs to be treated — what needs to be confidential within a given group, what is personal, what can be standardised across the organisation, what has to be customised to specific users, etc.

2 *Task and user analysis methods:* it is not sufficient to ask users to describe their work and to hope that this

will yield an agreed set of requirements. The process has to be supported by formal methods of analysis which will help users to describe the critical features of their work. Several methods exist which attempt to go beyond functional and quantified analysis to describe more of the organisational reality. Checkland's 'soft systems' methodology *(EAS13)*, for example, offers a step-by-step procedure for capturing a 'rich picture' of the organisation which is qualitative rather than quantitative. The sociotechnical analysis tradition is embodied in Pava's method *(EAS3)* and in the ETHICS methodology *(EAS14)*. In these methods explicit attention is given to the social systems in organisations and to the values, beliefs, satisfaction and stresses of the work role holders within the social systems.

These methods are useful for developing a broad view of the organisation, but do not provide formalised support when it is necessary to specify in detail the form and content of the information service to support each work role. It is our view that as systems development proceeds there is a need to work from a coarse-grained analysis to progressively finer levels of detail. It is necessary to do this with respect to functional requirements and to the 'non-functional' requirements that support the work, for example confidentiality, non-monitoring, autonomy, control, etc. Eason and Harker *(EAS15)* have developed the Open Systems Task Analysis (OSTA) method as a means of carrying sociotechnical principles into the analysis of the information requirements associated with a specific work role. Eason *et al (EAS16)* provide a case example of the conduct of a task analysis which starts at the broad level and proceeds to the fine level needed for interface specification. Throughout this analysis process the role responsibilities and needs of the user are sustained so that the requirements of managing the boundaries between the roles are a major aspect of the representation.

3 *The principle of minimum critical specification:* an important principle in sociotechnical systems theory is that as much autonomy as possible is left to the point where the work is undertaken. This maximises flexibility in the organisation and provides the autonomy and control which is so important in job satisfaction. The implication of this principle for the design of IT systems is that designers should avoid making judgements about the exact form and content of the service to be delivered to specific work roles. Rather they should concentrate upon the provision of a set of information handling tools relevant to the general character of the role.

In a survey of current design practice, Harker *et al (EAS18)* demonstrate that the form which a system takes on the end user's desk is often the product of several design processes. A generic systems design process may have produced the relatively general-purpose hardware and software that bespoke application builders use to develop a system for a specific organisational setting. It is the bespoke application builders who most obviously need the forms of task and user analysis described above. However, it would be wrong for generic design teams to ignore the character of the work roles their products are designed to serve. In order that the principle of minimum critical specification can be upheld, the products must contain sufficient flexibility in relevant parameters to permit later customisation to specific needs. This may mean, for example, that a report generator is needed to enable information to be combined and presented in many different ways. It may also mean that the system needs a built-in flexible security system which enables application designers to tailor access to support each work role.

Application designers also need to operate to the minimum critical specification principle in order that individual users or groups of users can adjust systems to suit their particular requirements, and can modify systems locally to suit changing needs. It only needs, for example, the local manager to decide that he wishes to reallocate responsibilities amongst his staff for the existing distribution of access for 'read' and 'write' rules to be outdated. A flexible means of adjusting these rules is necessary if the system is not to become unusable or a source of inertia which inhibits organisational change.

4 *Organisation design:* IT often provides organisations with the opportunity to countenance new forms of organisation which enhance their business opportunities. The design of the technical system is not therefore an exercise in making explicit the detailed role relations that currently exist, and then matching the technical system to the structure. Such an approach would lead to ossification. It is important therefore that user participation extends beyond description to include debates about the alternative organisational forms which the new technology may render feasible. The issues of which allocation of function between human and machine, and which allocation of duties between work roles, is desirable, is clearly a set of topics of considerable importance to potential users. The role of

prototype systems in specifying systems is becoming increasingly apparent. The use of a prototype in helping users to simulate and evaluate the different role structures they might adopt is one important avenue yet to be explored.

Sociotechnical implications for the interface

The development of interfaces that are easy to use and easy to learn has made rapid strides in recent years. However, these interfaces are primarily designed as though the world were organised into a series of discrete human/computer connections. What are the implications for the interface of recognising that the user is in various kinds of cooperative and conflicting relations with other users who may also have access to the same computer system? The following list of properties for the interface is a first attempt to specify what is required to cope with this situation.

1 *Easy-to-use security systems:* many easy-to-use systems are rendered unusable by the need to remember passwords and manage complex procedures which are designed to prevent unauthorised access. They often have the effect of discouraging authorised users. We need to help the system to recognise its user and the extent of the user's authorisation without burdening the user. Amongst other approaches the concept of the system holding a user model, which maps the rights and obligations of the user's work role, may be one avenue to explore.

2 *Authenticating messages to others:* most human systems by which people cooperate depend upon methods by which the receiver can be assured that the message is authentic. It may bear a signature, may be in familiar handwriting or the voice may be distinctive. How can the equivalent of a signature be conveyed electronically?

3 *Providing private to public gateways:* to support their own autonomy and their need to communicate easily with colleagues, users need the opportunity to transfer information from private files to semipublic or public messaging systems and files. They may also wish to move information in the other direction. Users may wish for these transactions to be easily accomplished but, at the same time, may require them to be secure so that unauthorised access to the private from the public is not possible. The public highways may need to be standardised, while users may like private sectors to be freely organised to suit their own purposes. Can this be accomplished while sustaining ease of exchange?

4 *The delegation of function:* as systems become more 'intelligent' they may be able to take on more information management tasks for users — for example they may be able to filter incoming messages to remove 'junk' mail, delete old files, do the housekeeping to keep files in an orderly fashion, automatically circulate certain classes of information to others, etc. A user model built into a system could develop these capabilities. It would be necessary, however, for the user to retain control so that any of these functions could revert to manual or the automatic functions be reset. All of these activities need to be easily undertaken by the non-specialist user if they are to be successful.

5 *Controlling access according to expertise:* it may be expected that most access rules will be based upon the right to know of the work role in question. This may, however, give access to people who do not understand how a system is structured and who may, in their ignorance, do considerable damage. Another criterion for access may therefore be the expertise of the user. This would once again require a user model on the part of the system. Since this procedure could debar senior people from a system they have purchased, this criterion would have to be carefully handled. It should not, for example, prevent access but should not make available those facilities which could damage the integrity of the system.

6 *Modifying rules of access, 'read' and 'write':* social structures are not static and it must therefore be possible to continually revise the authorisation parameters of the system. This may be a question of individual users making available the work they have completed, or it may be a broader question of enabling new people access to facilities and files. The interface must have a mode which shows the current status of security arrangements and permits the modification of these arrangements. Defining who has access to this mode is likely to be a critical local issue and protecting it from unauthorised entry is an important technical design issue.

Conclusions

The recognition that users operate within a sociotechnical context promises to be a major new point of departure in the development of IT systems. It provides many new opportunities for systems to support complex cooperative work amongst, for example, people who are geographically distant from one another. As this paper has pointed out, however, the current methods of analysis and design are not well geared to the additional complexity caused by the sociotechnical context. The methods of analysis are beginning to emerge, but are not fully developed as methods of representing user requirements in a form which would make explicit the needs of each work role. The list of interface issues with which the paper ends is not exhaustive and is no doubt a simplistic representation of the mapping of social relations inside the technical system. Nevertheless, it is sufficient to indicate the work that needs to be done before interfaces are easy to use — to support people who wish to cooperate and protect those who do not.

4: Methodologies for designing User/Computer Interfaces (UCIs)

A Gardner

HUSAT Research Centre
University of Technology
Loughborough
Leicestershire
UK

This paper discusses the essential requirements of a methodology for the human factors design of User/Computer Interfaces (UCIs) and concludes that it would have to give advice on human factors methods and attributes and also on management processes for controlling the design. Currently available sources of advice are reviewed and described against these criteria. The distinctions between human factors-oriented methodologies and the computer-oriented methodologies are highlighted.

© A Gardner 1988

A Gardner
Arthur Gardner graduated in 1964 with a BSc in Psychology from Hull University and in 1972 took the MPhil in Occupational Psychology at Birkbeck College, London. He is an Associate Fellow of the British Psychological Society, a Member of the Division of Occupational Psychology and serves on the Postgraduate Admissions Committee. Since 1964 he has worked, mainly, on system design and training for the UK Ministry of Defence. In 1983 he was seconded to HUSAT Research Centre to lead a team producing a new handbook in human factors in system design — initially for the Ministry of Defence and, later, for the Department of Trade and Industry. In 1988 he resigned from the Civil Service and joined The HCI Service, based at HUSAT, as a Principal Consultant.

Methodologies for designing User/Computer Interfaces (UCIs)

Introduction

The author has recently been involved in the production of a new handbook for the UK Department of Trade and Industry (DTI) and the Ministry of Defence (MoD (PE))*. The new handbook 'Human factors guidelines for the design of computer-based systems' *(GAR1)* — HF Guidelines for short — gives advice on incorporating human factors into all stages of the system life-cycle. This paper draws upon the lessons learned during the writing of the new handbook. It describes the 'state of the art' in human factors methodologies for the design of interfaces. The Invited Paper in this Report by McKenzie *(GAR2)* gives specific advice for User/Computer Interfaces (UCIs).

Methodologies for human factors

Definition of methodology

The definition of the term 'methodology' is a source of confusion — a 'methodology' for one person is a 'method' for another, a 'technique' for a third, a 'tool' for a fourth, and so on. The differences are a matter of breadth or narrowness of focus. An entirely different view is given by those who reserve the term to mean 'the study of methods in a particular subject'.

To avoid further confusion, this paper adopts the definition used in the STARTS Guide *(GAR3)*:

> ... *A methodology not only includes technical methods to assist in the critical tasks of problem solving, documentation, analysis, design ... (etc) ... but also includes management procedures to control the development process, and the deployment of the technical methods.*

The STARTS Guide is concerned with software engineering in large, real-time systems. Such systems are notoriously complex and costly and benefit from a formalised approach to their specification and design — hence the emphasis that the STARTS Guide gives to both technical methods and management procedures. Sound technical methods are essential, but these have to be integrated into a coherent management plan if they are to be effective.

Figure 1 tries to capture this dual interest by showing message and material flows between two parallel sets of processes — management processes of plan, monitor and control; and practitioner processes of analyse, design, document, etc. Applying this way of thinking to the design of interfaces leads to a search for advice on both management and practitioner processes.

---

*The views expressed in this paper are those of the author and do not necessarily represent those of the DTI, the MoD(PE) or Loughborough University of Technology.

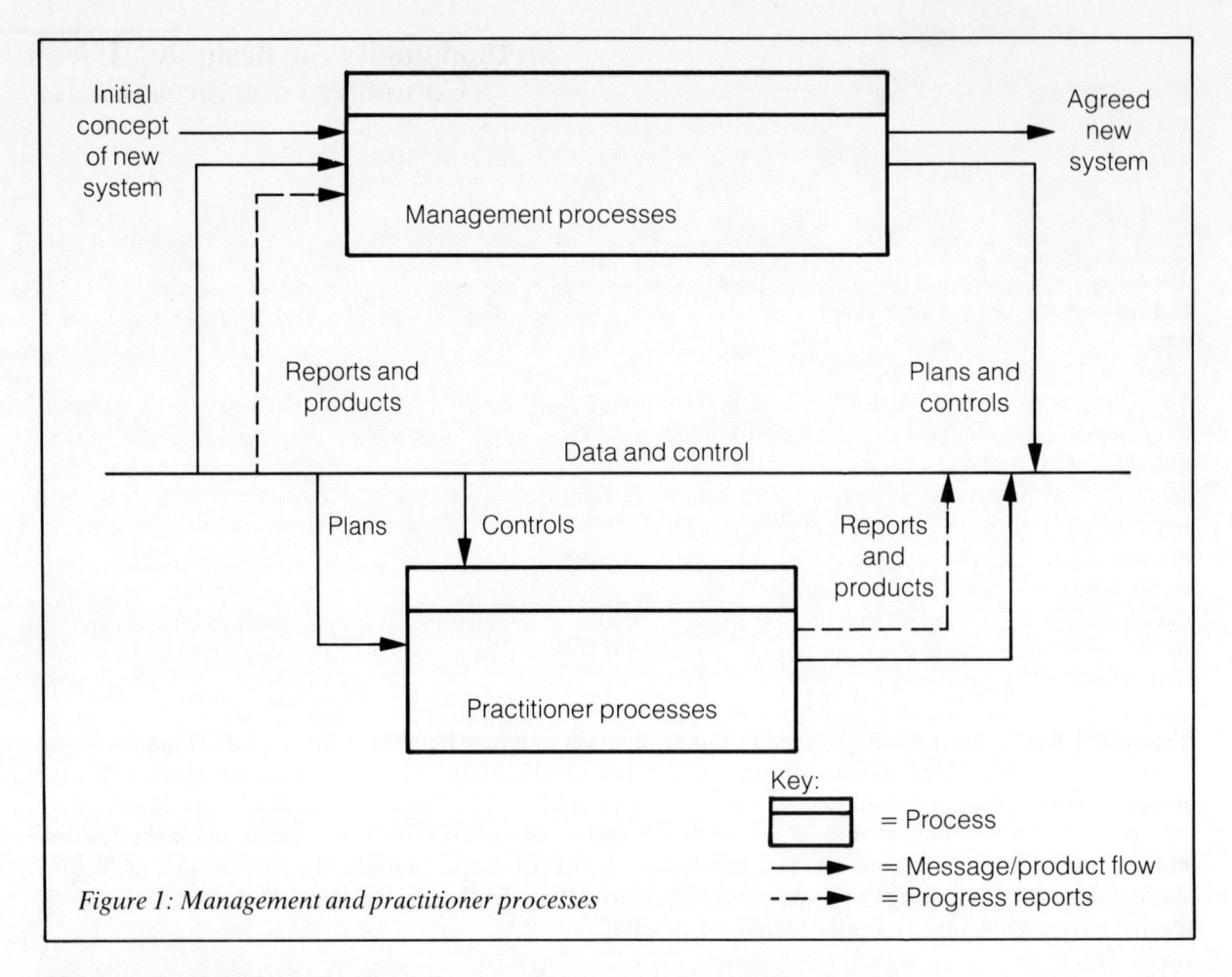

Figure 1: Management and practitioner processes

Key:
☐ = Process
⟶ = Message/product flow
--⟶ = Progress reports

Human factors practitioners

An extensive review of recent handbooks on interface design, carried out during the course of producing the HF Guidelines, showed that there were many excellent sources of advice on methods and data relevant to human factors practitioners *(GAR4-GAR12)*. All of these books are worth reading, but each has its own focus of attention and range of convenience of use.

Two issues, in particular, need to be considered:

1 *Who are they aimed at?* Most handbooks are written for specialists in human factors (for example people with a training in psychology, ergonomics or human engineering). By analogy with the medical profession, these deep specialists are 'consultants' of human factors. In contrast, most of the decision making in design teams will be made by people without this deep specialisation.

   In the opinion of the author, many of the most valuable sources of human factors advice for the 'consultant' are too technical for the non-specialist with a background in physical sciences, programming or engineering. By analogy, what is needed is a set of methods suited to the 'general practitioner of human factors'. The conclusion is that equipping the general practitioner is the priority target for handbooks and training courses.

2 *Integrated methods?* Most handbooks exist in a design vacuum — they do not concern themselves with what precedes the detailed design of an interface (for example task analysis and task allocation) or with what might follow the design of an interface (for example the design of user tasks, jobs, work organisations or the problems of user training, system installation and in-use support). Also, most describe 'facts' to be taken into account (for example anthropometrics of user populations) rather than methods of how to use such facts. In general, they describe attributes rather than procedures. *(GAR12)* is a notable recent exception in that it tries to show the flow of decisions throughout the whole system life-cycle and to give a mass of factual details. Unfortunately, each chapter is written by a different author using different concepts and terminology so it is impossible to trace the flow of ideas from one chapter to the next. Because their methods are not integrated these otherwise excellent

books cannot be offered to general practitioners as a *methodology*. Experienced consultants in human factors may have an internalised overview of the various methods and how they can be integrated, but general practitioners do not. The conclusion is that the integrating overview needs to be made explicit and integrated with the procedures and attributes.

Management of human factors

To elaborate on the last point, it is not enough to integrate the various human factors methods in a technical sense — they must be integrated, too, with the methods used to manage the project as a whole.

To give an example, an early draft of the HF Guidelines described a set of human factors methods in which great care had been taken to integrate the methods technically by using common terminology, by providing an extensive index and by providing cross-referencing in the text. This was sent out to many general practitioners and consultants for use and comment. The most telling reaction was from people with responsibility for project management. They understood what was on offer and saw the potential value of the human factors methods. What they could not see was when to use these methods and how to fit them in with the other 'factors' (for example programming and Quality Assurance (QA)) that they were more used to managing. The conclusion is that management plans for incorporating human factors into system design need to be made explicit.

Figures 2-4 try to make clear the management plans for human factors in the design of interfaces. They are described below.

System life-cycle

Figure 2 shows the major stages in the system life-cycle (project initiation, requirements specification, etc) as practitioner processes. The third stage 'Full development and build' is the stage at which the detailed interfaces are designed. This makes it clear that there are practitioner activities to be scheduled prior to and after 'Full development and build'. The design of the total system involves a lot more than just the design of the UCIs.

Human factors plans

Figure 3 looks specifically at one activity within 'Full development and build' — a practitioner process dealing with the detailed design of the UCIs (taken from the HF Guidelines). It shows that there are two component activities — the first identifies the logical need for a UCI and the second specifies how this is to be implemented in terms of a UCI protocol. These two steps are explained below. The point to be made, here, is that Figure 3 is, in summary, a management plan for incorporating human factors into the design of the interfaces. It says that these are the processes which the human factors practitioners are to follow, these are the inputs they must have available to them and these are the outputs they will make. As such it is a declaration:
- To management of what ought to be done
- To the practitioners of what management expects them to do.

In both cases, explicitly declaring such plans allows them to be considered and, if necessary, amended to meet project requirements. As far as the author knows, no other general-purpose handbook does this as thoroughly as the HF Guidelines. (Impressive examples for specific projects can be found in *(GAR13)* for the computerisation of the DHSS and in *(GAR14, GAR15)* for the US Federal Aviation Authority.)

Human factors Quality Assurance (QA)

What managers and practitioners need, also, is guidance as to how the activities specified in the plans are to be checked for the purposes of QA (see *(GAR16)* for a definition of terms). Figure 4 is an example from the HF Guidelines. Three sets of questions are asked dealing respectively with:
- The quality of the project plan
- The quality of the progress
- The quality of the final output.

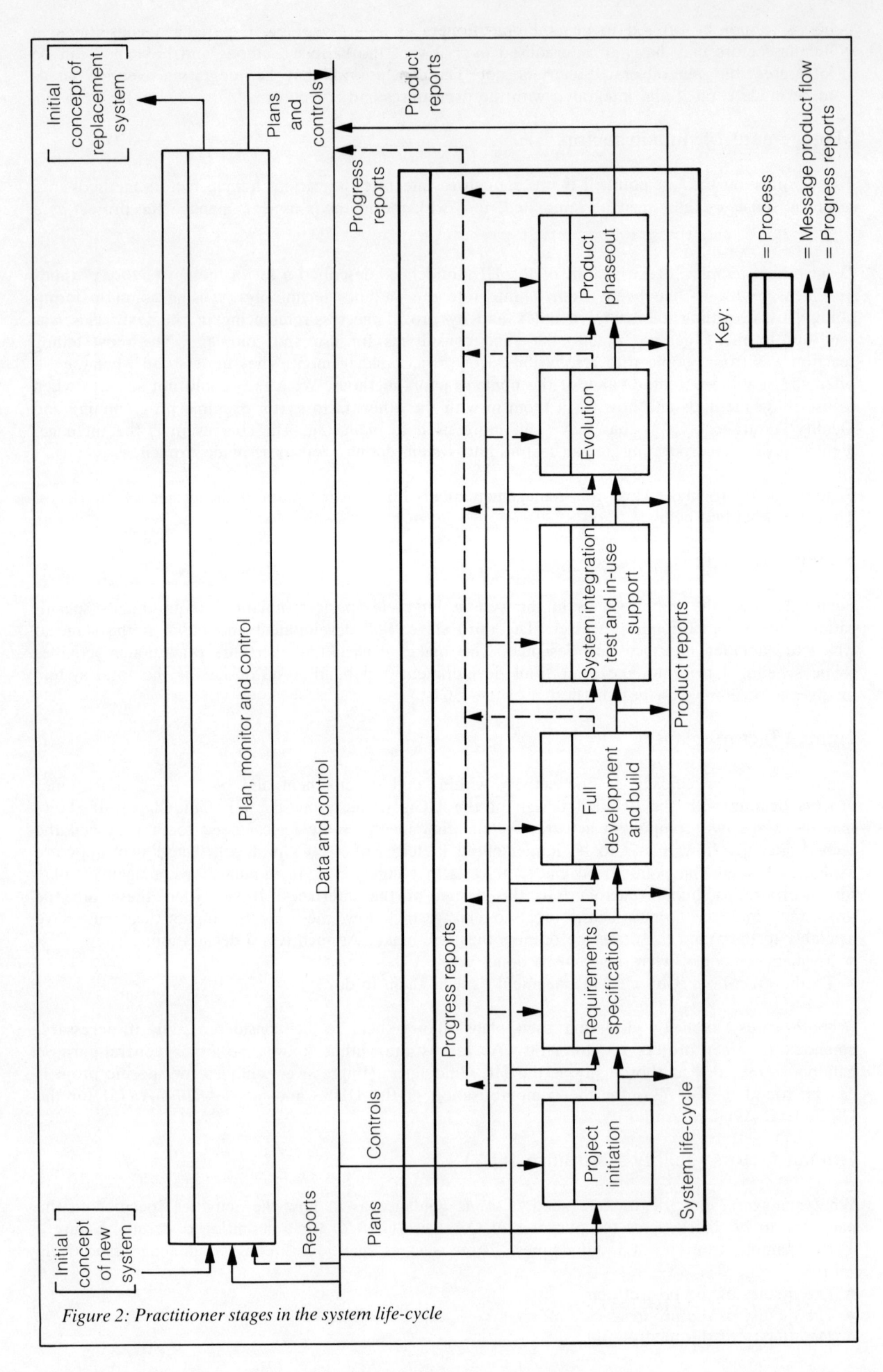

Figure 2: Practitioner stages in the system life-cycle

Figure 3: Human factors in the design of UCIs

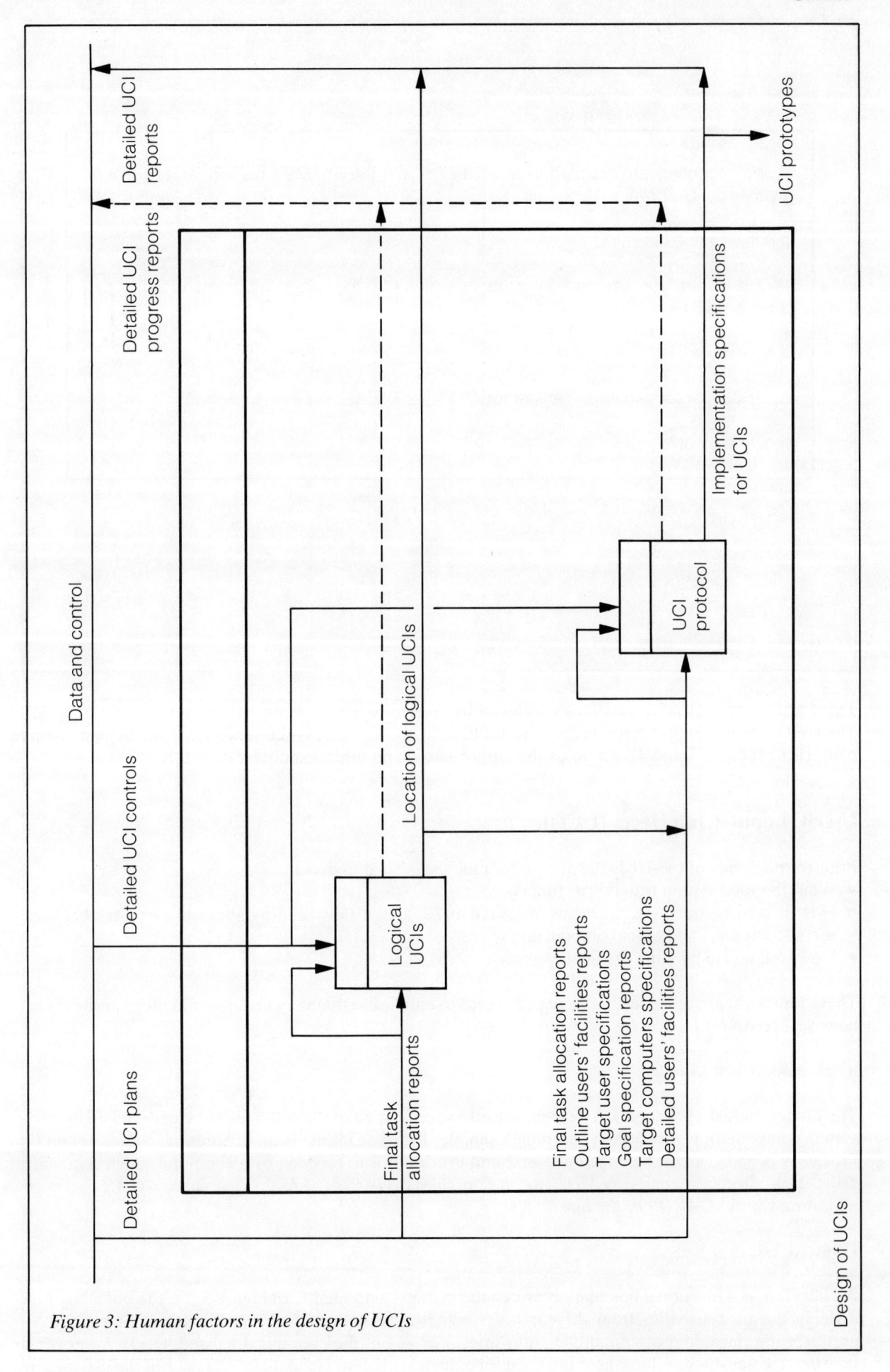

> 'Is the proposed project plan in accordance with the <relevant human factors plan(s)> given in the Guidelines?'
>
> 'If not, why not?'
>
> 'Is the contractor carrying-out <the activities> in the ways recommended in the Guidelines?'
>
> 'If not, why not?'
>
> Is the Contractor's <output> satisfactory?'
>
> 'If not, why not?'

Figure 4: General-purpose QA questions

These are general-purpose questions which can be applied to any stage or activity at any grain of detail. The HF Guidelines supply a comprehensive list of such questions cross-referenced into the human factors plans (for example Figure 3). As far as the author knows, no other handbook does this.

User/Computer Interfaces (UCIs)

Prior to the design of the UCIs the analyst and the users need to decide:
- What the total system is to do (its functions)
- How it is to be done (its processes, message and material flows and its allocation of tasks between users, computers and other components)
- How well it is to be done (its quality goals).

These topics are not discussed in this paper except to emphasise that they are essential prerequisites (see, however, *(GAR1)*).

Task allocation charts

The process of task allocation will have produced a specification of the activities to be undertaken by each system component. Figure 5 shows a simple example: Process D is made up of Subprocesses A, B and C; Processes A and C are to be done by User 1 and Process B is to be done by a computer. Such charts are called task allocation charts *(GAR1)*, jobstream charts *(GAR13)*, job process charts *(GAR17)*, work allocation charts *(GAR18)* or the like.

Logical UCIs

An interface is a functional boundary between the system components. In Figure 5 it is the boundary line dividing the user activities from the computer activities. (Other logical interfaces may be needed — user/user interfaces and computer/computer interfaces — but they are not discussed here.) Wherever a flow line crosses this interface there is a need for a 'logical UCI' to facilitate the transfer of the message or

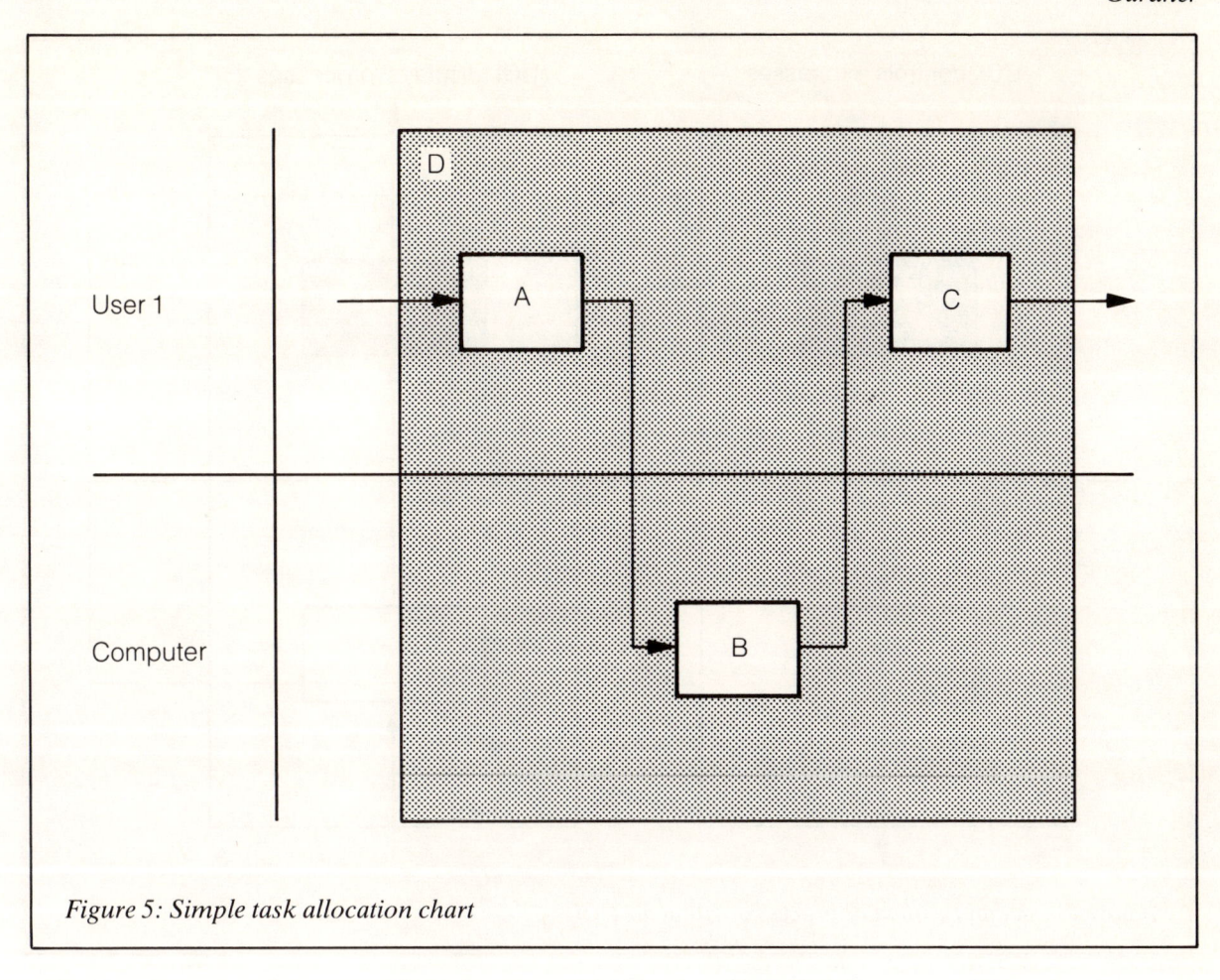

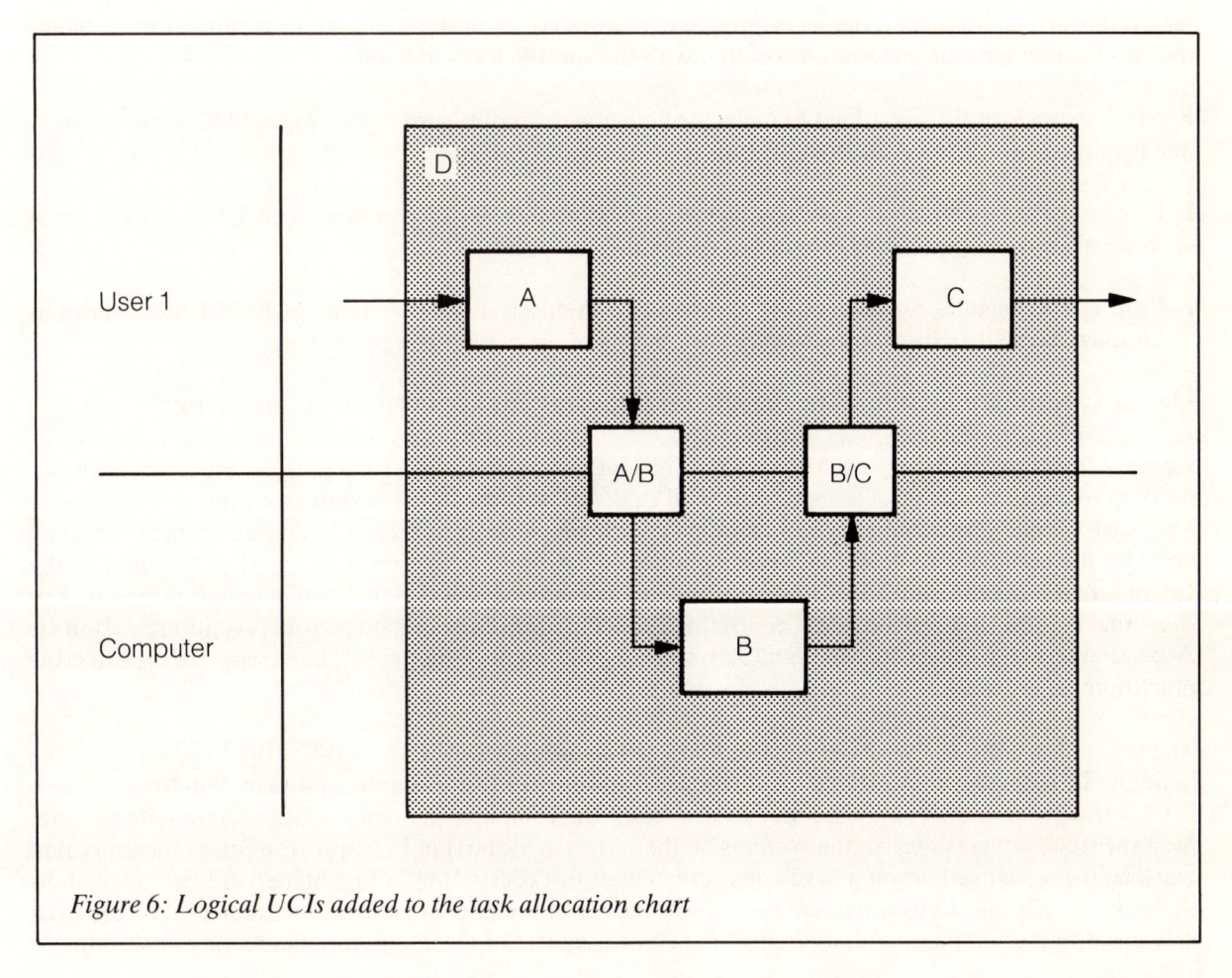

Figure 5: Simple task allocation chart

Figure 6: Logical UCIs added to the task allocation chart

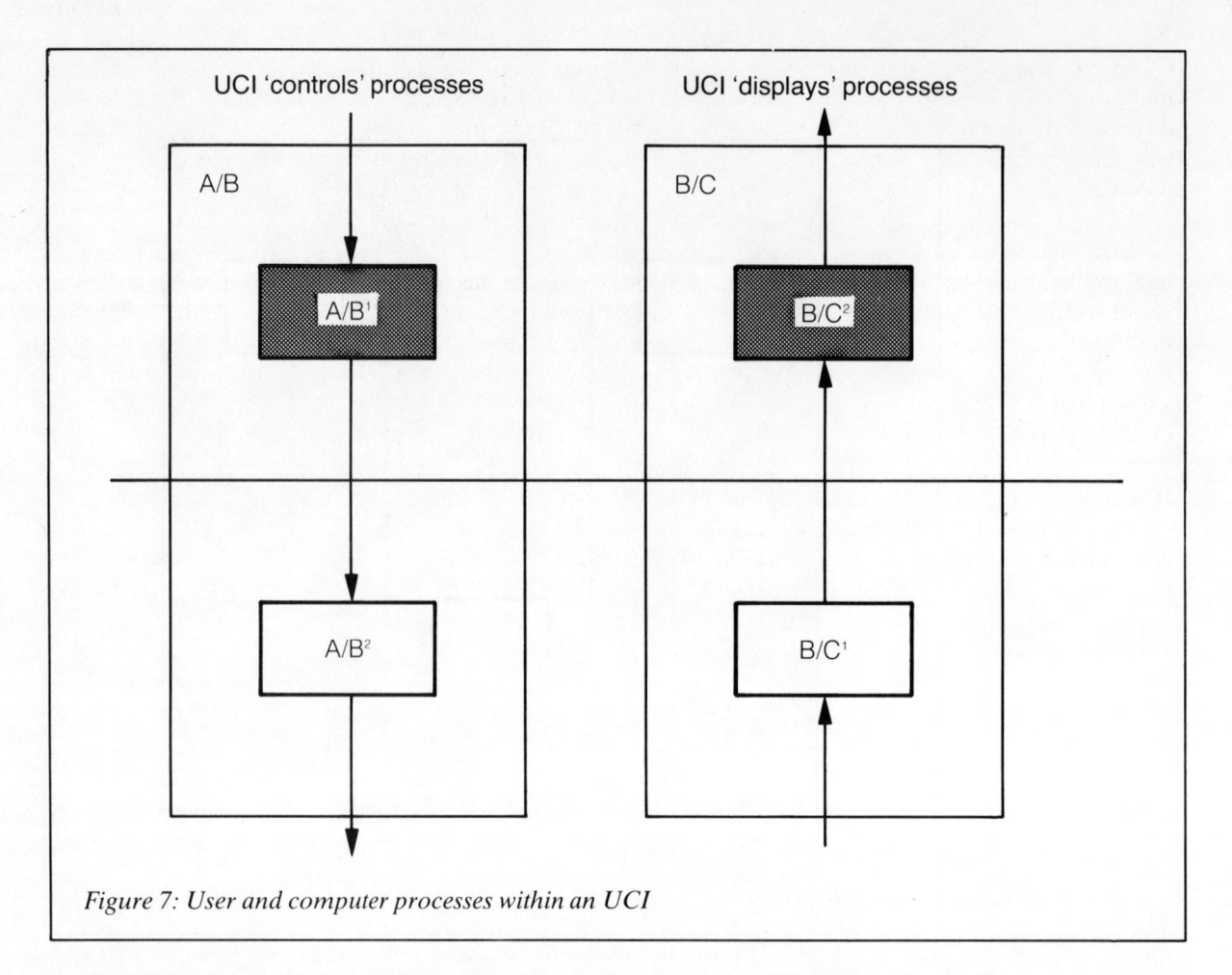

Figure 7: User and computer processes within an UCI

material. Each logical UCI is the set of processes required to allow the user and the computer to exchange the specific messages or materials associated with the specific tasks in hand.

Figure 6 shows logical UCIs added to the task allocation chart of Figure 5. Two logical UCIs are shown — one for each of the flows A to B and B to C:

1 Process A/B handles flows from the user to the computer. By convention, such UCIs are known as 'controls' since they enable the user to control the computer.

2 Process B/C handles flows from the computer to the user. By convention, such UCIs are known as 'displays' since they display to the user the outputs of the computer's processing.

Demarcation between human factors engineering and computer engineering

Figure 7 looks inside Processes A/B and B/C of Figure 6. The logical UCI A/B, in Figure 7, is shown decomposed into two subprocesses — A/B^1 and A/B^2. A/B^1 is the processing done by the user to achieve a physical output to the computer (for example muscle movements to press a key). A/B^2 is the processing done by the computer to detect the user's physical output and transform it into a physical input to the computer (for example an ASCII code for the key pressed). Process A/B^1 is highlighted in Figure 7 to show that it is the user functions which are the subject matter of the human factors practitioners. Process A/B^2 is internal to the computer and, as such, is the subject matter of the computer engineering practitioners.

The logical UCI B/C is shown decomposed into two subprocesses B/C^1 and B/C^2. B/C^1 is the processing done by the computer to achieve a physical output to the user (for example a bit map data for a screen). B/C^2 is the processing done by the user to transform the computer-generated displays into a meaningful message (for example perceive the symbols on the screen as a chart) or to extract the computer-generated material (for example tear off a hard-copy screen dump). Process B/C^2 is highlighted in Figure 7 to show that it is the user functions which are the subject matter of the human factors practitioners. Process B/C^1 is internal to the computer and, as such, is the subject matter of the computer engineering practitioners.

Of course, the demarcation being made here is between 'roles' — a general practitioner of human factors may be, also, a consultant in programming in which case the same person may undertake both roles. The distinction is useful, however, since the sources of advice on these aspects tend to be written by people with an emphasis on one or the other — indeed it would be a remarkable person who was equally expert in both!

This distinction between human factors and computing (the 'bits above the line' and the 'bits below the line' in Figure 7) lies at the heart of much of the confusion in this area. Ask a typical computer engineer about suitable methodologies for design and the answer will tend to be in terms of computer-oriented methodologies such as Structured Systems Analysis and Design Methodology (SSADM), Jackson and Controlled Requirements Expression (CORE) *(GAR3)*. Ask a typical human factors engineer and the answer will tend to be in terms of user-oriented methodologies such as those described in the HF Guidelines *(GAR1)*.

It is easy to think of these differently oriented methodologies as being in competition but they are not — they are complementary. The human factors methodologies address issues which are outside the range of convenience of use of the computer methodologies and vice versa. The task allocation chart is the point in the design process where they come together.

UCI protocol

A 'protocol' is a set of rules or conventions which prescribe how something is to be done. In the context of computer-based systems the term is used most often in the sense of a communications protocol (that is a set of rules defining how one system component is to communicate with another). This is the sense used in this paper.

Open Systems Interconnection (OSI)

The best known recent communications protocol is that produced by the International Standards Organisation (ISO) (ISO 7498) for 'Open Systems Interconnection (OSI)' *(GAR19)*. The OSI protocol deals with the standards for computer/computer communications and, as such, is not directly relevant to human factors practitioners. Nevertheless, the OSI protocol has properties which have influenced thinking about protocols for user/computer communication and these are worth noting:

1. The OSI protocol is *layered*, by analogy, like an onion — the whole is made up of distinct structures (layers) which are independent but nested.

2. Each layer is *defined* independently of the next inner layer and without explicit reference to it.

3. Each layer is *implemented* by means of the layers below it (in OSI jargon each inner layer provides a set of services for the layer above it).

The OSI layers and explanations of their functional interrelations are listed below *(GAR20)*:

7. The Application Layer (the top layer) supports the application processes, for example by providing a file transfer service.

6. The Presentation Layer resolves the differences between the representations of data used by the end systems.

5. The Session Layer handles the organisation of the dialogue between users. Synchronisation and recovery facilities are provided.

4. The Transport Layer provides an end-to-end service which makes optimum use of the supporting network services to provide the user with the required quality of service.

3. The Network Layer provides for transmission of data between end systems possibly separated by any number of relay systems and data links. The functions of the Network Layer include addressing and routing. The service provided to the end system is independent of the particular technologies used in the intermediate elements.

	Name	Exchanged units of information	
7	Goal	Real-world concepts	External to the computer system
6	Task	System concepts	What kind of objects are in the system, and what can we do with them
5	Sementics	Detailed functionality	Concrete objects in the system and specific operations
4	Syntax	Sentences	Sequences in time and space (1 or 2 dimensional) of the communicated tokens
3	Lexical	Tokens	Smallest information-carrying units, eg words, numbers, icons, screen coordinates
2	Alphabetic	Lexemes	Primitive symbols (hardware dependent), eg letters, colours, lines, phonemes
1	Physical	Physical information	Hard I/O, eg light, sound, movements

Figure 8: Summary of the levels in Nielson's protocol

2 The Data Link Layer is concerned with the reliable transfer of data across a physical link. This involves the provision of error detection and correction etc.

1 The Physical Layer (the bottom layer) deals with the transmission of a bit stream across a physical medium.

It will be seen that the OSI layers are concerned with machine issues rather than user issues. It might be argued that the 'Application' and 'Presentation' layers can be interpreted as referring to user tasks and that these layers can be expanded to act as a user/computer protocol. The counter-argument, in this paper, is that a user/computer protocol will need to take account of issues well outside the intended scope of the OSI protocol. The OSI layers are regarded as inadequate for human factors purposes.

A linguistic model for a UCI

The best known approach to defining a separate UCI protocol has been to emphasise the function of an interface as conveying messages and, hence, to define the interface, mainly in terms of the linguistic properties of the messages (Nielson's protocol) *(GAR21)*. Nielson's protocol is shown in Figure 8. Layers 2-5 are making linguistic distinctions which are missing from the OSI model.

Nielson's protocol (and others quoted by Nielson) identify issues beyond the scope of the OSI protocol and, as such, are an improvement. They suffer, however, in that they over-emphasise the linguistic issues. They make no mention, for example, of the intended routing of the messages, the characteristics of the users or the physical displays and control through which the UCI will be implemented (note that Nielson's 'physical' layer refers to the physical attributes of messages rather than the physical devices which will convey them).

UCI protocol from the HF Guidelines

The HF Guidelines *(GAR1)* take the view that a UCI protocol for human factors should be a user-centred list of features which together make up a detailed human factors implementation specification for an UCI. Such

UCI dynamics

Routing
Control
User guidance
User sensory modality
User action modality
User effector

UCI imagery

Language type
Grammar
Vocabulary
Accent

UCI devices

Displays
Controls

Figure 9: Summary of main features in UCI protocol

a protocol does not describe the internal working of the computer. In accordance with the distinctions made earlier (Figure 7), the UCI protocol deals with the human factors engineering (specifying the 'bits above the line' — what the computer is to be able to receive from or send to the user) rather than with computer engineering (the 'bits below the line' — how the computer is to process messages from the user and reply to the user).

Figure 9 summarises the main features of the UCI protocol. There are three layers dealing with dynamics, imagery (which covers linguistics) and devices. Within these are finer-grain distinctions as shown.

There is no space in this paper to describe the UCI protocol in detail. McKenzie *(GAR2)* gives some further explanation, but for a full account see *(GAR1)*.

Conclusions

The point being made here is to argue that a true methodology for the human factors design of UCIs has to provide advice on task allocations (as in the task allocation charts), on the logical and physical properties of the interfaces (as in the UCI protocol) and on the management of the design process (as in the human factors plans and QA checklists).

The HF Guidelines attempt to do all of these and do so more fully than any other handbook known to the author. This is not to say that the HF Guidelines are complete or perfect — they are not!

The important point is that the direction in which the discipline is heading is towards a more explicit integration of facts and methods to form a true methodology of human factors. How this can be made to integrate with the complementary computer-oriented methodologies to which it inputs and with which it has to work is something that has to be studied further.

Acknowledgement

The author acknowledges the substantial contribution made by Jim McKenzie to this paper.

5: Developments in Human/Computer Interaction (HCI) hardware

M Maguire

HUSAT Research Centre
University of Technology
Loughborough
Leicestershire
UK

This paper considers the ergonomic aspects of current HCI hardware including keyboards, displays, pointing devices, printers, scanners, voice I/O, portable computers and optical storage. The advantages and disadvantages of alternative devices are discussed together with their suitability for various task types. There is also a brief look at hardware developments in the modern integrated office.

© M Maguire 1988

M Maguire
Martin Maguire was trained at Loughborough University in computer science and ergonomics. His PhD thesis, from Leicester Polytechnic, was based upon the design of human/computer dialogues for inexperienced users with an emphasis on public information systems. He then worked in the Computer Laboratory at Leicester developing test programs for the GKS computer graphics standard. He is now at the HUSAT Research Centre working on an ESPRIT project which aims to produce and disseminate human factors tools for software designers.

Developments in Human/Computer Interaction (HCI) hardware

Introduction

Natural communication between human beings (talking, listening, writing, reading, drawing, gesturing, seeing, etc) is very different from the electronic communication that takes place between items of computer equipment. To overcome this fundamental mismatch, there is a diversity of hardware for building high-quality human/computer interfaces. This paper describes the various kinds of hardware available, their current state of development and situations in which they might appropriately be used. The following topics are considered:

1 Computer input:
- Keyboards
- Pointing devices
- Paper-based input
- Voice input
- Other means of input.

2 Computer output:
- Displays
- Voice output
- Hard copy.

3 Portability, storage and integration:
- Portable computers
- Optical storage
- Integrated office equipment.

Computer input

Keyboards

General considerations
Keyboard design is an important factor in user productivity. Compared to their mechanical predecessors, electronic keyboards are not only more reliable and cost effective, they also allow a much wider variation in design. Keys can be better placed in relation to each other resulting in less user hand movement, fewer errors and faster keying. However, certain useful properties have also been retained such as tactile feedback and key 'travel' — particularly important for touch typists who concentrate on the source document rather than the screen. For these reasons, membrane keyboards with a non-moving touch-sensitive surface are unacceptable for touch typing. However, they are durable and therefore effective for public usage such as in information centres, libraries and amusement parks.

Certain keys such as the space bar, ENTER, SHIFT, or CTRL are made larger to allow easy, reliable access, while mode keys such as CAPS LOCK and INSERT or OVERTYPE can be made to physically lock in a lowered position or contain an embedded light to show what position they are in. A further useful feature is that two of the middle row keys (for example D and K) may have a deeper concavity or a small raised dot to reassure users that their fingers are properly placed.

The traditional QWERTY keyboard layout was devised by Christopher Latham Shole in the 1870s. It is said that the placement of letters on his typewriter was intended to slow the user down sufficiently to avoid key jamming. He did this by placing frequently used keys far apart, thereby increasing finger travel distances. In the light of this inefficiency, many alternative layouts were developed. The Dvorak keyboard, for instance, is supposed to allow expert typists to work at speeds of between 150 and 200 words per minute *(MAG1)*. Despite these attempts, QWERTY has increased in popularity and has become the *de facto* standard for computer keyboards. It is now an official International Standards Organisation (ISO) standard.

There is little controversy over the basic dimensions of keyboards and manufacturers now accept the following guidelines *(MAG2)*.

Keyboard height above desk (middle row)	30 mm (max)
Inclination	5-15°
Distance betwen key tops	17-19 mm
Resistance of keys	400-800 mN
Key displacement	3-5 mm

It is also accepted that users prefer detachable keyboards which can be positioned on the work surface as desired.

In order to enforce general ergonomic requirements for VDTs in offices, the British Standards Institution (BSI) has developed a six-part draft standard *(MAG3)*. Part 4 deals with keyboard requirements and defines methods of testing whether a candidate keyboard meets the standard. For instance, in addition to simple error testing, a sample of users who have performed a series of typing tasks will be asked to subjectively assess the acceptability of both the keyboard under test and a 'reference' keyboard (known to conform to the standard).

Split and tilt keyboards
Traditional keyboard design based on parallel rows of keys has for a long time been recognised as less than ideal in terms of user comfort. The hands are held parallel to the keyboard, the wrists and arms rotate and the hands twist in a sideways movement. This often causes physical discomfort and in some cases inflammation of the tendons in the hands and forearms *(MAG2)*. This reaction is an example of a whole class of problems related to repetitive work known as Repetitive Strain Injuries (RSI).

To overcome this awkward posture, Kroemer *(MAG4)* proposed splitting the keyboard into right and left halves and laterally angling them down on either side to allow a more natural hand position (like a handshake as opposed to palm down). His prototype (called the K-keyboard after Klockenburg who criticised the standard keyboard) featured keys arranged in straight columns but curved to fit the different finger lengths on each hand. The space bar was also curved to fit the thumb. Various tests performed on the K-keyboard produced some evidence that users experienced less aches and pains and made less typing errors as a result.

Grandjean followed the same line of research with his STR-keyboard developed for Standard Telephone and Radio. He studied preferred settings of the angle between the two keyboard halves, the distance between the halves, the lateral sloping and use of a forearm/wrist support attached to the front. Typists found the split keyboard acceptable and favoured a lateral tilt of 10° with an angle between the two halves of 25°. The use of the wrist/forearm support was also welcomed and is thought to help improve typing posture. The STR-keyboard won a design award at the Ergodesign conference in 1984.

A more recent design (see Figure 1) has been developed by Ilg *(MAG5)* and his colleagues at the IAO in Stuttgart. This also won an Ergodesign award in 1986 and an IBM AT-compatible version now sells for about £300.

Figure 1: A keyboard designed by Ilg (MAG5)

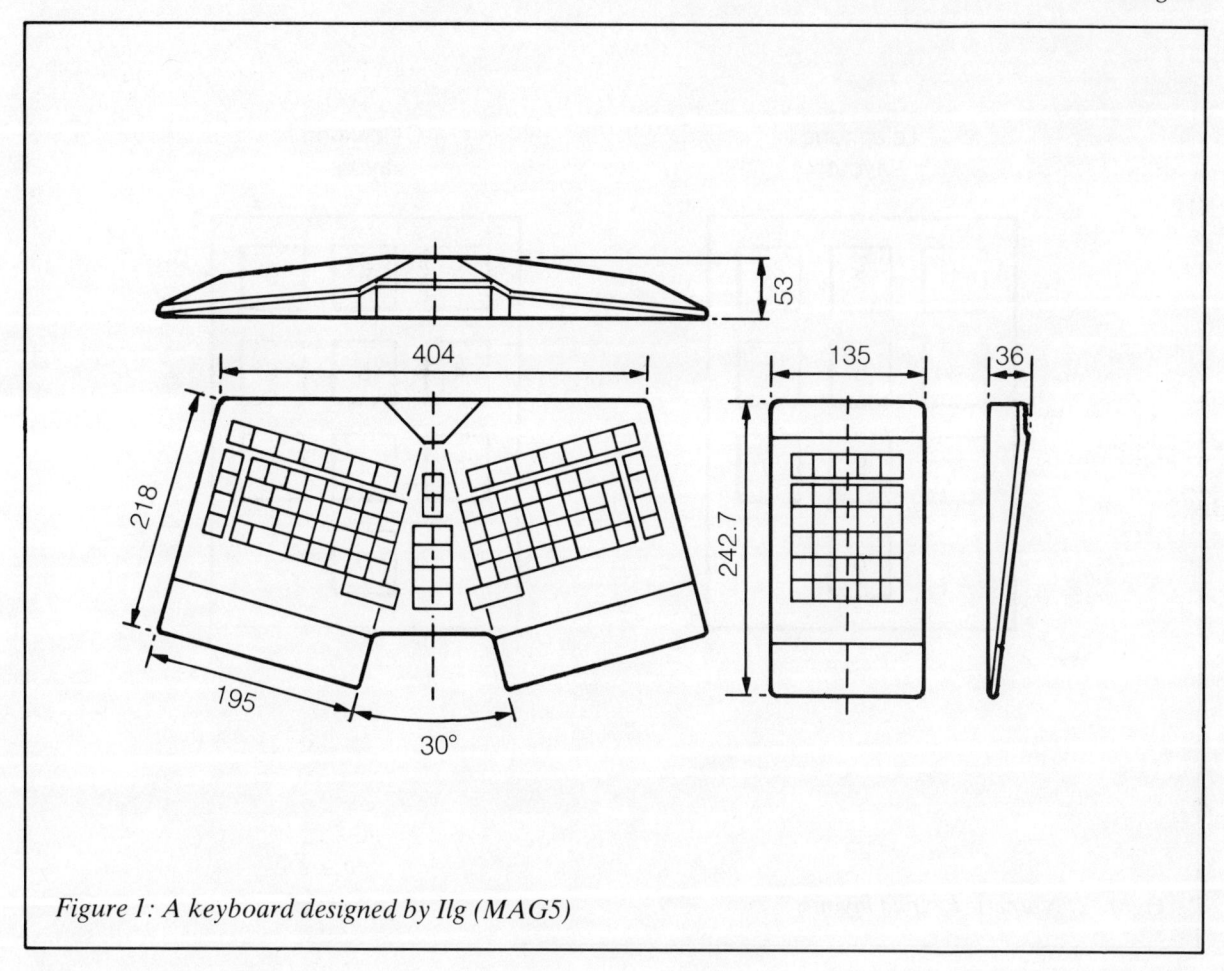

Another innovative keyboard is the PCD Maltron which combines a split-halves design with a variation on the Dvorak layout. For example the vowels, a source of error with the Dvorak layout, are located further apart to avoid confusion. Initial tests by Maltron themselves showed the design to result in comfortable, efficient typing while a 'changeover key' also allowed the user to switch to a QWERTY layout if preferred. Interestingly each keyboard is hand-built and costs £295. (See *(MAG6)* for a background article on the inventor, Stephen Hobday.)

Koffler's review *(MAG7)* of office systems ergonomics includes a detailed review of alternative keyboard designs.

Soft function keys

Most keyboards now contain a set of 'soft' function keys which can be programmed by the applications designer. In striving for IBM PC compatibility, many keyboards have two vertical rows of five function keys down the left-hand side. However, a horizontal row across the top can be more easily linked to labels across the bottom of the screen. Further benefit is provided by grouping the keys in, say, blocks of three or four. The programmer can then group the screen labels in the same way thus providing the user with a more distinct correspondence between label and key giving faster performance with fewer errors.

Numeric pads

For numeric keypads, there are two widely accepted layouts. Telephones have the 1-2-3 keys on the top row of a 3x3 layout while calculators put the 7-8-9 at the top (see Figure 2).

Conrad and Hull *(MAG8)* have compared the two types and found the telephone layout to be significantly better, providing a higher degree of accuracy. Although the 'calculator' keypad has been shown to be faster for engineers and technical people, the 'telephone' layout is faster for non-technical people. This may be related to whether the user expects the zero to precede 1 or follow 9 as a number concept. Although most computer keyboards currently use the 7-8-9 layout, the trend towards interfacing computers with telephone systems will probably result in more widespread use of 1-2-3. This would particularly benefit frequent users of both computer keypads and telephones. Some terminal

Figure 2: Numeric keypad layouts

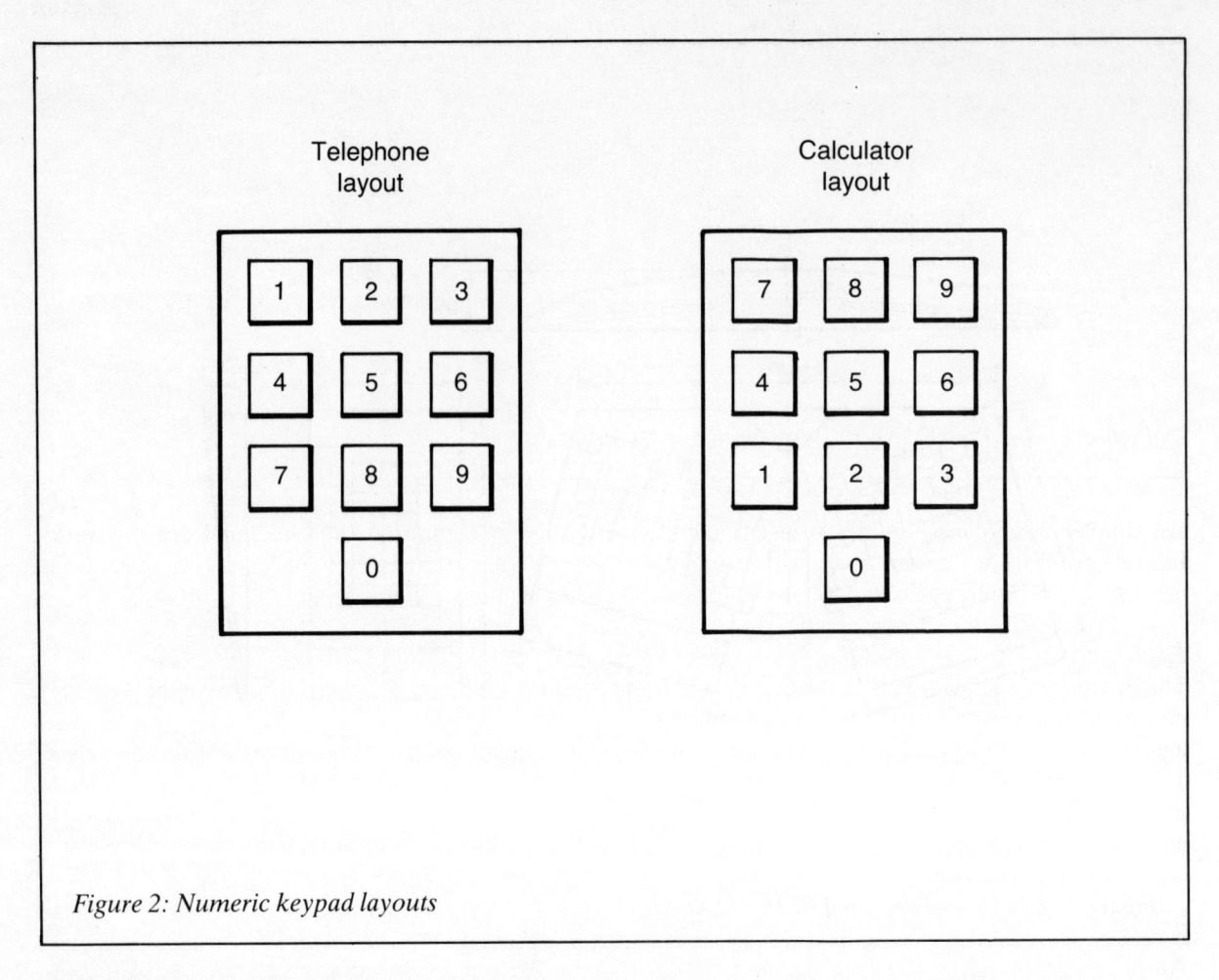

manufacturers now supply an alternative set of key tops so that the layout can be modified and the terminal settings changed to generate the corresponding key codes.

Cursor keys

The use of four 'arrow' or cursor keys has become a central feature of many applications such as word processing and form-filling. For substantial text input, many typists prefer to use cursor keys, thereby keeping their hands on the keyboard, rather than moving the cursor with, say, a mouse. In graphical applications, cursor keys can be a useful supplement to the mouse or roller ball. Single key presses provide a means of one pixel-at-a-time cursor movement, while the mouse or roller ball allow for rapid movement of a less precise nature or over a wider screen area. Cursor keys are generally more effective when placed in a 'North, South, East, West' configuration (see Figure 3) rather than in the configurations shown in Figure 4. Cursor keys usually require an auto-repeat facility for continuous movement on screen, while some systems also incorporate a 'SHIFT cursor key' function to speed up autorepeating.

Concept keyboards

A concept keyboard consists of a flat membrane-covered board, drawn up into an array of cells. As with soft function keys, each cell can be programmed to output a key code or sequence of codes when pressed. A paper overlay, customised to the particular application, shows the keyboard layout. This might, for instance, contain a map of marked locations which the user presses in order to display related information on screen. Large keys can also be created for novice users or users with poor motor control by programming adjacent cells to send out the same code. The simplicity of concept keyboards makes them popular in schools where attractive, colourful overlays can be created. The interface also becomes highly simplified — for instance the overlay might contain pictures of wild animals and the instruction: 'TOUCH AND EXPLORE'. User programming of the concept keyboard does however depend on the provision of suitable software and this should be checked prior to purchase.

Pointing devices

The two main categories of pointing device are 'direct', which allow the user to point directly to items on the screen, and 'indirect', where the user manipulates a screen cursor or pointer. Direct pointing devices

Figure 3: 'North, South, East, West' configuration of cursor keys

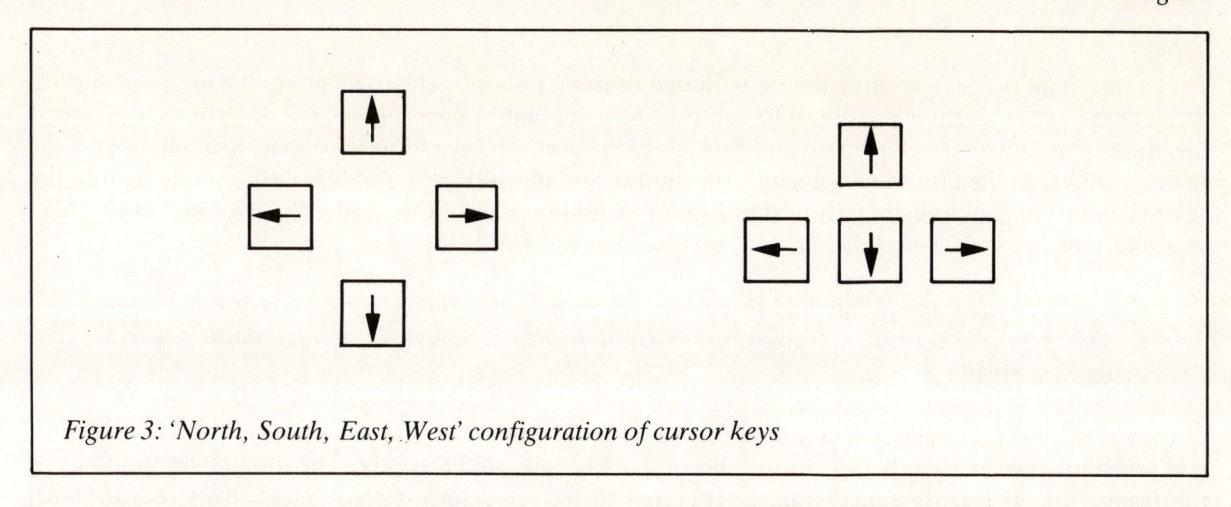

are simpler for novices and allow direct hand/eye coordination, important for freehand drawing tasks. Indirect pointing devices are more comfortable for usage over a period of time, but require more cognitive processing and hand/eye coordination to locate the cursor on the required target.

Lightpens

The lightpen is a device which allows the user to point *directly* at the screen to both indicate choices (perhaps in a menu or tree structure) or to manipulate items (for example graphical objects). The main problem with lightpens is that prolonged use on a vertical or near-vertical screen can be extremely fatiguing for the wrist or arm. Users may also find that lightpens lack sufficient control for 'dragging' operations. Thus they tend to be more effective for simple item selection. For example, Haller *et al (MAG9)* found the lightpen faster than the graphic tablet, mouse, tracker ball, cursor keys and speech recogniser for locating (positioning a cursor over) typing errors on screen.

Touch screens

Another *direct* pointing device is the touch screen. There are two main types:

1 'Actual' touch on an electrostatic surface where the finger creates an active circuit.

2 An infrared grid in front of the screen, the input being recorded either as the finger enters or leaves the grid.

Touch screens have some advantages over light pens. Users do not need to pick up a pointing object — they simply point at the screen with their finger. Touch screens can therefore provide a pleasant and simple means of input for naive users who may find the use of a physical input device more daunting. They have been successfully used as a basis for public information points in banks and information centres. However, as with light pens, the arm can quickly become fatigued and the hand hides part of the screen which may also become obscured by fingermarks unless cleaned regularly. Pointing is also fairly imprecise and so touch screens are perhaps most appropriate for simple selection. Finally, users sometimes need reassurance, thinking that they might receive an electric shock when they touch the screen.

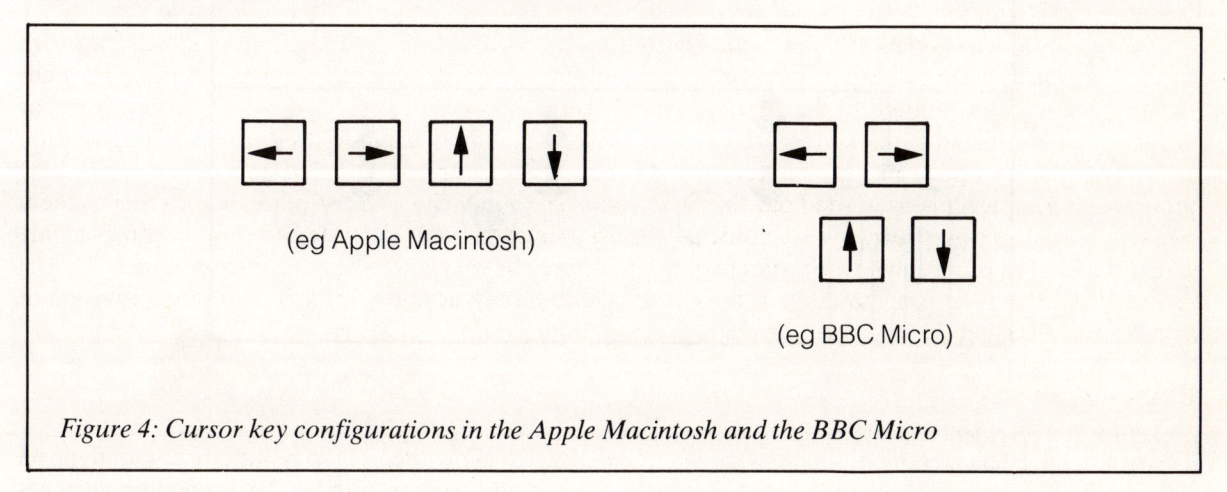

Figure 4: Cursor key configurations in the Apple Macintosh and the BBC Micro

Mice

The mouse is an *indirect* pointing device with one or more buttons. The user moves it over a flat surface (sometimes a special mat is provided) to control a screen pointer, pressing one of the buttons to trigger a specific action. It works well at close quarters, since the user can lift and reposition it, without moving the screen pointer. In the office environment, the mouse has almost become the standard complement to the keyboard, forming an integral part of the popular Windows, Icons, Mice and Pull-down menus (WIMP) user interface. Bewley *et al (MAG10)* sum up the main value of WIMP:

> *Seeing something and pointing to it is easier for people than remembering a name and typing it. This principle is often expressed in the psychological literature as 'recognition is generally easier than recall'.*

Card *et al (MAG11)* compared a mouse, a rate-controlled isometric joystick, cursor keys and text keys for text selection. The study took account of distance, target size and learning. The mouse was found to be the fastest for all experimental arrangements and to have the lowest error rates. Roberts *(MAG12)* confirmed this, but also found that cursor keys were faster over small distances. Mice are thus appropriate for fast selection and manipulation of items on screen (for example dragging an object by holding down the button) and can easily be used for 'structured' drawing, say, of charts and diagrams. However, it is less suitable for freehand drawing or writing on screen. Cursor keys may be preferred by experienced typists wishing to keep their hands on the keyboard.

Apple machines now allow the user to select the movement characteristics of the mouse, for example speed of pointer movement, double-click speed, etc. This increases the overall flexibility of usage (see Figure 5).

Roller balls

The roller or tracker ball is another *indirect* pointing device, comprising a rotating ball that can be moved with fingertips for fine positioning or the palm of the hand for gross movements. It occupies a small area and can be fixed to a worktop. This may be important if conditions are unstable, such as on board ship,

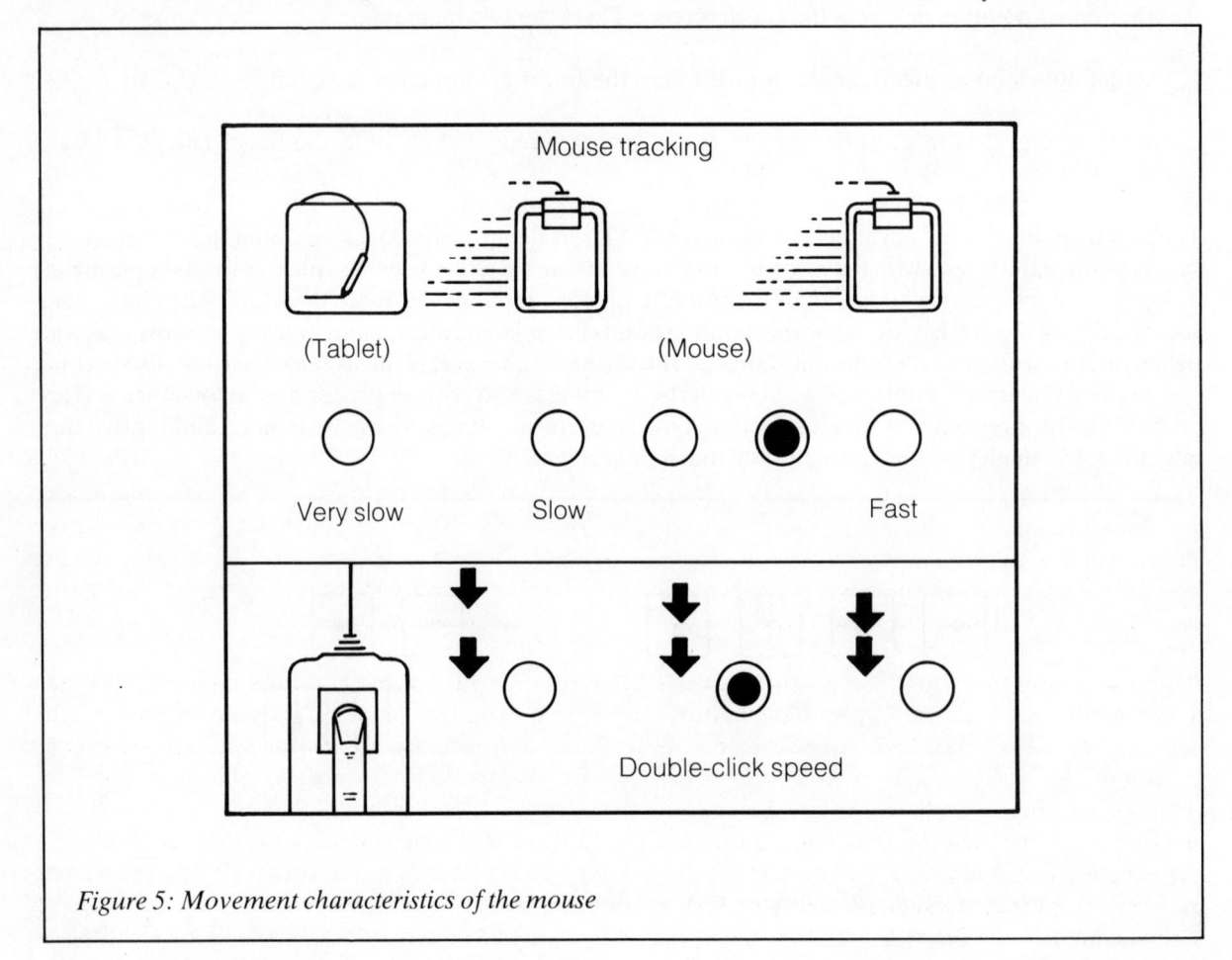

Figure 5: Movement characteristics of the mouse

where a mouse could easily roll onto the floor! Roller balls have the advantage of high resolution, ease of location by touch alone and unlimited movement in any direction. They are good for rotation movements but very poor for freehand drawing. Until recently, another drawback was the absence of selection buttons as on a mouse. The latest devices now include buttons and are angled for more comfortable usage, although holding down the button to 'drag' objects on screen (as with a mouse) would probably require two hands.

Joysticks

Joysticks have become the standard input device for control applications such as flight simulators. The firm grip and easy movement they provide allow the user to comfortably maintain continuous control in a real-time situation. Joysticks work best if the displacement of the stick controls the *rate* of movement, so that the further the joystick is pushed the faster the controlled object moves. Where vibration is a problem (for example in a helicopter) 'force' joysticks which react to pressure may be needed. The public's familiarity with joysticks in home computer games has added impetus to the development of cheap, high-quality products. The instructions for a recent computer game advise the user to 'plug in your best joystick!'.

Figure 6 provides a summary comparison of a range of devices for pointing and graphical input.

Paper-based input

Digitising tables and graphics tablets

The input of coordinate data from engineering drawings or maps is usually performed via large digitising tables. Smaller tablets are also available and can be more easily transported between graphics terminals, although they still occupy a sizeable portion of the desk space.

The choice of hand device is largely task dependent. A *puck* consists of a small frame containing a transparent viewer and incorporating a cross-hair cursor. This permits accurate positioning of the cursor in relation to the drawing. If therefore digitising is the main task, a puck may be the best choice. Buttons on the edge of the frame signify different functions such as 'store a point', 'store a line' or automatic 'stream' input (for example record one data point per half second). The buyer should take note of both the number and function of the buttons as this will strongly affect the ease of use of the complete device.

Alternatively a *pen* or *stylus* can be used for either drawing or pointing. Instead of buttons, pens have a switch activated by pressure on the tip. Thus 'pen down' means record a point or series of points as a line. For drawing, the force required to close the 'down' switch must be low enough to correspond with the user's perception of having the pen in contact with the paper. If heavy pressure is required, the drawing task can be seriously impeded.

When performing a digitising task, it is also desirable that the controlling software gives a continuous display of the data being input. This allows the user to check and correct mistakes during the input process.

Character recognition

The ability to optically read alphanumeric characters from the printed page would clearly be a major breakthrough in efficiency of computer usage. Gone would be the need to laboriously copy-type large documents in order to transfer them to computer. Currently Optical Character Recognition (OCR) equipment is available, which will read *typed* alphanumerics with near 100 per cent accuracy, and postal services are beginning to utilise this technology for sorting letters by post code.

The cost of accurate OCR equipment has traditionally been high, but basic devices now cost less than £1000 and there is also OCR software that works with PCs and simple image scanners. Typically, the accuracy of recognition is about five errors per page, so correction with a word processor is usually required. The problem is the wealth of fonts that may be encountered. Most scanners have templates for a limited number of fonts, usually of the monospaced or 'typewriter' variety. However, scanners are now coming onto the market that can 'learn' fonts and therefore deal with a wider range *(MAG13)*. Recognition of proportional spaced text (as produced by laser printers) is a further problem which some recognisers cannot handle. A new Kurzweil machine uses Artificial Intelligence (AI) techniques to emulate human reading skills. It offers highly accurate, although not error-free, recognition of both fixed and proportionally spaced text in any font. The cost is £8000 *(MAG14)*.

Device	Comment
Cursor keys	Accurate but slow for pixel positioning Effective for positioning within text Can keep hands on keyboard
Lightpen	Allows direct hand/eye coordination Fast for positioning (eg menu selection) Arm/wrist fatigue with prolonged use Need to lift pen for each set of inputs Can obscure screen with hand
Touch screen	Allows direct hand/eye coordination Best for simple selecting Arm fatigue with prolonged use Can mark or obscure screen with hand
Mouse	Becoming a standard keyboard complement Efficient for selecting, dragging and manipulating objects Works well at close quarters Poor for freehand drawing
Rollerball	Palm of hand for gross movement, fingertips for fine positioning Good for rotational movement Can be fixed to worktop Poor for dragging or freehand drawing
Joystick	Comfortable for control tasks over long periods Pressure joysticks useful in vibrating environment
Graphic tablets or digitisers	With stylus: good for freestyle drawing With puck : good for accurate digitising Requires substantial floor or desk space

Figure 6: Comparison of devices for pointing and graphical input

```
62 ⑴⒋ 78⑴
```

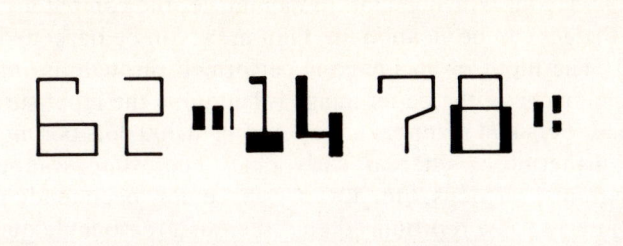

Figure 7: MICR and OCR fonts

The banking industry uses equipment that can accurately read characters written in 'magnetic ink', that is Magnetic Ink Character Recognition (MICR). Special MICR and OCR fonts are also used, giving near 100 per cent accuracy (see Figure 7).

The ability to read *handwriting* would be another major breakthrough in computer input. Commercial systems are now available but they constrain the writer in some ways, for example individual letters must be printed rather than joined. The BBC TV programme 'Tomorrow's World' recently showed (31 March 1988) a more advanced system developed by the National Physical Laboratory as part of the Electronic Paper Project. This system uses pattern recognition techniques to identify key characteristics in normal handwriting (loops, sticks, descenders, crosses, dots, etc). Using an 800-word vocabulary, it was shown to correctly recognise a long word such as 'important' and to associate a short word such as 'must' with either 'must', 'most' or 'mast'. It seems likely that as such systems are developed further, they will become increasingly used.

Mark recognition

It is easier for computers to read handwritten marks than handwritten alphanumerics, since the range of possible inputs is much reduced. Optical Mark Sensing (OMS) equipment has been available since the late 1970s. Such systems usually require the writer to put short lines on a preprinted form as a waiter or waitress might do in taking an order. The cash register then reads the form and automatically produces a bill.

The use of *bar code readers* to recognise printed marks is widespread in shops, warehouses, distribution organisations and libraries. Every item is given a label containing a printed set of lines of varying thickness (see Figure 8). Each label can then be quickly read by running a light pen or stylus across it. Such systems are very efficient for recording high volumes of, for example, items sold or books issued. Accuracy is very high and the checking procedures built into the bar code system give the user immediate feedback (a short bleep) when a code is misread. This allows them to re-input the code and correct the error. Supermarkets now use laser-based technology to read bar codes, the cashier simply passing the item over the laser reader. This speeds up the process, since the user is freed from manipulating a stylus in conjunction with varying shaped objects.

Figure 8: Example of a bar code

Image capture

An important factor in the growth of desktop publishing is the ability to capture camera images and to merge them into a textual layout. Having captured an image, the computer can then be used to reshape and enhance it. Ragged edges can be cleaned up, faint areas can be darkened and monochrome pictures can have colour added. The input of an image is performed through an *image scanner*. Working in a similar way to a facsimile machine, the paper image is laid upon the input surface and captured in digital form by the scanner head. Personal scanners are operating at 300 dots per inch — the same resolution as many laser printers. Furthermore, whereas early black and white scanners were only suitable for capturing drawings, diagrams, cartoons, etc, advances have now been made in grey scale representation enabling photographic images to be reproduced on screen to a reasonable quality.

As an alternative to paper scanners, an image can be input directly into the computer from a camera. This is of course a major component of image recognition in the field of robotics.

Image capture equipment is now relatively cheap and basic systems are available for approximately £500.

Voice input

With voice input, the user enters data or commands into the computer via a microphone fixed to the work surface or attached to the body. Although much has been expected of voice input systems, the technology has some way to go to fulfil its potential. Successful systems have been designed, but they are limited in their performance and restricted to specialist applications.

Most voice input systems (also known as speech recognisers) are based on template matching. Speech samples are provided by each intended speaker and stored digitally for comparison with user inputs. Usually 3-10 samples of each word in the vocabulary are required. Each inputted work is thus either matched with the correct word, matched with an incorrect word, or rejected as not matching any word closely enough. If the application allows the designer to choose the vocabulary, it is desirable that each word should sound substantially different from the rest. During trials of a simple recogniser at HUSAT, the word 'stop' was occasionally confused with both 'start' and 'help', so it was decided to replace it with the more distinct word 'finish'. Systems normally allow the user to set the threshold for closeness of match before a word is accepted. Thus a higher threshold will tend to increase recognition accuracy but more words will be rejected as matching none of the templates.

There are two major categories of speech recogniser — *discrete word* and *continuous speech*. Most commercial systems are *discrete word recognisers*, requiring the user to speak in a series of isolated words with a short pause between each. Thus the words in the phrase 'bread and butter' would need to be complete entities in order to be recognised. However, some discrete systems allow connected speech, the user being able to speak continuously, provided the words do not vary as they run together: 'breadandbutter'. The other major category, *continuous speech recognisers*, have the potential to interpret fluent speech: 'breadnbutter'.

Performance figures for speech recognisers are normally given as a percentage of utterances correctly recognised. For discrete word recognisers, manufacturers usually quote 95-97 per cent with lists of between 50 and 150 words. In practice, system performance tends to be lower due to:
- Speaker inconsistency
- Background noise
- Similarity of vocabulary words.

Despite the apparently limited vocabulary size, the total vocabulary can be much larger, provided the number of templates needed at any one point during interaction is less than the figures quoted. In fact recognition systems work best when there are very few input possibilities at each stage. Currently one of the most reliable devices is Marconi's connected speech system, 'MacroSpeak', which can operate on a vocabulary of a few hundred words.

For continuous speech recognisers, most of which are still at the research stage, performance figures are much lower, ranging between, say, 50 and 80 per cent. Nevertheless, manufacturers' claims remain high and, in 1985, Kurzweil Computer Products announced an experimental system able to handle a 3000-word vocabulary for continuous speech — a significant step, perhaps, towards speech-driven text entry.

Recognisers can also be either *speaker dependent* or *speaker independent*. The more usual speaker-dependent systems require the user to train the system beforehand with each of the words in the vocabulary. However, there is now a move towards 'easy' training where the user simply reads aloud a representative passage of text and the system identifies key vocal characteristics. There has also been some success with speaker-independent systems (no training required) — a level flexibility essential for general public usage over a telephone. For example AT&T recently announced a system capable of 99 per cent accuracy with a limited vocabulary.

The cost of speech recognition systems varies widely, ranging from a few hundred pounds for basic discrete word recognisers to, say, £20 000 for continuous speech systems.

Speech input could be of value in the following kinds of situation:
- If the user's hands or eyes are busy (for example operating machinery, baggage handling, driving or flying — see *(MAG15)*)
- In a darkened environment
- Interaction over the telephone
- Input device for the physically handicapped
- Input of highly structured and error-prone data when the user has poor typing skills.

Speech has, however, been found to be of limited value for common keyboard tasks such as cursor movement *(MAG16)* and text editing *(MAG9,MAG17)*.

In conclusion, most current speech recognisers require the speaker to train the system, use discrete words, keep to a restricted vocabulary and to wear a head- or lapel-mounted microphone. Users must also speak in a consistent manner, often difficult if the system is performing badly. Perhaps the two most important pieces of advice when using speech input technology are to:

1. Keep the bounds of the system within the bounds of the technology, for example use a small vocabulary.
2. Try out the system in the intended working environment beforehand.

Talbot *(MAG18)* and Mariani *(MAG19)* give an overview of speech technology for both input and output, while Joost *et al (MAG20)* and Cooper *(MAG21)* look at current human factors research in the area.

Other means of input

Gesture

Gesture recognisers consist of a wrist- or finger-work sensor and a fixed infrared radiator. In a typical system, the three-dimensional digitiser returns the position of the sensor with respect to the radiator 40 times a second. They are often used in research as a means for the user to remotely point to objects on a computer screen. In one system, 'Put that there' gesturing is used as a supplement to speech input to position and move ships around on a map of the Caribbean *(MAG22)*. It is argued that because speech input systems are never likely to be 100 per cent accurate, the computer can overcome recognition failures by determining where the user is pointing instead.

An alternative gesture device is the 'sensory glove' described by Zimmerman *et al (MAG23)*. Analogue flex sensors on the glove measure finger bending, while ultrasonics or magnetic flux sensors measure hand position and orientation. Piezoceramic benders provide the wearer with tactile feedback. The authors suggest that the glove could be used in conjunction with a host computer driving a three-dimensional model of the hand to allow the glove wearer to manipulate computer-generated objects as if they were real. The system could also be used to interpret finger spelling, evaluate hand impairment or provide an interface to a visual programming language.

Weber *(MAG24)* has developed a gesturing system for blind users, providing star map information. Input is achieved by the user tracing a 'gesture path' with their finger on a touch-sensitive screen. Output of star maps is via a paperless braille display consisting of a flat surface with 7000 pins which can be raised and lowered. The value of gesturing, particularly for the blind, is that index finger movement is accurate enough for user input without visual feedback.

Eye movement
Eye-tracking systems have been in existence for some years and are available in two forms — head mounted and remote systems. Head-mounted equipment contains an image sensor which detects the reflection from the cornea of an infrared LED. This measures the orientation of the eye, which is then combined with data about the observer's head position in space to determine the viewpoint on the computer screen. The alternative remote tracking approach is less intrusive but more expensive. Both provide a high degree of accuracy.

Bolt *(MAG25)* considers that computer/eye movement interfaces could be used for the following kinds of task:
- Selection of items to zoom in on or be given help on
- Allocation of bandwidth or processing only to the portions of the display the user is looking at
- Gaze-contingent vocabularies in voice-controlled graphic displays
- 'Travel' by head and eye in graphics scrolling and zooming
- Eye contact in teleconferencing for the chairman to control the proceedings.

For some time, eye-activated systems have been installed in fighter planes, allowing pilots to quickly call up information on 'head-up' displays. This technology has recently been employed by Marconi Defence Systems in collaboration with the Royal National Orthopaedic Hospital to develop a communications system for the disabled. Called the Eyewatch System, it utilises impulses between the temples resulting from eye movement to assess eye pointing direction. This allows paralysed people to type at speed and to control their own environment *(MAG26)*.

Computer output

Displays

General considerations
The trend in displays is towards bit-mapped devices which display one or more bits of information for each position or 'pixel' on the screen. A simple colour display, for example, might use four bits to display 16 colours simultaneously. These displays are displacing both specialised line drawings displays for computer graphics and the simpler text-only displays. They have the advantages of being able to display many sizes and typefaces of text, solid as well as line graphics, to mix text and graphics and to display both grey scale and colour images. The common preference for a 'positive image' format can also be well supported with dark characters being displayed on a pleasant neutral background. In contrast, the use of inverse video, on traditional terminals (for example black on green or black on orange) gives a totally different and glaring effect.

The use of high-resolution bit-mapped displays is less advantageous for functions such as scrolling where the need to quickly redraw hundreds of thousands of pixels can place a heavy strain on the computer. However, with the advent of more powerful processors and special hardware for scrolling and region manipulation (for example Block Image Transfer (BIT) or 'Blitter' chips), the problem has largely been overcome.

The draft BSI standard for VDTs, described earlier under keyboards, also contains a section on the ergonomic requirements of displays (see *(MAG3)*: Part 3 — Visual display requirements).

Large screens
Graphical applications such as Computer-aided Design (CAD) and scientific modelling have always benefited from the use of large display areas. However, the demand for large screens has increased further since the advent of Desktop Publishing (DTP) software — enabling people to see as much of the page as possible (A4 size) or even a double page spread (A3). A key issue is the screen resolution since the more dots that are shown on screen, the more accurate is the image of the material being laid out. Large screens may start at about 800 x 600 and go up to 1024 x 1024 (a 'mega-pixel'). Indeed the new series of Sun 4 workstations offers a resolution of 1600 x 1280. It has been found, however, that on some large screens characters can become distorted towards the edges, typically becoming squashed at the top and bottom. Other problems are the desk space needed to accommodate the larger screen and the possible need to sit further away, to avoid the 'front row of the cinema effect'.

A flicker-free image is also important which, for displays in general, can be achieved with a scan rate of at least 70 Hz for positive images (that is light background), 55-60 Hz for negative images (dark background) with green phosphors and 50 Hz for negative images with white or yellowish-green phosphors *(MAG27)*. However, for large displays it becomes difficult to scan the screen fast enough to maintain, say, a 70 Hz refresh rate. Therefore to artificially speed up the scan rate, 'interlacing' is sometimes used with the electron gun scanning alternate lines of the screen. Although this tends to make the character edges jitter, it can be masked with long persistence phosphors. The arrangement is satisfactory for static images such as page layouts, but it can give a smearing effect when scrolling or when animated graphics are needed.

Hammond *(MAG28)* reviews a range of PC-compatible large screens.

Flat screens

The Cathode Ray Tube (CRT) display remains a relatively bulky component of a computer system and so considerable advantages can be gained from flat screens. They can be carried around more easily and can also be fitted into confined spaces such as car dashboards. Although work is underway to produce 'flat' CRT devices, the following alternative kinds of flat screen technology exist:

1 *Liquid Crystal Displays (LCDs):* these use voltage to change the reflectivity of tiny capsules of liquid crystals, turning some spots darker when viewed by reflected light. A light behind the screen can enhance their readability. LCDs are flicker free, but the size of the capsules limits the resolution. Portable computers use LCDs because of their light weight and low power consumption. Display size goes up to 24x80 characters and simple colour versions are now available. Recent LCD displays known as 'Twisted-Nematic' achieve greater readability by twisting the liquid capsules to an angle which increases their reflectivity. On a PC, it is also useful if the LCD screen itself can be angled to obtain maximum viewing comfort. In contrast to the 'passive' LCD display, which relies on reflected light, display types 2-4 are 'active' in that they produce their own light.

2 *Light-emitting Diode (LED) displays:* arrays of light-emitting diodes are assembled to form characters. Since the power requirements of LED displays are relatively high, their usage tends to be limited to applications requiring only restricted text output, for example dates, times, voltages, etc.

3 *Plasma displays:* these are based on neon-gas-filled glass capsules which produce an orange, flicker-free image. Again the size of the capsules limits the resolution and the high level of power consumption means that PCs with plasma displays rely on mains supply and cannot be battery powered. Regarding size, displays have been built of up to 62 lines by 166 characters.

4 *Electroluminescent displays:* these contain yellowish-light-emitting phosphors. They can be of high resolution, thin and lightweight. As yet the cost of producing large displays prevents them from being used widely in computers although they are often used for pocket televisions and information display boards. Another variation is the *vacuum fluorescent display* which is also phosphor based but emits a blue-green colour.

Voice output

There are basically two kinds of voice output technology:

1 *Digitised speech* requires a person to prerecord all messages, which are then digitised and stored in data files. The quality of the output is very high, being almost equivalent to the original speaker. However, the approach is inflexible since changes to the spoken messages usually require the original speaker to re-record them. Considerable data storage is also needed if the messages are lengthy or numerous.

2 *Synthesised speech* is speech generated by the computer itself. In *synthesis-by-analysis*, a finite vocabulary of speech sounds are analysed and corresponding parameters representing pitch, energy and type of speech sound are stored in Read Only Memory (ROM). Typically a 64-Kbit ROM will hold a 200-word vocabulary. Speech generated in this way is usually spoken accurately but often sounds robotic in quality. Such systems are low cost and are used in cards, home computers and toys. In *synthesis-by-rule*, the computer can apply rules to any text stream sent to it by an application program. Under good listening conditions, all current text-to-speech systems are understandable, but some sound more natural than others. Newer systems include intonation and thus sound better in producing

longer passages of speech. Text-to-speech systems are, however, likely to mispronounce uncommon words and proper nouns. To overcome this the software should incorporate a 'dictionary' of exceptions to normal pronounciation. The Infovox speech system is typical of this kind, costing about £1200.

Although synthetic speech is of much lower quality than digitised speech, research shows that increased exposure to synthetic speech results in greater intelligibility as far as the user is concerned. Applications based on synthetic speech are more flexible than digitised speech and can be changed fairly freely. Long passages of speech can take a considerable time to transmit and so it should also be possible for the user to interrupt the output and for untransmitted speech to be flushed from the output buffer.

Speech output can potentially be used in the following situations:

- When the user is heavily loaded with visual stimuli, where speech output grabs the attention quickly
- When manipulating data on screen, where speech can be used to transmit related instructions or help
- To precis passages of screen text
- To prompt for input and give auditory feedback if the user is unable to look at the screen
- For users with a visual handicap.

A recent development by the Transport and Road Research Laboratories (TRRL) is a voice-controlled in-car navigation system, called Autoguide. The user types into a small computer his destination coordinates, the computer gives voice instructions (turn-left-turn-right) and a direction arrow on a two-inch dashboard screen points the way (see Figure 9). The system will be self-correcting so that if the driver misses a turn, it will automatically put him back on the correct route. The driver can be led to within 50 yards of his destination. The system is directed by a series of computerised beacons fixed to traffic lights. Each beacon stores a map of an area with all the relevant traffic information which can be transmitted to the car. Outside beacon range, a compass system takes over as a guide. The system is expected to be operational in the UK by 1992 (and parts of Europe by the mid-1990s). The cost will probably be about £250 plus an annual fee of £30-40 *(MAG29)*.

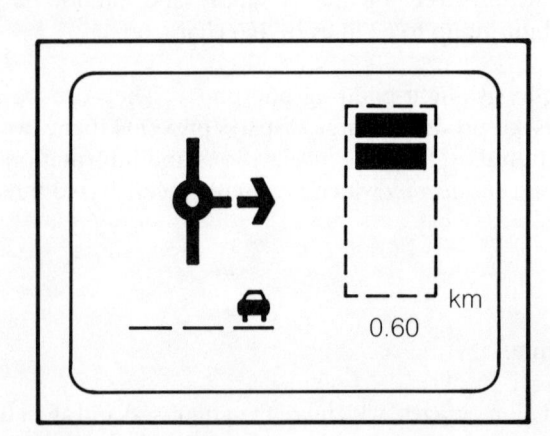

Figure 9: Autoguide, a voice-controlled in-car navigation system

Hard copy

Printers

The standard form of hard copy output from a computer is the printer. The most common type is the *matrix* or *impact printer* which employs a matrix of pins to impact the shape of letters through an inked ribbon onto paper. They have the flexibility to use either single sheets of paper or continuous stationery. Traditionally matrix printers have been fast and cheap but lacking in print quality. Most are based on a vertical column of nine pins creating a 9x9 character box. In Near Letter Quality (NLQ) mode, some printers can make a second pass with the paper slightly advanced to give a higher resolution output. This does of course slow the process considerably. The newer 18- and 24-pin matrix printers produce high-quality text output without a drop in speed. They incorporate print heads with two columns of nine or twelve pins, slightly staggered so that an NLQ effect can be achieved in one pass. The least expensive 24-pin matrix printers currently cost less than £400 and offer dual print speeds of say 150 characters per second (cps) in draft mode and 50 cps in quality mode *(MAG30)*. Higher specification machines can produce drafts at 300 or 400 cps. The use of multicolour ribbons can also produce reasonably good colour images. Matrix printers can be noisy in an office environment and so silencer hoods may be needed. However, quieter models now operate at a level of 55 dB. A long-standing irritation to printer users has been the need to fiddle with DIP switches to select different fonts, print modes or carriage behaviour. However, many printers, such as the Star range, now have control panels which greatly ease the selection process.

Laser printers have been called 'photocopiers with brains'. They work by receiving data from the computer and building up a bit map image of a complete page in memory. Then, in a similar way to photocopying, a laser beam creates an electrostatic copy of the image onto a light-sensitive drum. The drum then picks up a black powder called 'toner' which is transferred to the paper. Printing is of the highest quality with resolutions of up to 400 dots per inch (dpi) for personal machines and up to 1200 dpi for typesetting machines. The appearance is hard, black and visually 'perfect'. Laser printers also operate quickly with many manufacturers claiming speeds of eight to twelve pages per minute, comparable to the fastest matrix printers running in draft mode. However, in practice, speeds may be much lower since delays occur while page images are being prepared. This may range from a few seconds for 'text only' pages, to several minutes for complex graphics. The operating motors of laser printers are fairly quiet, although the noise level is increased by associated cooling fans. Laser printers are rapidly falling in price but still start at about £1800 for desktop machines and replacement toner cartridges can also be expensive. Currently, laser printers are single colour only, although multicolour versions are anticipated in the near future.

Ink-jet printers offer an alternative print technology using the technique of firing a fine spray of ink at the page. Both single-colour and multicolour versions are available and they are capable of resolutions equivalent to laser printers. They are also very quiet and operate at speeds almost equivalent to lasers, reaching 450 cps in draft mode and 200 cps in letter quality. Cheap ink-jet printers are available for £400 although most machines cost upwards of £700. However, they have yet to firmly establish themselves in the commercial market. Stobie *(MAG31)* reviews three typical machines. The quality of ink-jet printing will tend to vary with paper type but a new solid ink technology firing hot (100°C) quick-drying ink onto the page overcomes this problem *(MAG32)*.

Daisywheel printers provide true 'letter quality' text which is higher even than the best matrix printer. Prices have also been falling and Lennox *(MAG33)* reviews four ranging between £200 and £500. As with matrix printers, they can handle continuous or single-sheet paper although appropriate feeder attachments often come at extra cost. The drawbacks are that daisywheel printers are low (normally 8-40 cps), fairly noisy and restricted to textual output. The range of type styles and sizes are limited and require the user to change the daisywheel manually. However, on the newer models, this is normally quick and easy. Some daisywheel printers provide the option to add a keyboard so that they can act as a normal typewriter.

Thermal transfer printers work by melting dye from a special ribbon onto paper. As with matrix and most ink-jet printers the characters are formed from a matrix of dots. They use special paper which may be expensive and inferior in appearance to normal printer paper. On the plus side they are compact, inexpensive to manufacture, quiet in operation and, as they require little power, often battery powered. The cheaper machines, in the £100-150 bracket, are normally only suitable for draft output of either text or graphics. However, the technology is improving, and a more expensive model, such as the IBM Quietwriter III, offers excellent print quality at 60 cps for around £1000.

Type	Claimed speeds	Noise	Print quality	Additional coments
Matrix	100-300 cps (draft) 40-100 cps (quality)	55-65 dB	Draft mode: acceptable Quality mode: fairly high (esp. 24 pin)	Flexible and inexpensive Low running costs Colour available Can use carbons and multipart forms
Laser	6-10 pages/min (8 p/m = 300 cps)	44-55 dB	Very high	Expensive but falling in price Can use ordinary A4 but not continuous paper No colour
Ink-jet	100-300 cps (draft) 40-100 cps (quality)	45-55 dB	High	Fairly expensive but prices falling Colour available Running costs quite high May need special paper
Thermal	10-60 cps	45-55 dB	Fairly high	Cheap and compact Special paper needed Colour expensive Ribbons short-lived
Daisywheel	8-40 cps	60-68 dB	High	Can use carbons or multipart forms Text only Wheel change needed to change font

Note:
Print speeds claimed by manufacturers are usually theoretical maximums, ignoring carriage returns, line feeds, page preparation, etc. In practice they tend to be significantly lower. Nevertheless the figures are useful for comparative purposes.

Figure 10: Characteristics of the different types of printer

Figure 10 compares the major characteristics for each printer type described. The figures quoted represent typical rather than extreme values.

Plotters

For precise graphical output onto paper (for example technical drawings) or for continuous display of analogue data (for example electrocardiographs), the standard output device is a plotter. Plotter technology is well established, being based on grip wheels or a drum to move the paper along one axis while the pen moves in the other, or a flat bed where the paper remains stationary and the pen moves in both axes. Human factors in relation to plotters include:
- The number of pens available in the palette (1-16)
- Speed (for example 200 mm/sec)
- Ability to draw solid colour, which for business presentations looks better than hatched patterns
- Accuracy — scientific applications may need high accuracy and repeatability, business applications may not
- Work space needed
- Quietness of operation
- Pause facility to halt pen in mid-operation if necessary.

Some plotters have a digital read-out to set scaling or windowing points and to debug a program that the user may have written to control it. Others, incorporating cursor keys on the control panel, can also be used as a simple digitiser. An eight-pen, A3-sized flat-bed plotter costs from about £900 upwards.

Portability, storage and integration

Portable computers

Portability in computer systems has always been a desirable feature from a human factors point of view. They can easily be transported between home and work and can also be used on the move. They can be used in meetings for taking notes or in the field where electrical supplies may be unavailable. A number of factors have enabled portable machines to become commercially viable and very popular:
- The production of full-sized flat screens of 80x25 characters
- The creation of more readable flat displays such as 'supertwist' LCD, electroluminescent and gas plasma screens
- Displays with a range of colours and intensities
- Built-in graphics capability
- Built-in floppy disk drives
- Built-in small and lightweight hard disk drives
- IBM PC compatibility.

The sizes and weights of portable machines vary widely. The heavier 'luggable' machines such as the Compaq 386 and Toshiba 3200 weigh about 20 lb. Although costly (for example £5000) the power of such machines is higher than many desk-bound PCs. The lighter 'laptops' weigh approximately 6-10 lb although those in the upper range would be uncomfortable on the lap! The lightest is currently the Cambridge Z88, weighing a mere 2 lb, A4-sized and about one inch thick. Other leading manufacturers are Toshiba, Sharp, Tandy and Zenith. 'Hand-held' computers such as the Husky Hawk and the Psion Organiser, tend to have smaller screens, no disk storage and non-standard key layouts. However, they come into their own when the user is truly on the move, for instance making duty-free sales on board an aircraft *(MAG34)*.

The increasing capacities of floppy disks will add further impetus to the portable computer revolution since buyers may be able to dispense with both the extra cost and weight of a portable *hard disk*. Toshiba have now started to market a 3.5-inch floppy drive with a storage capacity of 4 Mbytes and costing the equivalent of $320. This has been achieved using the technique of 'vertical' data recording where the magnetised elements of the recording surface (oxide grains) are oriented perpendicular to the disk surface like blades of grass rather than end-to-end like a line of dashes. Toshiba's new drive, the PD-210, also has the flexibility to cope with existing 1-Mbyte floppies as well as the new 4-Mbyte versions *(MAG35)*.

Optical storage

The standard medium for on-line mass storage is the magnetic hard disk drive. Both its storage capacities and access speeds are increasing while costs are falling — a PC with a 20-Mbyte hard disk can cost less than £1000. However, optical storage, while somewhat slower and more costly, provides the potential for much larger storage. This enables innovative user interfaces to be developed which combine normal computer text and graphics with video pictures and sound sequences. There are three main forms of optical storage, Compact Disk Read Only Memory (CD-ROM), Write Once Read Many times (WORM) and laser disks.

CD-ROM

CD-ROM is rapidly becoming a retail product, offering mass storage at low cost. A single CD-ROM disk can hold 550 Mbytes or 270 000 pages of A4 text — enough books to fill over 50 feet of shelf space. CD-ROM is very similar to standard audio CD, consisting of a 4-inch (12-cm disk) of plastic with a metallised layer sandwiched in the middle. Digital data is stored on a spiral track as a sequence of tiny pits in the reflective metallic layer. A laser beam scans the tracks, reading each pit as 'one bit' and each reflective space as 'zero'. As its name implies, CD-ROM is a read only medium and the user cannot store his or her own data on it. However, because of its immense capacities and relatively low cost, it offers a serious challenge to on-line databases and microfilm for supplying data which does not change rapidly. CD-ROM is also finding a niche in the field of electronic books. Already books exist covering such diverse topics as American history (with animated maps, time lines and 'hypertext' links) and the 'Electronic cadaver' (a dynamic textbook on the human corpse). Microsoft offer a range of standard reference books on a single CD including a dictionary, thesaurus, dictionary of quotations, works on writing style, an almanac and a guide to business information sources. The cost of such products range from under £100 to a few thousand, depending on sales volume. CD-ROM also offers a new publishing medium which can integrate text with static or animated graphics as well as sound or speech. A CD can hold up to 30 minutes of video material, opening up the possibility of interactive video for applications such as computer-aided learning. Recording information on CD is relatively expensive, the data preparation and mastering process costing up to £4000 for a one-off order of 1000 disks. Initially the cost of a CD player for computer interaction is expected to be approximately $1000 (or Sterling equivalent) but audio CD players with digital input and output ports will also be upgradable, allowing the user to play the CD through a domestic television *(MAG36)*.

WORM

Data is stored on WORM disks in a similar manner to CD-ROM. The disks, at 5¼ inches, are slightly larger and the metallic layer is sandwiched between sheets of glass in a protective cartridge. The metallic film is designed to evaporate when exposed to laser light. Whereas CD-ROM is essentially a means of cheaply and easily distributing large amounts of information, the WORM disk is a mass data storage device which will probably be most useful in creating information and data archives, where they will be used to replace paper and microfilm. Although the user can write data onto a WORM disk, it is impossible to change the data once it has been written without writing a new copy — hence the name WORM (Write Once Read Many times). This means that systems utilising WORM disks will store a full record of all changes made to a database — an attractive feature to financial users since it will automatically provide them with data security and a full audit trail. Erasable versions are expected in the very near future from both America and Japan.

Hampshire *(MAG37)* reviews CD-ROM and WORM technology in depth.

Laser disks

Laser disks provide an alternative form of 'read only' mass storage. As opposed to the digital storage of CD-ROM and WORM, it uses an analogue recording technique (pulse with modulation) which gives even greater capacities. It would be possible, for instance, to record more than 100 000 images on a single 12-inch laser disk. A 'jukebox' of such disks has been described by Hammond *(MAG38)* which contains the mind-boggling memory capacity of one 'terabyte' (or 1024 gigabytes) — capacity enough for the digital capture of over 12 years' worth of X-rays, CAT scans and ultrasound examinations for a 250-bed hospital! One of the first and most striking applications in the UK has been the Domesday Project where a national survey was carried out by schools, similar to the original survey by William the Conqueror. Children's essays and photographs, combined with Ordnance Survey data provide an exciting record of life in the modern era. The user simply points to places on a map of the UK and then zooms in on the information for each local area. Further general information is accessed by 'walking around' a picture gallery, while on-line tutorial help is effectively provided in both a visual and verbal form. The high costs of both laser disk players and disk production itself is currently a limitation to the technology becoming widely used (the cost of the Domesday Book system is about £4500).

Integrated office equipment

The modern office now contains a range of hardware for handling information, producing and copying documents, and communicating both locally and to the outside world. There is now a movement towards combining these functions into a single computer-based unit.

Most organisations have facsimile (FAX) and telex machines for sending messages and documents but the procedures involved in using them can be cumbersome and restrictive to the individual. However, add-on boards are now available enabling PCs to provide either FAX or telex functions. The computer's printer can then be used for hard-copy output. The user can prepare their message with a word processor and then send it directly rather than (as for FAX machines) producing it on paper first. A scanner can also be added (for about £1000) so that existing paper documents may be transmitted in the normal way.

Another possibility for integration results from the mechanical similarity between laser printers and photocopiers. A single machine could therefore incorporate both these functions and could, with some extra intelligence, also operate as a scanner and FAX box. Sharp have now introduced their MZ-IV01 machine which provides the functions of a FAX machine, an A4 image scanner, a thermal printer and a photocopier. As well as being cost effective and convenient, such machines represent a great saving in space within a small office.

The introduction of the Integrated Services Digital Network (ISDN) standard for digital telephone networks will allow computers and telephones to work together more closely and transform the humble telephone. The Bellcore consortium, for instance, has a prototype voice dialling system. The caller can speak the number they wish dialled or simply say 'Ring John' or 'Ring home'. The system will recognise the words 'John' or 'home' and retrieve the previously stored number. Voice recognition can also be used for security purposes so that only authorised personnel can use certain phones (hopefully not mimics!). Advanced message handling is also possible so that for instance all but certain incoming callers can be diverted, perhaps to a secretary or an answering machine. Text messages received via electronic mail can also be listened to using voice synthesis. Such telephones will routinely send data as well as voice and, with a screen incorporated, will act as a fully fledged computer terminal. This would allow wider use of on-line databases, teleconferencing and teleshopping. The higher transmission rates of ISDN raise other possibilities. Voice transmission will become clearer, FAX communication faster and video phones will also become workable. The user should of course be given the option to keep the screen turned off!

An interesting series of articles on the subject of office integration is introduced by Moody *(MAG39)*.

Conclusion

An outstanding feature of HCI is that there is not as yet any alternative to the computer keyboard for textual input. Sholes' prototype is so well matched to human characteristics and requirements that it is hard to see it being replaced in the foreseeable future. For direct manipulation in the office environment, the mouse appears to be about to become equally dominant. Voice input technology is improving but is not yet capable of supporting a large vocabulary of words without speaker training, as would be required for word processing. Other factors such as the lack of privacy in having to speak aloud, possible disruption to others and the need for quiet working conditions may also limit market acceptance.

On the output side, competition is much fiercer and the impetus for portability and compactness has transformed LCD and plasma screens into genuine alternatives to the still dominant CRT display. The same is true for printers with impact, laser and ink-jet technologies all becoming faster, cheaper and of higher quality.

Hardware standards are of crucial importance and the BSI's initiative *(MAG3)* is to be welcomed as a means of ensuring high-quality products. Another important point of reference are the HF Guidelines developed for the Ministry of Defence and Department of Trade and Industry *(MAG40)*. As part of the design process, these guidelines advise on desirable *attributes* of suitable hardware for procurement. The authors note, however, the problems of laying down *performance* standards in a project-independent way, as the BSI standard attempts to do.

Nevertheless, the development of computer input and output devices is proceeding rapidly and people's expectations are rising accordingly. Whereas a short time ago graphical displays were restricted to computer-aided designers and specialised graphics laboratories, every PC user now expects graphics on his desktop. This is no bad thing and great benefits in efficiency and job satisfaction can result. We must, however, bear in mind the human factors implications of new hardware and be sure that it is being employed appropriately to suit the user, the task and the working environment into which it will be placed. The overheads in using the hardware should also be considered, such as the cost of ink cartridges, special paper, the effort needed to link it to a software package, time spent in correcting OCR errors, etc. It is also important to consider whether users will need special training to learn how to handle new equipment (such as non-standard keyboards) and how much training time will be needed.

Careful consideration of all these factors will help to ensure that new hardware is of genuine benefit to both the user and the organisation. Prospective buyers should try to obtain new and expensive equipment on approval so that it can be evaluated properly. Most dealers realise that a happy customer is a long-term customer and should be happy to oblige.

As a general reference the book 'Designing the user interface — strategies for effective human computer interaction' by Schneiderman *(MAG41)* has been found to be useful.

Acknowledgements

The author would like to thank Gordon Allison, of HUSAT, for his assistance in producing this report. Of particular value was his ability to see the human factors wood when the author became bogged down among the high-technology trees.

6: Guidelines and principles of interface design

J McKenzie

HUSAT Research Centre
University of Technology
Loughborough
Leicestershire
UK

This paper examines the type and sources of existing information for the design of the User/Computer Interfaces (UCIs). It then offers a UCI protocol for use by system developers as an aid to identifying the appropriate human factors decisions and their timing within the system life-cycle of products. It suggests areas where further research may be appropriate.

© J McKenzie 1988

J McKenzie
Jim McKenzie joined HUSAT five years ago after graduating in Ergonomics from Loughborough University. He has gained experience on a variety of short-term consultancy and longer term research projects. His research experience has included detailed task analysis work with civil emergency services and public utilities. He has been involved in requirements analysis for potential applications for various computer and communication systems within large organisations. Since 1984 he has contributed to both Ministry of Defence (MoD) and Department of Trade and Industry (DTI) guidelines on human factors in the design of computer systems. Jim's contributions to consultancy projects have included such hardware and software areas as terminal design, screen layouts, database systems and office automation, for both manufacturers and user groups. He has jointly authored several papers in conferences including INTERACT '84 and Milcomp '85. He has also contributed to the six-part HF Guidelines commissioned by the MoD and the DTI.

Guidelines and principles of interface design

Introduction

The basis for many of the ideas behind this paper is work carried out in the production of a handbook for the UK Department of Trade and Industry (DTI) and the Ministry of Defence (MoD(PE))*. This handbook provides guidance on incorporating human factors into all stages of the system life-cycle. It attempts to provide guidance in several ways:
- Methodologies for human factors
- Principles and guidelines for human factors
- Suggested solutions for specific human factors problems
- Human factors Quality Assurance (QA).

It is not possible in this short paper to review the entire scope of the handbook *(MCK1)*, but some guidelines and principles of User/Computer Interface (UCI) design are given, with examples where relevant and possible. A paper by Gardner *(MCK2)*, in this volume, describes the 'state of the art' in human factors methodologies, the place of UCI design in the system life-cycle and the place of the UCI protocol within the design process. It should be read as an introduction to this paper.

Guidelines and principles

In order to understand what sort of advice is available, it is useful to begin by describing what sorts of advice are possible.

The process of generating and giving advice can be thought of as a progression from the specific to the general, and back to the specific (Figure 1).

Designers have personal experiences of design solutions (for example they find a method that works well and, spurred on by this, they may try it again in other applications. If it holds up then it may become embodied into a 'standard' or a 'guideline'. Standards and guidelines tend to be context specific. The initial experience may then be abstracted or generalised further into a design 'principle' (implying that it is relatively context free).

The process continues in that these fundamental principles may suggest new standards or conventions derived not from direct personal experience but by reasoning from the fundamental or 'first' principles. In turn, the designer faced with new problems may derive new design solutions consistent with these higher order principles. For example, Marshall *et al (MCK4)* describe their experiences of deriving guidelines for the design of UCIs from an empirical basis in cognitive psychology.

---

*The views expressed in this paper are those of the author and do not necessarily represent those of the DTI, the MoD(PE) or the HUSAT Research Centre.

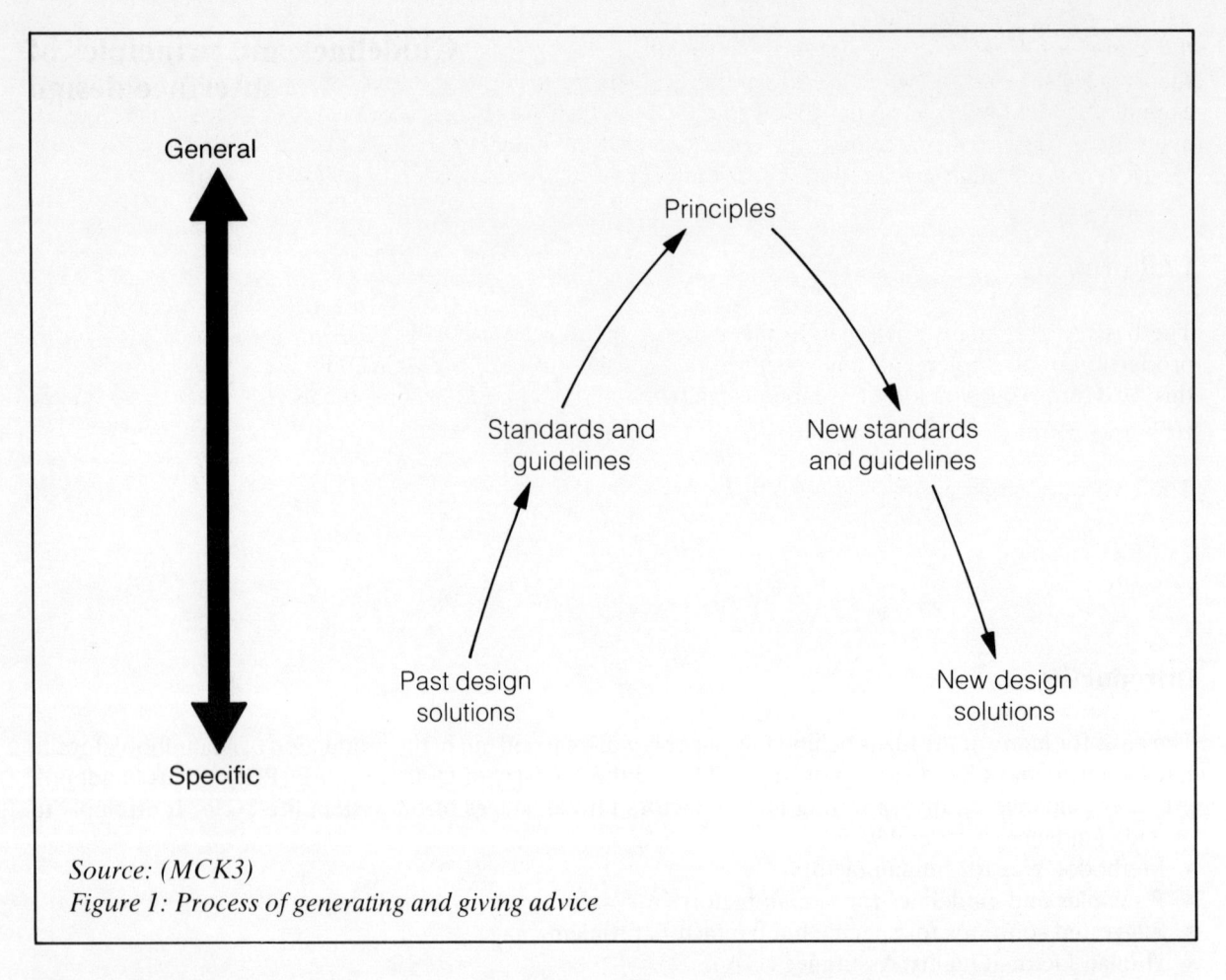

Source: (MCK3)
Figure 1: Process of generating and giving advice

This paper does not attempt to give guidance on new design solutions; this is only possible by the development team that knows the precise circumstances they face (users, tasks, goals, scenarios, etc). Additionally it is not possible in this short paper to summarise all existing standards, conventions, guidelines and principles. There are many good works that provide advice in this way *(MCK5-MCK7)*.

This paper describes a UCI protocol, which is aimed at providing system developers with a methodology for new UCI design solutions, making use of, where appropriate, existing principles, guidelines and solutions.

The use of the UCI protocol attempts to support some high-level principles:

1. *Match interface characteristics to the user:* users are going to vary in their requirements for a UCI — this should be considered in design.

2. *Match interface characteristics to the task:* the task will place requirements onto the design of the interface over and above those from the user.

3. *Consistency:* consistency with what the user is already familiar with is important in all aspects of the design.

4. *Flexibility:* the system should be flexible enough to cope with variations between users and changes in the way in which they may want to interact with the system over a period of time.

5. *Feedback:* users should be provided with a level of feedback on their own actions and on the actions of the system, commensurate with their level of experience and the particular task requirements.

6. *Control:* the focus of control should lie with the appropriate partner (user or computer) in the system depending on the circumstances for each logical UCI.

This is not meant to be an exhaustive list, but rather a list of those principles most frequently 'broken' in the design of some current systems. These high-level principles could be further decomposed into subcategories, or added to. A useful comparison can be made to the work of several other authors, for example Schneiderman's 'eight golden rules' *(MCK8)*, Galitz's 'desirable qualities of a system' and his main areas identified under 'current directions and guidelines' *(MCK7)*, Coutaz's 'nine golden rules' *(MCK9)* and the 'high-level objectives' at the beginning of each section of *(MCK5)*.

UCI protocol

The basis for the main discussion in this paper is the development of a UCI protocol to be used in the production of an implementation specification for a UCI. Gardner *(MCK2)* discusses the relationship of this UCI protocol with other computer/computer and user/computer protocols; for a full account see *(MCK1)*.

The UCI protocol is summarised as follows:

1 UCI dynamics:
- Routing
- Control
- User guidance
- User sensory modality
- User action modality
- User effector.

2 UCI imagery:
- Language type
- Grammar
- Vocabulary
- Accent.

3 UCI devices:
- Displays
- Controls.

It takes a layered approach to produce a user-oriented list of features which should be considered in the make-up of a detailed human factors implementation specification for a UCI. The UCI protocol aims at producing a recommended minimum set of features which ought to be considered in most projects. Additions and improvements could be made to the list by system developers. The UCI protocol is user oriented in that it considers only those factors that will directly influence user/computer interaction and not those affecting the internal workings of the computer system.

It is intended that the procedure for defining a UCI protocol for a logical UCI should follow a top-down approach. The UCI protocol requires the designers to specify the logical/functional features first (that is the dynamics and the imagery) before specifying the physical devices by which these will be implemented. This approach can be compared to the recommendation of Sperandio *(MCK10)* of choosing the most suitable sensory motor channels prior to choosing the most efficient input/output devices. Also, Coutaz *(MCK9)* describes a five-stage methodology for the design of UCIs, which considers user characteristics, task characteristics, system-dependent notions, dialogue structure and, *finally*, interaction style. It has often been the case that poor UCI design has originated from an initial choice of the target display and control and then a fitting of the imagery and dynamics to them.

The use of the UCI protocol by more experienced human factors specialists or consultants may result in a concurrent specification across several of the layers. This is because the human factors specialist will be able to deal with a greater number of contingencies between the layers of the UCI protocol than can the 'general practitioner' *(MCK2)*.

UCI dynamics

This section summarises the dynamics aspects of the UCI protocol. The information resulting from the definition of the dynamics aspects will be used in the later stages to help define the imagery and devices.

Routing
The following list summarises the main features in routing that need to be defined for each logical interface:

1 Source (who from?).

2 Destination (who to?).

3 Security:
   - Broadcast (for all to receive)
   - Private (point-to-point).

4 Prearrangement:
   - Sent with prior arrangement (connected)
   - Sent without prior arrangement (connectionless).

5 Receipt to be acknowledged.

6 Priority.

7 Capacity:
   - Dynamic (for example frequency of message and rate of transmission)
   - Static (for example size of maximum message).

8 Subject matter of message.

This list utilises and checks for completeness of information that has been collected in previous task analysis. Further, it allows an analysis of all the messages that a user is expected to receive or send so that similarities and conflicts can be identified at an early stage.

Control
The following list summarises the main features to be considered in 'control' that need to be defined for each logical interface:
- User initiates the communication
- Computer initiates the communication
- Timing of the communication.

It is worth noting that the source of the initiating communication is required to be identified. For some systems, knowledge-based systems being a good example, it is recognised that in the partnership of computer and human there is a requirement that 'both parties initiate interaction (ask questions, or set goals) and respond (answer, or carry out investigations)' *(MCK11)*. It is important that these decisions are made explicitly for each situation rather than resulting from an inappropriate choice of dialogue styles.

The subject of the timing of the communication is one that has produced much guidance in the literature. It is worth noting the various aspects that go to make up a system response time (Figure 2). Specific response times will be totally system dependent (both users and computers). Guidance on specific response times can be found in *(MCK1, MCK5-MCK8)*.

User guidance
The user guidance provided by the computer to the user should be defined for each logical interface. A major feature of this is the choice concerning which dialogue type should be made use of within each logical interface. A second major feature is that of error feedback. The following list summarises the main features of user guidance by the UCI:

1 Structured dialogue — guidance as to:
   - Duties involved
   - Activities involved
   - Message and material routing
   - 'Paragraph' construction
   - 'Sentence' construction
   - Vocabulary.

2 Freestyle dialogue.

3 Hybrid dialogue:
   - Question and answer
   - Form-filling.

4 Error feedback.

It is necessary to specify which of the dialogue types, 'structured' (as typified by 'menu-based' interfaces), 'freestyle' (as typified by 'command language') and 'hybrid' (as typified by 'question and answer' and 'form-filling', which combines features of both structured and freestyle) will be used for each of the logical interfaces. At this stage it is not yet suitable to make decisions as to how the dialogue type is to be implemented — decisions as to how the user is going to physically interact with the system should be made first (see remainder of section on 'UCI dynamics').

With structured dialogues the user is provided with considerably more guidance than freestyle, with a screen prompt (for example available menu items), an indication of the 'legal' vocabulary and the sentence and paragraph grammars (for example an indication of the range of message options and the rules for constructing a message) and a terminator (labelled 'keys' such as 'return' or 'enter' are examples). Menu-based dialogues are not limited solely to alphanumeric messages or to screen displays, since there are systems with graphical forms of menu and separate function keys.

Other forms of more recent menu-based dialogues which provide a considerable form of user guidance are 'pop-up' and 'pull-down' menus where guidance can be provided by the system as required by the user, or the user can enter a keyboard command where guidance is not required. These forms of menu provide guidance at several layers of command (for example select 'format' to see option of 'bold, italic, underline, etc'). Maguire *(MCK12)* suggests the use of a 'look-ahead' facility in providing user guidance to several levels of pop-up or pull-down menu simultaneously.

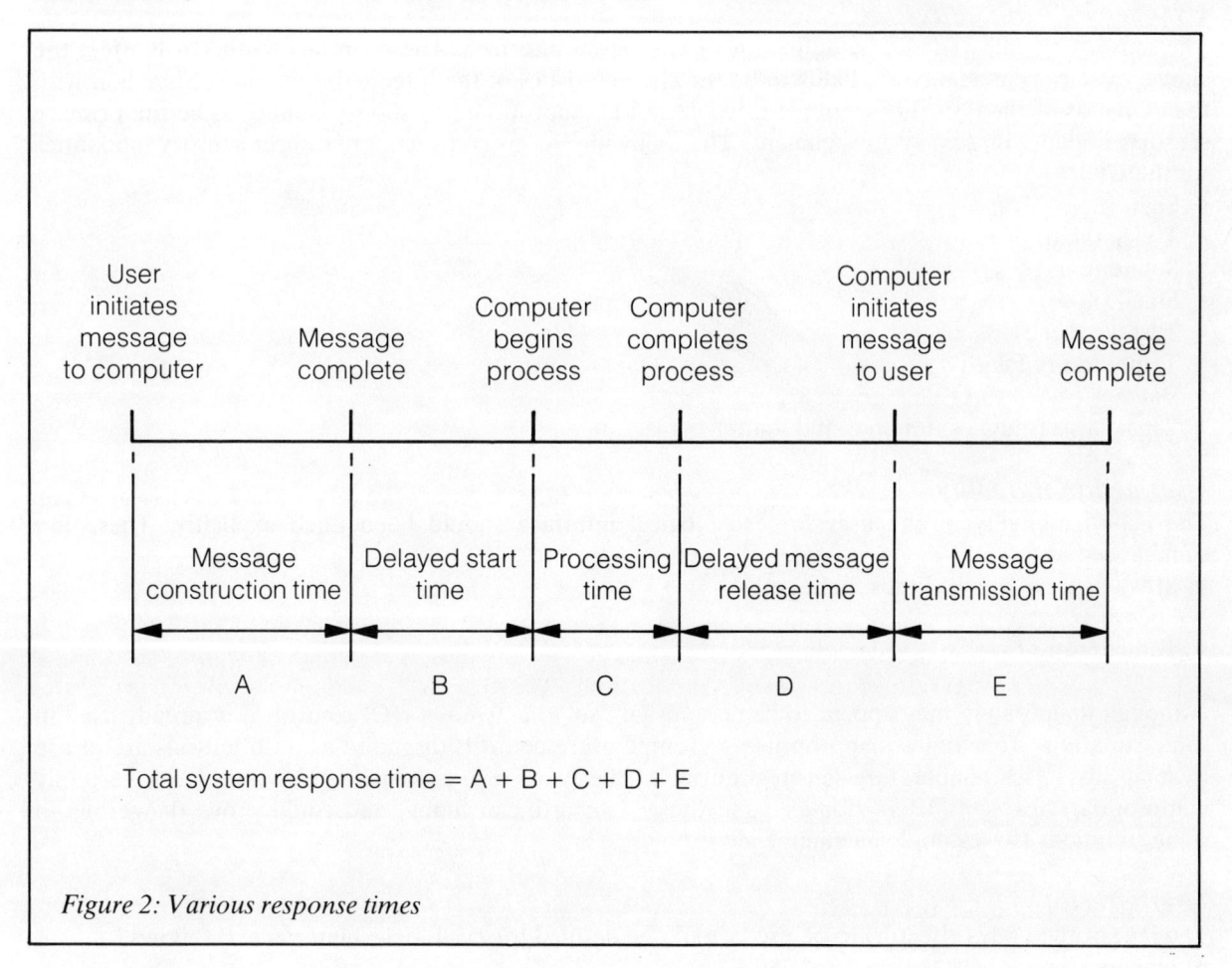

Figure 2: Various response times

There is much additional information in the literature concerning dialogue types, good examples including *(MCK5,MCK7,MCK8)*. Where possible the provision of several types of dialogue should be provided in order to account for such variances among users as skill levels, experience levels or simply personal preferences. What appears to be an easy-to-use system to an infrequent user may appear to be slow and cumbersome to a more experienced person who does not require the same level of guidance or feedback on his actions. To simplify the learning of systems with several types of dialogue, it is important that as far as it is practicable, compatible vocabulary and grammar is used in each of the dialogues, in order to allow switching from one type to another as user experience or preference changes. Making the vocabulary and grammar at the interface compatible with the task vocabulary and grammar already familiar to users is one of the major ways of ensuring that the new system will be consistent with the old one.

The terms 'paragraphs', 'sentences' and 'vocabulary' refer to how much guidance the interface is to provide on the construction of 'complete' commands as opposed to simply which vocabulary is valid. Some systems attempt to not restrict the grammar of the command while in other systems the order in which a command is structured is very rigid (for example copying files in MS-DOS follows rigid rules of grammar).

Error feedback is an important aspect of providing user guidance. Feedback is essential for controlling most user activities, but it can be difficult and costly for system designers to provide (for example the in-built test needed to detect an error, diagnose its cause and generate a helpful message to the user might be impracticable or impossible to implement).

It is important that error messages are as informative as possible and not only indicate to the user what has caused the error, but also attempt to provide information on how to put the error right. This becomes more important for infrequent and important actions by the user rather than frequent and minor ones. Where possible the user should be informed as to the valid vocabulary (for example 'The valid sizes are 1-6') and grammar (for example 'The correct date format is DD-MM-YY').

User sensory modality
The sensory modality should be defined for each logical interface. The main factors that will affect the choice of sensory modality are likely to be the characteristics of the intended users, in conjunction with the demands of the task. For example it would not be appropriate to choose 'sound' to be the primary sensory modality in a noisy environment. The following list gives a summary of user sensory modalities for the UCI:
- Sight (eyes)
- Touch (skin)
- Sound (ears)
- Smell (nose)
- Taste (tongue)
- Temperature (skin)
- Balance (inner ears)
- Kinesthesis (muscles, tendons and joints).

User action modality
The action modality of the user for each logical interface should be defined explicitly. These are summarised as follows:
- Movement (of hands, limbs, head, etc)
- Speech
- Temperature (warming and cooling).

Although temperature may appear to be an unusual way to activate a UCI control, it is already used in some situations, sometimes inappropriately. Temperature controls disguised as push-buttons are in use in some lifts. This temperature-sensitive device in the place of a pressure-sensitive device is certainly inappropriate for some users (for example those with artificial limbs) and could prove dangerous in some situations (for example an emergency stop).

User effector
The part of the body (effector) to be used should be defined for each logical interface as follows:
- Fingers

- Hands
- Feet
- Vocal chords (and associated organs)
- Tongue
- Mouth (and lips)
- Head.

Again this explicit definition may highlight inappropriate choices for some users and task situations.

UCI imagery

This section gives advice on interpreting the imagery aspects of the UCI protocol. The decisions made concerning the required dynamics for the UCI protocol will influence to an extent decisions concerning the imagery. Together the dynamics and imagery will aid the choice of suitable control and display UCI devices.

Language type

The type of language to be used in constructing the messages should be defined explicitly for each logical interface. The choice of language type (or types) should be strongly influenced by the characteristics of the tasks and the intended users. The UCI language should be chosen to enable the users to think and communicate in terms that are familiar and acceptable to the users. The following list summarises the main features of UCI language types (further subdivisions could be made):
- English prose
- 2D pictures (for example histograms and icons)
- 3D pictures
- nD pictures (for example animated solids)
- Mathematics
- Computer languages.

One common representation that is gaining place in office automation is that of the visual metaphor of the 'desktop'. In trying to match the language of the interface to the user's cognitive model of office work, icons of symbolic telephones, documents, wastepaper baskets, etc, appear on an office desk. Such models and metaphors are highly task specific. In office automation the desktop has proved to be a successful metaphor to the extent that users already possess an effective cognitive model of an office desk and the objects/activities which it presumes. These can improve if different applications consistently reinforce the cognitive model. However, these standard metaphors are not likely to carry successfully to other environments — other metaphors will be needed, such as map displays in a military environment or mimic diagrams in process control.

The inconsistent use of a visual metaphor, or the use of an inappropriate visual metaphor, is likely to decrease the usability of the application. Many have suggested that it is an area where further research is required *(MCK13,MCK14)*. Indeed, it may be the case already that *de facto* standards are beginning to emerge prior to the research being completed, with the obvious danger of imposing a suboptimum (see *(MCK15)* for a fuller discussion).

Grammar

Defining the grammar to be used in constructing the messages is an important stage in the UCI protocol for each logical interface. The main features are summarised in the following list:

1 *'Sentence' construction* (that is the arrangement of vocabulary primitives into meaningful message units). Examples of 'sentences' are sentence in English prose, diagram in graphics, equation in mathematics.
   - Complexity (meta-rules): examples are one 'idea' per sentence, maximum number of embedded clauses and maximum length of noun phrases.
   - Format: an example is <sentence prompt> <message> <sentence terminator>.

2 *'Paragraph' construction* (that is combination of 'sentences' into higher order message units). Examples of 'paragraphs' are sequence of processes and products arranged as a flowchart or a proof in geometry.
   - Complexity (meta-rules): an example is one logical sequence of sentences per paragraph.
   - Format: an example is <para prompt> <sentence> ... <para terminator>.

The 'grammar' of the interface is the arrangement of the vocabulary primitives (for example words, abbreviations, icons, etc) into meaningful message units. As in the English language, other languages have rules (or grammar) that dictate what makes a meaningful combination. In this protocol, all such functionally equivalent message units are called 'sentences'. Continuing the analogy, a 'paragraph' is a larger, more complete, more meaningful, unit of information than is a single 'sentence'.

Every proper language has its own corresponding grammar. Languages such as English, mathematics and computers have grammar which are well established. Other languages are less well established (for example graphics) and in the absence of well-founded research, the best approach is often to be consistent with the 'grammar' that is most familiar to the intended target users.

One aim should be a situation where users can send and receive messages in as complete or 'high' a form as possible (sentences and paragraphs). This will tend to emphasise the functional completeness of the messages, to give guidance to the users as to the legal grammar, to reduce ambiguity for the computers and to reduce the memory load on the users.

Vocabulary

The vocabulary to be used in constructing the messages should be defined explicitly for each of the logical interfaces. The main features which should be considered are summarised as follows:

1 *'Words'* (the whole range of words, numbers, mathematical symbols, map symbols, lines, points, colours, etc that are the primitives of sentences). Meta-rules for defining legitimate words may be included. Special categories are:
   - Prompts (to signal that the user or computer is ready to send or receive a message)
   - Actions (for example verbs and arithmetic operators)
   - Objects (for example noun phrases, numbers and map symbols)
   - Conjunctions (for example 'and' and '( )')
   - Punctuations
   - Terminators (to signal the end of a message or part of a message).

2 *Abbreviations* (shorthand words).

3 *Characters* (the sub-units of words).

Again the analogy with the English language is used, which as with mathematics and programming languages has vocabularies which are well defined. The vocabularies of graphics are less well established and are likely to require more research.

The use of abbreviations ia an area where there is much conflict and confusion. The task of the user, or limitations in interface technologies, may encourage their use, but care should be taken in their creation. For more information on this topic see *(MCK1,MCK8)*.

Accent

Features such as the emphasis, or tone, used in constructing messages should be defined for each logical interface. The main features can be summarised as follows:

1 *Typography* in written messages (for example fonts, use of upper case/lower case, justification, pagination).

2 *Pronounciation* in spoken messages.

UCI devices

This section summarises the device aspects of the UCI protocol. The displays are summarised as follows:
- Screens
- Indicator lamps
- Headphones
- Loudspeakers
- Telephones.

A summary of the controls is also given in the following list:
- QWERTY alphabetic keys
- Chord keyboards
- QWERTY number keys
- Number pad
- Touch screen
- Cursor keys
- Mouse
- Tracker ball
- Joystick
- Light pen
- Fixed function keys
- Variable function keys
- Graphics pad
- Digitiser
- Voice analyser.

It is important that suitable combinations of UCI devices with the chosen UCI dynamics and imagery are made. The choice of dynamics and imagery will place requirements on the UCI devices (for example screen resolution or need for, and properties of, a pointing device). It is important to note that this is the most appropriate way to make decisions concerning the UCI protocol, as opposed to the initial choice of UCI hardware influencing the dynamics and imagery. For more details on the choice of UCI devices and their main features for the chosen UCI dynamics and UCI imagery there are several useful sources *(MCK1, MCK5, MCK6, MCK8, MCK16, MCK17)*.

Standard UCIs

It is obvious that a great deal of time and effort will be saved if designers and users can decide in advance on standard features or preferred solutions to particular types of application. With regard to the choice of standard UCI devices, there is a wealth of existing and proposed national and international standards *(MCK16, MCK17)* as well as many useful guideline documents *(MCK5, MCK6)*.

Much of the information contained in these documents gives advice on *attribute standards*, that is specific physical or functional features or attributes of the displays and controls that the human factors community believes are likely to be effective and acceptable. However, it should be noted that there is some movement towards *performance standards* which advise on how well the displays and controls must perform with users. The draft BS on Visual Display Terminals (VDTs) *(MCK17)* is a notable example of this type of standard.

At present, there are no national or international standards covering the dynamics or imagery of the UCI. This is an area where much research may still be required. In their work on window management systems Hopgood et al *(MCK13)* believed that more work was needed to match user types and window manager design, but they encouraged the 'configurable toolkit' approach to provide an 'extensive set of defaults to provide a house style'. The major aim was to encourage consistency across a range of applications.

This is an area where computer manufacturers appear to be pushing the case for consistency in the dynamics and imagery of the UCI. Cohill *(MCK18)* describes how the variety of interfaces between systems left users 'frequently confused and frustrated' and how, within AT&T Communications, work was currently underway to develop a common interface for those computer systems that would be open to 'direct customer access'. Dysart et al *(MCK19)* in encouraging the use of user interface guidelines developed within Hewlett-Packard state the goal of 'making software easier for our customers'. ICL 'Human factors in design' guidelines *(MCK20)* aim to help the designer to produce more acceptable dialogues in order to increase the efficiency of the product.

Probably two of the most interesting recent examples of attempts to standardise on UCI dynamics and imagery have come from Apple and IBM. Rose *et al (MCK21)*, in introducing the user interface guidelines for the Macintosh, state that 'applications should be easy to learn and use' and 'should build on skills that people already have, not force them to learn new ones'. They put forward the concepts of 'responsiveness', 'permissiveness' and, most important, 'consistency', in the development of user interfaces. Interfaces should be 'responsive', in that user's actions tend to have direct results, 'permissive' in that the system allows the user to decide what to do next (as long as it is reasonable) and 'consistent' in order to share the interface ideas of Macintosh applications.

In IBM's 'Common user access' guidelines *(MCK22)* the concept of a three-dimensional 'consistency' is considered to be paramount. 'Physical consistency' refers to features such as the keyboard layout or properties of the mouse (cf 'devices' level of UCI protocol). 'Syntactical consistency' is used to refer to the sequence and order of appearance of items (or elements) on the screen and the sequence of action requests (cf 'language type' and 'grammar' levels of 'imagery' in UCI protocol). 'Semantical consistency' refers to the meaning of the items that go to make up the interface (cf 'vocabulary' and 'accent' levels of 'imagery' in UCI protocol).

Within the IBM document the benefits of this consistency are said to include the reduction of 'learning time' and 'frustration level' for users, while for programmers the rapid production and changing of applications and reuse of 'panel design' are considered most relevant. A major aim of the IBM guidelines is to establish a 'consistent set of concepts', where in the use of the system the user's 'conceptual model of the interface is reinforced'.

The Apple and IBM examples of attempts at user interface standards for dynamics and imagery highlight the possibility of the emergence of a *de facto* standard among manufacturers (cf the development and adaptation of the QWERTY keyboard as a *de facto* standard). It is possible that system designers may adopt these standards in unsuitable scenarios. Thimbleby *(MCK14)* warns against the development of 'pseudo-generative' principles and quotes the 'desktop' model and the WYSIWYG model as examples. He warns that the generalising of some principles such as these in nonsuitable situations will primarily encourage 'systems research' (for example towards improved technology such as higher resolution displays) rather than 'either an improved user interface or research towards one'.

Conclusions

This paper reviews what the author considers to be the main issues involved in designing UCIs. It suggests that whereas there are many good sources of guidelines for UCI design, system developers still fail to make the relevant human factors considerations at the right stage in the system life-cycle of products. It offers the use of a UCI protocol for use by system developers as an aid to identifying which human factors decisions need to be made and in what sequence they need to be made.

It is concluded that whereas there is a wealth of suitable standards and guidelines available when considering the features of UCI devices, the same level of advice is not available for standardising UCI dynamics and imagery. It is suggested that this is an area where further research is required. Without further research, there is a danger that manufacturers will impose *de facto* standards which may be suboptimum, just as happened with the QWERTY keyboard.

Acknowledgement

The author acknowledges the substantial contribution made by Arthur Gardner to the content of this paper.

7: Developments in computing and the user interface — emerging issues in end-user interface design

M A Norman

Department of Computer Science
University of Hull
Hull
North Humberside
UK

This paper considers the new issues that are facing designers of end-user interfaces. It is unlikely that the question 'How do I design a suitable interface?' will diminish in importance for the designer, since 'suitability' helps to determine the value and acceptability to the user of a system. There are also emergent technologies for which answers to this question have to be established. In order to face up to these challenges the designers will need to be aware of the way in which interface design can be integrated into the design process, the effect of technological innovation on the design issues and the directions that are evident and being followed to provide support for the user and the designer of IT systems. These issues, and their implications for future work in interface design, are considered.

© M A Norman 1988

M A Norman
Mike Norman had 25 years experience in the computer industry with LEO computers, UNIVAC and various user organisations, prior to moving to the academic world. He presently holds the Rank Xerox Chair in Information Technology and is responsible for the Interactive Systems Design Group at the University of Hull. Over the past six years he has served on advisory and research committees for Alvey/SERC, Bide and Department of Trade and Industry IT initiatives concerned with Human/Computer Interaction (HCI). Professor Norman established the first Alvey MMI R&D centre in Scotland before taking the appointment at the University of Hull. His present research interests are concerned with the provision of software aids for user interface designers.

Developments in computing and the user interface — emerging issues in end-user interface design

Introduction

The development of information systems is a matter of achieving some balance between *exploration* and *constraint*. There is, on the one hand, the exploration of the boundaries of available technology in the pursuit of a solution to some system problem and, on the other, constraint of the multitude of possible design solutions in order to provide one which is suitable for the users and the task which is to be carried out. The designer's task has always been like this, but it is becoming increasingly onerous as the variety and complexity of the technology and the sophistication of applications progress.

One response to this increasing complexity is the adoption of a more disciplined approach to the crafting process, such that the resultant artefact — the designed object — is devised in a more manageable way. Since the focus for the realisation of designs is predominantly the construction of software, the disciplined approach that is most evident is that of software engineering — an approach which calls for, among other things, a clear requirements specification, the development of demonstrable and robust code (notated and capable of validation) and the provision of code which is certainly maintainable and potentially reusable. All this so that the resultant artefact can, notwithstanding its inherent complexity, be designed, shared, maintained and used.

The issues that have led to greater consideration being given to this approach have not materialised overnight. In many cases they reflect the distillation of bitter experience of implementing and managing information systems. In others they arise from concerns about the critical nature of particular application domains, the problems caused by the mobility of skilled and knowledgeable staff or the increasing costs of software production and maintenance. However, for all this, the end objective has been to deliver, through the technology, an application. To this objective there has now to be added another constraint — the need to deliver the application in a form *suitable to the user*.

The consequences of engineering the interface either well or badly are by now well known and evident. Conscious consideration of the design of the user interface has given rise to the Windows, Icons, Mice and Pull-down menus (WIMP) interface and the beneficial effects and endorsement of this are seen by the considerable and swift uptake of this type of system by users. The pressure that this has created within the industry should not be underestimated, and it contrasts quite starkly with user response to systems where the interface is neither appealing, easily learnt or consistent in operation. Other pressures exist for the designer to take more conscious and positive steps to design the user interface — the increasing number and range of end users, the increasing proportion of code that has to be devoted to handling the user system interaction and the improved display resolution that is now commonly available. The designer cannot leave to chance or intuition the design of the user interface. The problem this presents for design can be viewed from two apparently distinct standpoints.

Firstly, there is the need for human factors issues to be taken into account in the design of IT systems, a view which has been voiced for some time. A considerable number of studies and investigations have been carried out which would support this view, and yet the information produced by these studies seems to have been ignored or overlooked. In part a separation of concerns has arisen because it has been seen that the interface is concerned with the superficial appearance of the system — the appearance, layout and presentation of the display — rather than the structure of the application. Improving this situation appears to be a problem of process, of providing the means for the two different cultures of the human factors expert and the designer to be brought together. It is only comparatively recently that it has been recognised that User Interface Design (UID) issues are central to design and cannot be somehow 'grafted' on as a separate and latter stage *(NOR1)*. Such a simple statement belies, however, the difficulties in achieving that step forward. Much of the focus and direction for human factors work has been concerned with the evaluation and assessment of existing systems and, no matter how well meaning or well informed such judgements are, they are typically made and given with hindsight. Good design, or at least improvement of present practice, is accomplished through foresight and foreknowledge. At the heart of the matter is the timely provision of information and support for the designer and, through the design of the user interface, support for the user.

Secondly, there is the need, from the designer's view, to be able to take account of the potential of technology-based developments. In particular there is a need to know how these developments may be exploited in the context of providing some systems solution. It is arguable that historically the developments to which the designer has had to respond have, in computing terms, been dominated by concerns of processing power and storage capacity coupled with dramatic changes in economic justification. In terms of the artefacts that have been produced there is a strong sense of progress amounting to more of the same but quicker and better connected, leading naturally to a focus on the issues of managing large complex software environments. In terms of the user interface the changes have been modest. The command-driven model of computing has given way to menu selection (less effort for the user, less to remember, but structurally the same as command-driven systems) and, more recently, iconic manipulation (the easy-to-use desktop metaphor). However, the technologies affecting UID that are available now or evident on the horizon, particularly multimedia and innovative technologies, pose design issues of an altogether different form to previously. Moreover, it is not a neat pattern of progression and refinement of established design constraints. The user environment is becoming much richer, in terms of the interactional possibilities, and requires the formulation and resolution of design issues of an entirely different type, since the designer has to be aware of more than the forms of interface technology in order to suggest with any confidence that it may be appropriate as a potential solution. The requirement is that the designer also understands the constraints on its applicability.

There are two viewpoints which give rise to apparently different pressures in relation to the design process for the user interface:

1 Provision of existing information about the principles of UID in a manner which relates to the needs of designers and is usable (dependable, valid, applicable and predictive).

2 Identification of the issues related to new interaction methods (applied singularly or in combination) and the definition and codification of these results to identify the principles and applicable rules for design.

However, in order to make UID more accessible the emphasis has to change from concern with evaluation *after* construction to the provision of constraint information which is *usable at some stage in design*. The issues for UID for the future are concerned with the applicability and predictability of design guidance, in relation to both existing technology and emergent technologies, so that UID can be incorporated into the existing design process and practice.

What is interaction?

Early models of systems were based on simple query/response views of the gathering of information by the system from the user, with equally simple and flat representations of the application provided for the user. Systems developed so that users could well have at their fingertips a range of applications — systems operating in different 'modes'. With this came the realisation that issues of consistency (for example the need that the effect of keystrokes should remain constant), of ordering (for example the sequence of commands and arguments), of memorability (for example the mnemonics used for command abbreviations) affected user performance. The further development of the menu-based approach saw the user selecting and choosing what to do. This raised issues of navigating through (for the user partially invisible) data and command sets, of context and current state, and of the view that the user formed of the system at large. Add to these issues the question of the user learning about the system (an issue for which there are not particularly well-formed theories), and the notion of the user and a system interacting together becomes a complex process. While various models of interaction have been proposed it is clear that the topic is a complex, if not confounding one, in relation to design. The deeper issues of human problem solving, of cognition, of intention and of language and meaning are unlikely to be resolved overnight and yet they all form part of a fuller understanding of Human Computer Interaction (HCI). The reality is that the development of technology will not stand still while we pursue these questions and, so far as design is concerned, we shall have to make use of 'engineering approximations' where we have only partial theories and understanding.

Exceptions to this state of affairs have been the development of Fitts Law *(NOR2)* (concerned with the time taken to move across a display space) and the more sophisticated Keystroke Model *(NOR3)* (concerned with task performance times). In the case of the latter, it was restricted to the prediction of error-free performance by an expert user and clearly the use of a standard mental operator — albeit defined by the use of a set of heuristics — was based on a composite approximation for a number of mental operations. The failure to provide other, more sophisticated, models with predictive capacity is indicative of the difficulty of the area rather than neglect on the part of researchers.

Engineering the user interface

Design principles and guidelines

The available approaches to UID range from sets of design principles to sophisticated software design tools. In one sense the principles that are stated for UID can be seen as trivial or commonsense — for example 'Know the user population' — but they have been used and shown to be advantageous, not surprisingly, since what is frequently claimed to be commonsense is not commonly applied. It would, however, make sense to have more detailed interpretations of these principles in relation to features of interactive systems, and more comprehensive and detailed guidelines have been developed. In contrast to the simplicity and compactness of design principles, design guidelines are detailed and lengthy — for example the guidelines proposed by Smith and Mosier *(NOR4)* identify more than 600 aspects of UID for which a design rule can be stated — but do provide specific advice. In the particular case referred to, the information has been *codified* and related to the achievement of specific design objectives for the user interface. The end result is a comprehensive reference, albeit a voluminous and somewhat daunting document. Maguire *(NOR5)* has pointed out that as guidelines become more comprehensive and detailed they can lead to conflicting and contradictory advice. This is not necessarily a difficulty since design is concerned with making trade-offs between conflicting requirements. In the case of UID, this depends on interpreting the constraints of user, task and system attributes, to arrive at a workable and implementable design. Further work is required to address the issue of the applicability of guidelines to characteristics of user and task, and should lead to a better understanding of the salient characteristics and features of interaction.

Prototyping

In the end some guidance for the designer is far better than no guidance at all, and the resultant system does not have to stand and fall by the deliberations of the designer alone. It is after all intended to be used, and a final arbiter of the usability of a system is the user. Some attention has been given to the need to provide alternative interaction methods and sequences, both initially and as the user learns more about the system. The difficulty of making changes to a system at later stages of the design cycle, with their attendant high costs, can be ameliorated by the use of prototyping as an approach to design.

Prototyping calls for the availability of a software environment (usually some form of User Interface Management System (UIMS) — for more detail see *(NOR6)*) that will permit the easy construction and revision of the interface to an application system (for example *(NOR7)*) (see Figure 1). The objective is to demonstrate and evaluate the user interface as a way of making good any deficiencies in the requirements specification or the designed interface. The difficulties arise from the amount of time that can be taken in this process, the amount of effort needed to construct the prototype and the reluctance of users to stop the process of refinement. On the credit side, the systems so produced appear to be more easily

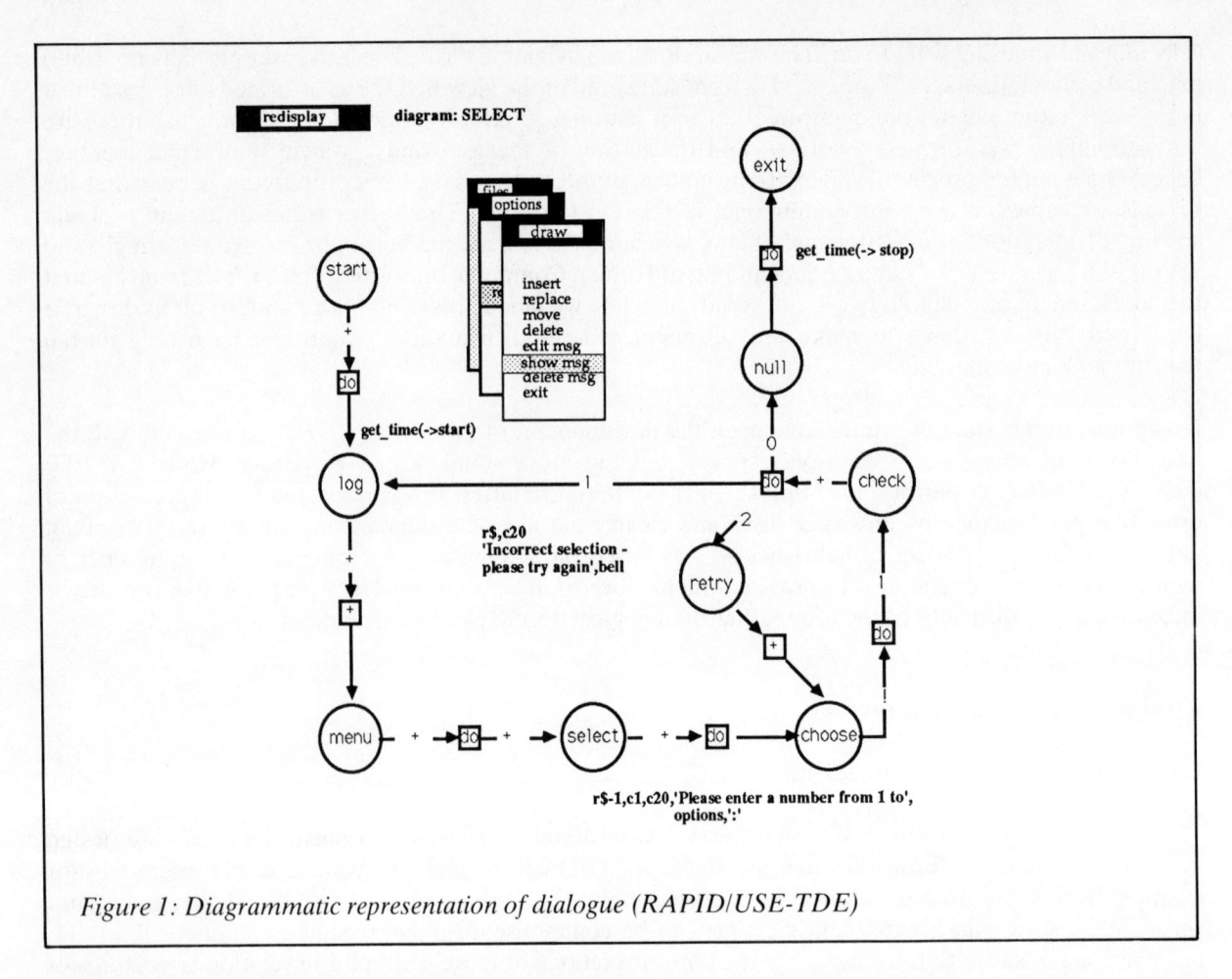

Figure 1: Diagrammatic representation of dialogue (RAPID/USE-TDE)

introduced and accepted. Of consequence is the fact that this approach reflects the essentially iterative nature of design, in contrast to other more rigid models of the stages in design, and separates out the interaction handling from the application.

Interface features and user tailoring

One consequence of this approach is the easy re-engineering of the interface, which has generally been assumed to be the province of the designer/implementor. However, there is no logical reason why the re-engineering should not be undertaken by the user or why this process should not be available throughout the life of the system. The further development that has encouraged this is the abstraction of interface feature handling into standardised software support environments — window management systems. Clearly, one of the ways to reduce the effort in providing the code for the user interface is to provide generalised support for a range of interface features — in much the same way that operating systems were designed to provide common and generalised device handling. Such a system typically provides support for window operations (Move, Resize, Scroll, Open and Close), menu definition and selection procedures, context information (currently available commands, current position in relation to total file size, help features, etc) and dialogue with the user (through definable dialogue boxes, which can be composite objects including sub-windows, selections and data entry — see Figure 2 for an example of a dialogue box).

Not only are such environments efficient — by reducing the amount of code that has to be devised and generated — they also provide methods of interaction for the user which are consistent and predictable, thus meeting in some measure the principles of UID. They also provide support for an approach to interaction that allows the individual user to obtain the behaviour they require or feel most comfortable with from the underlying system. Users can gain control of the way in which the task is carried out through defining the following preferences:
- Operational preferences — registration of keystrokes, setting 'alarm' bell, etc
- Position preferences — sizing, placement and relationship of active screen areas (windows)
- Representation preferences — file structures displayed in text or iconic form, displayed in sequence according to different attributes (time, space, alphabetic)

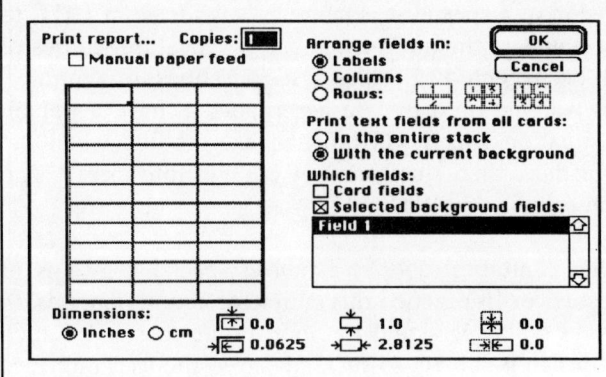

Figure 2: Sample dialogue box (HyperCard)*

Note:
In common with most dialogue boxes this example is a composite object which includes a scrollable sub-window, selection boxes, data entry areas and a layout area which is activated through direct manipulation to give visual and numeric feedback.

- Task preferences — command or menu driven, menus or soft keys to include users' composite task sequences as selectable items.

Potentially, the user can change all the attributes of the system's behaviour that are accessible to the designer, so that applications can be individualised to meet the user's particular needs.

In practice what has happened is that the features of the interface that designers have to deal with have been generalised and described in some formal and implementable way. Much of the work on UIMSs was based on directed graphs/transition diagrams as the underlying mechanism, and further work has been carried out to formally describe features of the interface. However, much of this is not accessible to the designer or the user since it describes the interface in terms which are more familiar to the computer scientist. Alternatively, one can look for paradigms which more readily model interaction and one such model which intuitively commands attention — even if there are not good theoretical grounds for such attention — is the object-oriented approach. Put at its simplest, it is based on the notion that it is the 'objects' of a system which are paramount and that user interaction amounts to invoking the 'methods' for these objects. The phrase that is usually used to describe this approach is 'direct manipulation', since actions can be invoked on the objects directly without the intermediary of an explicit command structure. Therefore, for example, the deletion of a file is accomplished by selecting the 'file object' and physically dragging it to a 'wastebin object'; similarly files are moved between directories (folder objects) by selection and physical dragging to the new directory. It is this approach which produced the Xerox Star system *(NOR8)* and continues to underpin its modern-day equivalents — the Xerox Documenter and the Apple Mac. The end result gives systems with 'universal' interaction tasks — copy, move, etc — invoked by some direct and visible action on the part of the user, a method of working that users seem to find intuitively easy. (The reasons for this are potentially many — the method of operation conforms to the way in which we generally act, the system is visible, the system provides immediate and positive feedback, task closure is facilitated and evident, less has to be remembered, etc.) Moreover, the 'objects' have properties which can be made visible to the user and are themselves selectable and can be changed. In this way both the interaction and its outcome can, to some extent, be determined by the user. In relation to the technology it is this approach which more readily allows the integration of the traditional medium of computing systems (text) to be integrated with other types of information — specifically graphics representations.

Integration of UID

It should be clear from these considerations that presently design practice will need to draw on a variety of information sources and aids in order to deliberately and constructively contrive a 'good' user interface. Much depends on pragmatic engineering considerations, although the range and variety of interaction tasks and features to which this has to be applied are such that there will be likely to be as many errors of omission as there have been errors of commission in the past. However, such a fragmentary approach will not serve the needs of the users, even if they can in the end enhance a system's behaviour by 'tailoring' it to their needs.

---

*Reproduced from HyperCard™ Version 1.01 © Apple Computer 1987.

One approach that has been advocated is the provision of a specialist, someone well versed in UID, to serve alongside the members of the design team. It seems to the author that the practical difficulties of achieving this end make it unlikely that it will be accepted. Besides considerations of 'cultural' differences, there is an implicit assumption that it will, in any case, be acceptable to have a person monitoring and reviewing the work of others, a situation which will only be exacerbated when the inevitable pressures of meeting deadlines arise. Further, there just are not enough interface design specialists presently trained or available to fulfil such roles.

An alternative approach has been to recognise this limitation and to establish specialist groups of designers who can be called on to supply specialist advice. In practice this course of action depends on the designers identifying for themselves the instances where it would be appropriate to call for such advice. It is of course possible to ensure that every design is subject to such advice — the user interface equivalent of the 'system walkthrough' review — and HCI specialists are beginning to provide comprehensive laboratory testing facilities to meet this need. It has also been recognised that this advisory/evaluative process needs to be supplemented by the early definition for designers of the user interface requirements — usually referred to as *usability criteria*. Clear statements of objectives are to be welcomed. They can be taken into account by designers and the proposed design can be evaluated against them. However, it does seem at the moment that, while they can be stated and evaluated, there are difficulties for the designer in knowing how to interpret and achieve them.

The main issue is not the need to take account of user requirements, nor the importance of user interface design *(NOR9)*. It is the question of the transferability of design information which inhibits the integration of UID with conventional design practice. The author gave an earlier reference to software support environments as aids to interface definition, and they are being increasingly used. Indeed, it is not surprising that support for the designer that is fashioned as a software artefact should be communicable, comprehensible, convenient and, above all, made use of. The author suggests that it is through this medium — the provision of software tools, techniques and methods — that taking account of the user as a component of the system (imposing his own constraints on design) will become as natural to the designer as any other aspect of design. This is not to deny the role of the UID specialist or of evaluation, it is rather to insist that the designer is dealt with on his own ground and on his own terms.

The issues that have to be dealt with to bring about this state of affairs in relation to the information we already have at our disposal are already evident and being pursued:

1 Descriptive methods which are accessible to the designer and end user.

2 The separation of concerns as between the application and the interaction.

3 Encapsulation of design information in software support environments and, in order to achieve this, beyond the purely pragmatic engineering approach.

4 Codification of existing design information which, in turn, depends on the development of fuller models and theories (see point 5).

5 Fuller models and theories (albeit partial) to account for and explain the process of interaction when carried out between a human and a computer.

Looking to the future

All that has been said so far relates to our present state of affairs and, although it may be thought that this provides sufficient challenge for UID, the issues raised by the prospective developments should serve to sharpen our resolve to deal with these issues. Inevitably in any review of the future there will be issues that are omitted, sometimes from a lack of foresight and sometimes from the lack of space to do justice to the particular topic. The author has attempted to tread a middle ground by selecting examples which serve to raise general issues. The issues are those of:
- Identifying and providing adequate design information for new application areas
- Evaluating and providing guidance for new methodologies — particularly the handling of information-rich multimedia systems

- Formulating communicable and implementable notations to express interaction
- Applying new techniques to the process of design.

In all these respects there is pressure to provide information for design, and urgency to devise methods of delivery for that design information through tools, methods and techniques. The attention and concerted effort that is required cannot be overstated, and with such attention we can provide practical solutions to the problem of including the user as a component of the system, making user interface design a matter of choice, not chance.

The application issue — group working and computer-mediated communication

There has been much emphasis on the provision and exploitation of computing support for the individual, through the PC or workstation and its software environment. However, one of the requirements in this era of electronic communications is to provide support in a variety of ways for people working together, but perhaps separated by time and place. The traditional method has been to use electronic mail, and this has been extended to less private and more open methods — electronic bulletin boards *(NOR10)*. In this approach the messages are organised in terms of 'topics' covered rather than the usual 'originator/recipients' model. This raises issues of the arrangement and management of such electronic message databases, optimisation of search and message scanning, mechanisms for designating subject matter associations between messages and groups of messages, etc. It also of necessity requires that we understand and provide adequate support for communication in its various forms. Thus, questions are raised which require new answers in a new domain, allowing us to derive functional requirements from some form of task analysis of user needs.

The methodology issue — hypertext

Hypertext provides a way of gathering together different types of information (text, graphics and animation) in the form of 'screenfulls' of information — designated as a notecard *(NOR11)* or hypercard *(NOR12)* — which are effectively arranged as a database which can be browsed through. Conceptually, the card consists of a collection of objects — for example the card itself, its background, selectable buttons and text frames — which may stand individually or, in the case of buttons particularly, may form part of some composite object. Besides providing a method of representation which is appealing and invites exploration (objects look like the thing they stand for, for example a page of a diary looks like the page from a diary), the various objects are active and can be used to form a variety of linkages through the collections of cards. Further, in the case of HyperCard as released by Apple, the actions associated with selecting particular objects are described in a programming language — HyperTalk *(NOR13)*. The approach is one of direct manipulation by the user of screen objects, which are defined in terms of their properties and methods.

The end result is a graphics-based system of considerable power, supported by its own development environment (including preprepared graphics objects) and applicable in a wide range of ways. The following examples show, respectively, HyperCards used as:

1 Pictures (from 'Clip Art'), giving an indication of the realism that can be achieved on modern high-resolution screens (see Figure 3a).

2 Sketch and diagram (Bill Sez), which is a replication with associated images of a talk given by the originator of the concept (see Figure 3b).

3 Electronic children's book (Inigo), where selection of one of the three available objects — the footpath, the bush or the tree — reveals other similarly active 'pages' of the storybook (see Figure 3c).

4 Representation of timetable (undergraduate course material), where the timetable topics are selectable leading on to views of the particular course material (see Figure 3d).

The design issues are multitudinous, in part because of the general-purpose nature of this application and in part because of the variety of media that can be handled. Representative questions would cover the following:
- The rules for screen layout and graphics design
- The need for consistent conventions for navigation, titling and operations of objects

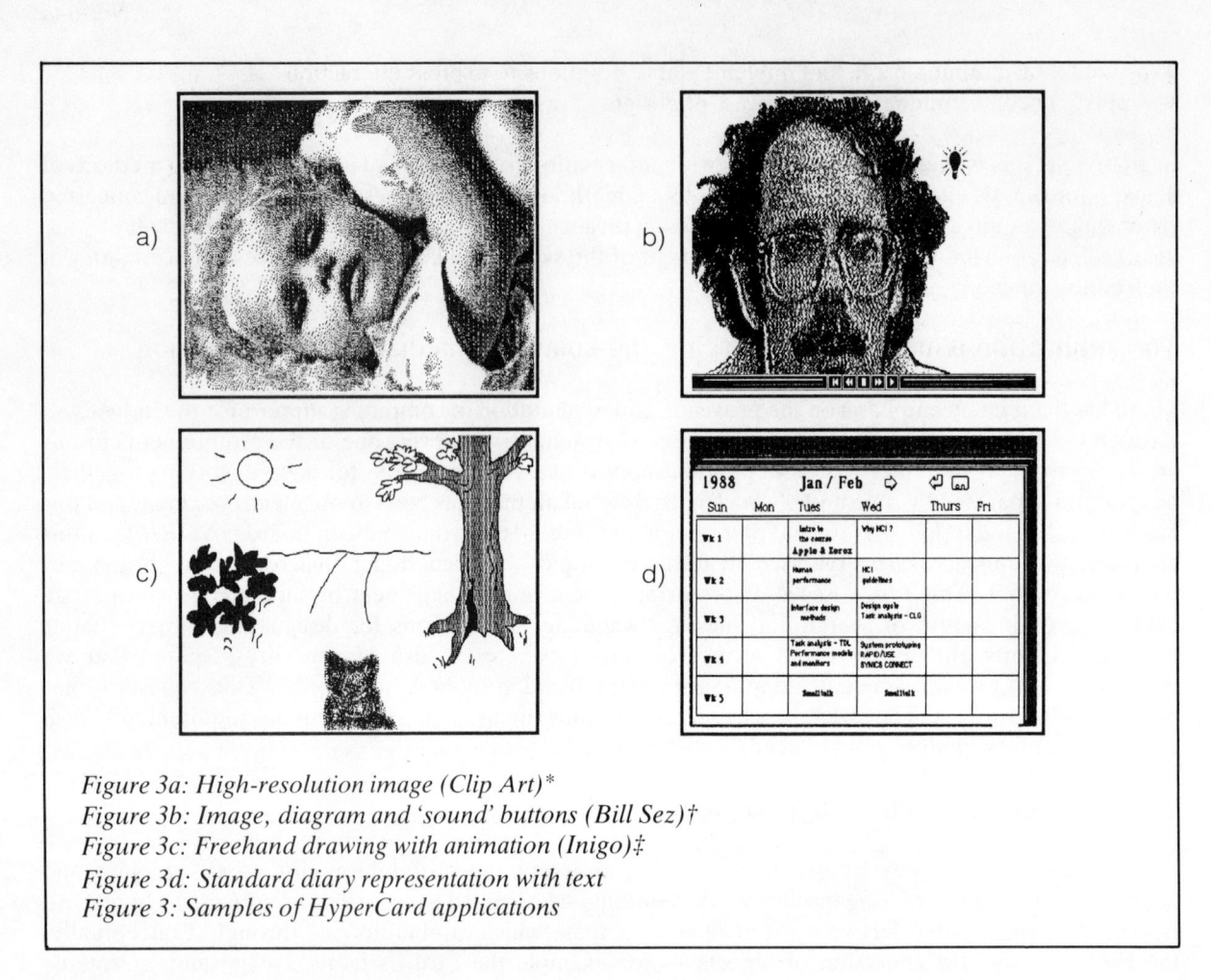

Figure 3a: High-resolution image (Clip Art)*
Figure 3b: Image, diagram and 'sound' buttons (Bill Sez)†
Figure 3c: Freehand drawing with animation (Inigo)‡
Figure 3d: Standard diary representation with text
Figure 3: Samples of HyperCard applications

- The best use of text, image and speech for information handling, and representation
- The use of programming language for control, monitoring and 'intelligent' responses.

It is to be noted that libraries of ready-made routines for menu handling, etc (for instance the widely available HyperCard 'Developer stack') are already being distributed, whereas information about the user interface design issues posed by this method of working are far less evident, but much needed.

The language issue — NeWS

The separation of the definition of the interaction from the application component has been tackled in a number of ways. However, a new approach is evident, based on extensions to the way in which 'print images' have been defined in PostScript *(NOR14)* and subsequently extended in the Network Extensible Window System (NeWS). In essence the change is from a mechanism to support interaction (UIMS) to the expression and definition of interaction through a 'language'. There are considerable debates yet to be resolved about the merits of this and other competing approaches. However, NeWS has one feature of particular consequence — the extensible nature of the definitions — which permits the easy and consistent development of high-level operations. This offers the possibility of moving beyond the standard interface support mechanisms — the windowing operations — to provide task-related operations. Since the NeWS scripts are interpretable, this offers the further possibility of portable and communicable software artefacts to support not just the interface operations, but also the interactions involved in a task. This is very much in line with the present move towards, where possible, providing standard definitions for application domains (for example the recently adopted Office Document Architecture Standard), and would provide a major step forward in the provision of a task-based framework to be used in common by interface designers and software engineers alike.

---

*Reproduced from HyperCard™ 'Clip Art' stack © Apple Computer 1987.
†Reproduced from 'The vision of HyperCard' (Bill Atkinson) — shareware/demonstration stack.
‡Reproduced from 'Inigo gets out' © Amanda Goodenough, Amanda Stories, Santa Cruz — shareware stack.

The technique issue — 'intelligent' HCI

There has been much interest in the development of 'intelligent' systems and, although this is a much misused term, there are evident techniques and methods related to the provision of intelligent interfaces which require further exploration *(NOR15)*. So far as this effects UID, the principal concerns are those of the internal representation or embedding of models of the user (including thereby a sense of history into current system responses to user actions), and the provision of context-sensitive responses (intelligent help systems, etc). Certainly work in this area highlights the need to adopt a wider view of interaction — to include, for instance, the issues of goal representation and explanatory and 'conversationally competent' features. One area that presently appears to be neglected is the application of these techniques to issues related to the user interface itself *(NOR16)* — an intelligent system seems to refer to intelligence in relation to the application domain rather than the users and their characteristics. The possibility of applying these methods to the 'uncertain' process of design, so that design choices may effectively be deferred or related to the characteristics of usage is something to be explored. Indeed a logical development of the user tailoring approach is to provide internal mechanisms to validate design choices and, if appropriate, automatically vary the behaviour of the system *(NOR17)*. The notions of context-sensitive help systems are extensible to include other attributes of an interactive system.

Conclusion

In all these instances there are new issues to be addressed and dealt with which collectively contribute significantly to UID. The importance of these issues for the exploitation of technology should not be underestimated, since they deal with concerns of development, acceptability and uptake of IT products, and much rests on our ability to respond to these challenges. At present UID skill is a scarce resource and difficult to integrate smoothly into the design process. Clearly the role and nature of the human interface designer needs to be defined and recognised, a process that will be much easier when the multidisciplinary nature of the skills required are stated and understood more openly *(NOR18)*. Mechanisms need to be found for the adequate communication of design information, particularly to harness this to existing software engineering practice. Lastly, adequate models of computation have to be devised to take account of the process of interaction. Resolving these matters is not a straightforward task and there is much to be done to be prepared for the future.

8: Introduction to the design of end-user interfaces

B Shackel

HUSAT Research Centre
University of Technology
Loughborough
Leicestershire
UK

For many users the computer in an IT system is remote and hidden; the terminal or workstation is effectively the computer as they see it. If good usability is to be achieved this computer interface must be made to match the needs and characteristics of the human user. In this paper the user's perspective of the interface is first emphasised. Some reasons for the frequent neglect of user interface design are suggested and some consequences of poor interface design are reviewed. The context, definition and quantification of usability are then considered at some length. Finally, the importance of usability and good interface design, especially in the European context, is discussed and some illustrations are presented of the benefits of bringing human factors and usability fully into system design.

© B Shackel 1988

B Shackel
Brian Shackel graduated in Classics from Cambridge University in 1947 and, after three years as a naval officer, returned to Cambridge to read Psychology. He joined the Medical Research Council's Applied Psychology Research Unit in 1952 and, from 1954, was Head of the Ergonomics Department at EMI Electronics Ltd. In 1969 he took up his present position as Professor of Ergonomics at the University of Technology, Loughborough. Professor Shackel is a Fellow of the British Psychological Society, a Fellow of the Human Factors Society (US), a Fellow and past Chairman of the Council of the Ergonomics Society, and currently Honorary Treasurer of the International Ergonomics Association. He has been an Academic Adviser to the Department of Employment and in turn Editor of the journals 'Applied Ergonomics' and 'Journal of Occupational Psychology'. He is a past Dean of the School of Human and Environmental Studies at Loughborough University, and has recently completed 10 years as Head of the Department of Human Sciences.

Introduction to the design of end-user interfaces

Introduction

The industrialised world is now an information society. This change occurred during the 1970s and early 1980s, and is now being recognised more widely. For example, in the US between 1940 and 1980 the percentage of blue-collar workers decreased from 40 to 32 per cent, whereas the white-collar percentage increased from 31 to 52 per cent *(SHA1)*. The process has been similar in other countries and today more than 50 per cent of Britain's working population work in offices *(SHA2)*. However, white-collar and office workers are not the only information workers; a fair proportion of the service industries, involving 13 per cent of the US workforce in 1980, are handling information rather than industrial products.

Most of these workers handling information will be provided with computing or IT equipment which is supposed to aid and support them in their various tasks. For most of these users the computer is essentially the terminal or workstation which they are using, and that is the central computer as they see it. However, only too often these users are seen as 'end users' by designers. This name may well betray an attitude which causes some of the bad design for users and failures in usability. Designers must see the user as the centre of the computer system instead of as a mere peripheral. This simple concept, easy to state but harder to achieve, is often expounded by ergonomists and human factors specialists. It has been emphasised by Nicholls *(SHA3)*:

> *In spite of changes in the nature of computing, remnants of old thinking remain with us. In former days, when the CPU was at the heart of a system, designers naturally talked of 'terminals' and 'peripherals'. I suspect it was in this period that people began to use the term 'end user'. The unconscious symbolism is both a symptom and a cause; the 'end' user at the 'terminal' was often the last person to be considered in the design of the system. It is important to develop a new view of computing systems, and to look at the user in a different light ... taking this view of computing, the centre of a system is the user.*

So, if we are to improve the usability of interactive computer systems, much attention will need to be devoted to improving the design of the end-user interfaces; this, in turn, may well require a considerable change in the orientation and approach of the designers.

What is the end-user interface?

It is evident that the end-user interface must comprise any feature with which the users may interact during their work. So the interface consists not only of hardware aspects but also of any relevant software and documentation.

The *hardware interface* comprises the displays, controls, terminals, printers, consoles and similar equipment having a fixed physical form. The *software interface* comprises those parts of the human/computer communication process which are not hardware, are more transitory and are varied by program control — for example, the format and layout of the messages between user and system, the logical structure and sequence of operation of the procedures for using a word processor or an accounting system, etc. The documentation comprises the initial training manual, the detailed operating manual, the maintenance and fault finding manual, the 'help' facilities, the memory aid card, etc, which should be supplied with any computer application to support the users during their learning and regular use of the system.

Information is transmitted from the computer via displays mounted on output devices — the latter is the whole unit whereas the former is the information transmitter, for example the screen and its contents are the display mounted on a VDU output device. Information is transmitted into the computer via controls mounted on input devices, for example the keys on a keyboard or the buttons on a mouse. A complete combination of displays and controls built into an appropriate workstation for human interaction with a computer is a *terminal*; a well-designed VDU may prove to be an adequate terminal but is not necessarily so, though often given that name.

It is important to remember the total context within which the interface and terminal reside. In essence there are two contexts, one organisational and the other operational (see Figure 1). The organisational context involves the task/job/organisation dimension and the operational context involves the terminal/workspace/environment dimension with which we are primarily concerned in this Report. While the organisational aspects are not dealt with in depth in this Report, it is essential for designers to recognise that no system design can escape that context; these aspects have to be the starting point for the contribution of the human factors designers, from which they then move on to provide their direct contribution to the technology design.

Regarding the operational context, the interface and terminal must be seen as a fully integrated part of this total working situation for the user. The *workspace* comprises all aspects of machine size, chairs, desks, adjacent structures, etc which affect the position, posture and reach of the human. The *environment* comprises the physical, chemical, biological, psychological and social aspects of the surroundings which may influence the behaviour, performance and satisfaction of the human. Quite often

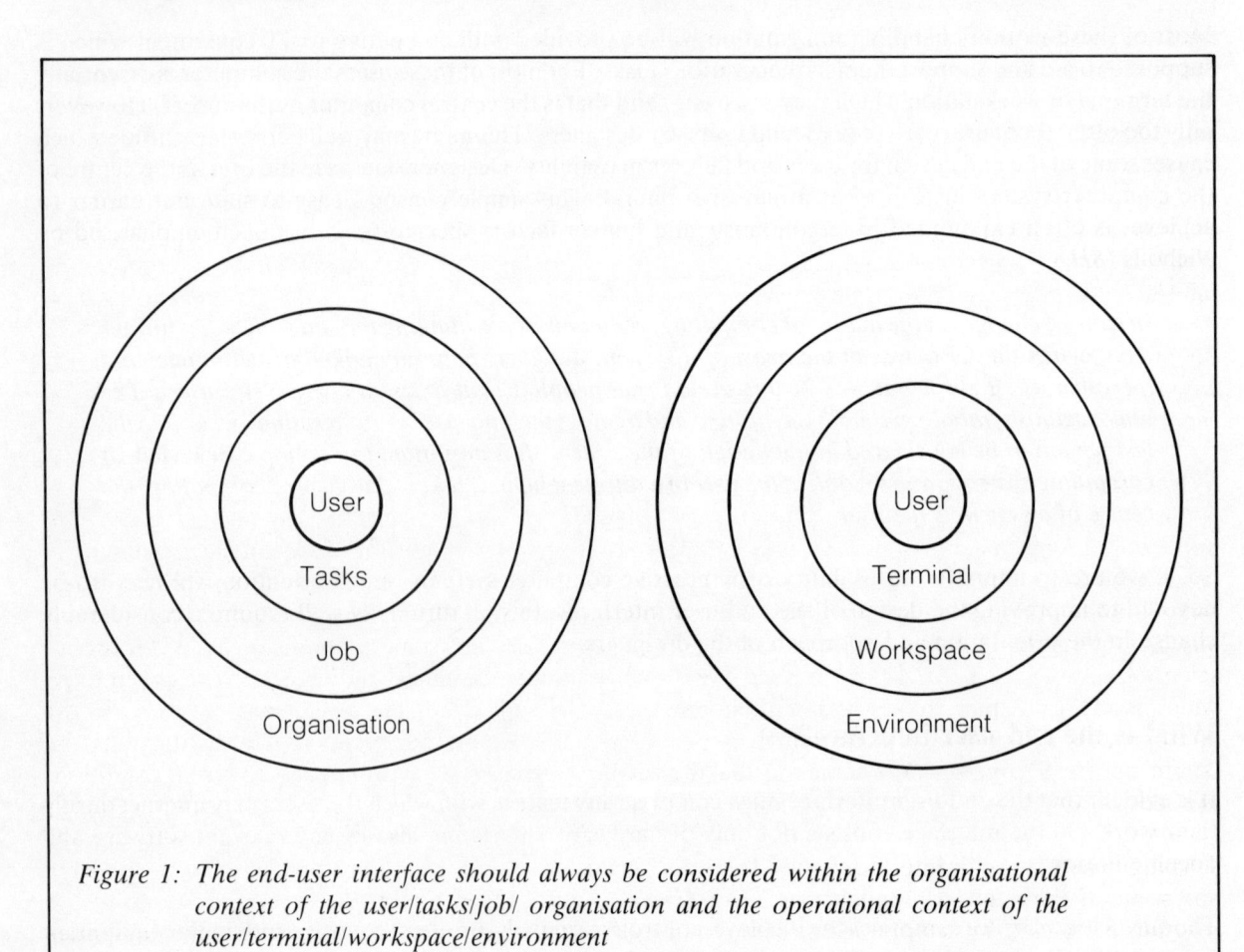

Figure 1: The end-user interface should always be considered within the organisational context of the user/tasks/job/ organisation and the operational context of the user/terminal/workspace/environment

the workspace aspects are discussed as part of the physical features of the environment, and quite often consideration of the environment is limited to the physical aspects, with the psychological and social aspects treated separately. However, in terms of ergonomics (human factors) the above are the correct definitions and more useful conceptualisation. When grouped in this way they help to remind us that all these factors may combine and interact variously to influence the final response of the human to his tasks, user interface, terminal and total working situation.

Why is the design of the user interface often neglected?

Many would perhaps argue that good system designers have always taken account of human/computer communication needs and have designed suitable interfaces. It is certainly true that *good* designers are aware of and do pay some attention to interface design, rather than simply neglect it, but that begs the question about less good designers and still leaves the question of whether even good designers actually achieve good interface designs. It is generally accepted today that many interface designs do not reach a satisfactory standard in relation to the needs of users and the requirements which can be specified from human factors handbooks and guidelines. Why is this so?

Several factors are working against the system designer. First, few system designers have enough knowledge about human factors to apply it to good effect. It is a fallacy to think that such knowledge can be acquired in the process of designing systems, unless the human factors of such designs are attended to explicitly as issues in their own right. Human factors is all about how beings operate and, as such, is an opaque and complex subject which cannot be learned by casual observation and chance reading. The second thing which prevents system designers from meeting human factors requirements to a satisfactory standard is simply time and money. Meeting these requirements successfully requires an explicit effort and management has not, in general, been prepared to spend time and money on that effort.

Another major reason is to be found in the nature and responsibilities of the computer system designer. Computer designers are primarily, and quite rightly, concerned to improve the performance of the computer hardware and software; they often forget that what matters most is the efficiency and performance of the total human/computer system, of which their computer contributions are only a part. Efficient performance can only result from proper attention to the needs and problems of the human users as well as the hardware and software aspects. However, the complexity and sophistication of modern computer technology often results in the designer being so busy with his own technical problems that he has too little time, and often too little knowledge, to deal with the human problems adequately. Moreover, the computer boom was so strong and rapid that the training of computer system designers could not, and still usually does not, include ergonomics and human factors. However, unless the human factor problems are foreseen in the design stage, and dealt with by appropriate methods to analyse, find and embody the relevant knowledge, a suboptimum interface and system is almost the inevitable result.

So the challenge to the computer professional is to learn new skills and new knowledge, to learn how to work with some new methods, some new advisers and especially with the users, in order to help computers and themselves to evolve to a new position as servants to society.

What are the consequences of poor interface design?

Some of the consequences of poor interface design have become common knowledge in the community at large. Only too often VDU terminals are just dumped on the existing user's desk, and the resulting aches, pains and complaints from awkward posture and bad interaction with local lighting conditions are obvious and easily predictable. Some problems have been overdramatised and some are non-existent under proper scientific scrutiny (see *(SHA4)* for a good overview). However, designers should not dismiss even these widespread installation causes as not their province; why should not the designer specify clearly the appropriate usage conditions within which users can reasonably expect the operation of the equipment to be comfortable and painless (in the same way that the range of physical and environmental operating conditions are specified)?

Turning to more specific interface issues, there are many examples in the literature of poor interface design and some of the many consequences *(SHA5-SHA7)*. Some of these are most revealing in terms of the resulting partial use, misuse or non-use of the equipment and the cash costs. These again illustrate the various types of user response to inadequate systems (see Figure 2, and *(SHA8)* for a further discussion).

Response	Meaning	Comments
Disuse	Reliance on and 100 per cent use of other information sources	Needs other sources and (senior) discretionary users
Misuse	'Bending the rules' to short-cut difficulties	Needs 'know-how'. May damage system integrity
Partial use	Use of limited subset of system capabilities	Users may not learn to use the most relevant facilities
Distant use	Use delegated to an operator	Typical response of managers to bad usability
Task modification	Changing the task to match capabilities of system	Typical for rigid tools and unstructured problems
Compensatory user activity	Compensation for system inadequacies by additional user actions	Typical with users of low discretion, such as clerks
Direct programming	Programming by user, to make system suit needs	Computer-sophisticated user, eg scientist or engineer
Frustration and apathy	Response of user when above actions are inadequate or unsatisfactory	Involves lack of user acceptance, high error rates, poor performance

Source: (SHA9), based on (SHA10)
Figure 2: Some typical user responses to inadequate systems

The planners and governmental sponsors of the large investment programmes in computing and IT research certainly recognise the problems of poor user interface design. The Alvey and ESPRIT programmes, and the equivalent work in Japan and the US, have all placed considerable emphasis upon human/computer interaction and the 'man/machine interface'.

The reason is self-evident from the fact that few if any IT applications involve computer specialists as the users (see Figure 3). While some IT users may well develop considerable expertise because they use the IT tool for perhaps half of each day (such as word processing secretaries, designers using Computer-aided Design (CAD), etc), others will only use several of the tools intermittently and will never become expert users. Above all, none will be computer specialists, able to understand its internal intricacies and therefore perhaps be more willing to tolerate inconsistencies and other difficulties.

These many new users have arisen because of the rapid change and growth brought about by the microcomputer. The result of this rapid growth is that both the market for the IT industry and the users of IT equipment are changing very rapidly. The market is becoming much more selective, partly through experiences of poor usability. The users are no longer mainly computer professionals, but are mostly *discretionary users (SHA11)*. As a result, the designers are no longer typical of, or equivalent to, users; but the designers may not realise how unique and therefore how unrepresentative they are.

Moreover, with the growth of IT, the many new users bring different needs to be satisfied. Earlier users were committed to using computers, either because of personal interest or job requirements. However, the potential new users are such people as managers, physicians, lawyers and scientists who are committed to their tasks but not at all to the computer. They have a choice and will only use computers if they are appropriate, useful and usable. The ultimate consequence of poor interface design for these users is that they will not use the poor designs and in the end they will learn to refuse the poor designs.

So the market now contains important new categories of users. Moreover, some predict that these *end users* will be the primary decision makers in the future about buying the equipment. Thus to be successful, the IT industry must improve the usability of interactive systems, and to do so the

Mainly 'expert' users (eg secretaries, designers, librarians)	Mainly 'non-expert' users (eg managers, students, the public)
Word processing	Simple word processing
General accounting	Electronic spreadsheet
CAD	Simple graphics
Computer-aided teaching	Computer-aided learning
Library systems	Viewdata/Prestel
On-line bibliographic search	Teleshopping
	Telebanking
	Electronic funds transfer
	Electronic mail
	Computer teleconferencing
	Electronic journals

Figure 3: Some IT applications involving extensive human/computer interaction. None of the users are computer specialists, so usability is the major problem

understandable orientation of designers in the early years must now be completely reversed; designing must *start with the end users* and be *user centred* around them. Therefore the human factors aspects and usability become paramount.

Usability context — the acceptability equation

This Report is concentrating upon the user-oriented issues of the end-user interface and many of these aspects are often encapsulated under the heading of usability. However, before concentrating primarily on usability, it is important to clarify its general context. When users and purchasers make decisions about systems, their decisions depend not only upon usability but upon an assessment balancing various factors; they probably consider how useful the system will be, whether they feel that it is suitable and that they would like to use it, and how much it will cost, both financially and in terms of the personal, social and organisational consequences. It is suggested that the relevant factors are associated in some form of trade-off paradigm such as that in Figure 4. This paradigm helps to place usability in its balanced position with functionality; as computers become cheaper and more powerful, it seems certain that usability factors will become more and more dominant in the acceptability decisions made by users and purchasers.

Thus, this paradigm suggests that whether I accept something depends upon whether I consider it sufficiently useful, usable and likeable in relation to what it costs me. If I do not accept something, then the combination of utility, usability and likeability are not sufficient for it to satisfy my wants in relation to human and financial costs. This paradigm helps to place usability in its balanced position with functionality; as computers become cheaper and more powerful, it seems certain that usability factors will become more and more dominant in the acceptability decisions made by users and purchasers.

Usability definition and quantification

Successful system design for usability requires much attention to various aspects of the user. However, the user must not be considered in isolation from other aspects of the situation; that would only be

> **Utility** — will it do what is needed functionally?
> \+
> **Usability** — will the users actually work it successfully?
> \+
> **Likeability** — will the users feel it is suitable?
>
> must be balanced in a trade-off against
>
> **Cost** — what are the capital and running costs?
> — what are the social and organisational consequences?
>
> to arrive at a decision about
>
> **Acceptability** — on balance the best possible alternative for purchase

Figure 4: The paradigm of usability and related concepts

perpetuating in reverse the all too common fault in the past of considering the technological tool in isolation from the user. Good system design depends upon solving the dynamic interacting needs of the *four principal components* of any user/system situation — *user, task, tool* and *environment*. Likewise usability, an important goal for good system design, depends upon the dynamic interplay of these four components.

With the framework of the four principal components in mind, we can now turn to the definition of usability. Usability depends on the following:

1 The design of the tool (the VDT and the computer system) in relation to the users, the tasks and the environments.

2 The success of the user support provided (training, manuals and other job aids such as on-line and off-line 'help' facilities.

We consider that usability for individual users will be judged by subjective assessment of ease of use of the design with its user support and by objective performance measures of effectiveness in using the tool.

Therefore, we can quantify the success or failure of an end-user interface in terms of the following criteria:

1 Success rate in satisfying (that is meeting the needs of) the specified ranges of users, tasks and environments.

2 Ease of use in terms of judgements of, for example, learning, using, remembering, convenience, comfort, effort, tiredness, satisfaction.

3 Effectiveness of human use in terms of performance (for example time, errors, number and sequence of activities, etc) in learning, relearning and carrying out a representative range of operations.

From the above suggestions, it is evident that usability considered in this way is not only conceived of as *ease of use* but also equally involves *efficacy*, that is effectiveness in terms of measures of (human) performance.

Therefore, the formal definition proposed for the usability of a system or equipment is: 'the capability in human functional terms to be used easily and effectively by the specified range of users, given specified training and user support, to fulfil the specified range of tasks, within the specified range of environmental scenarios'. A convenient shortened form of the definition of usability might be 'the capability to be used by humans easily and effectively', where 'easily' = to a specified level of subjective assessment and 'effectively' = to a specified level of (human) performance.

The definition of usability was probably first attempted by Miller *(SHA12)* in terms of measures for 'ease of use', and these were developed further by Bennett *(SHA11)* to describe usability. The concept of usability was first fully discussed and a detailed formal definition, as above, was attempted by Shackel *(SHA8)* and modified and developed by Bennett *(SHA13)*.

The problem with these definitions is that they are conceptually satisfactory but still only generalised in form; they do not specify what is usability in quantifiable or measurable terms. Therefore, the author has integrated and developed further these approaches into a proposal for a quantifiable definition of usability (see Figure 5). This definition is explained further and illustrated with a worked example in *(SHA14)*.

This definition has been formulated so that numerical values can be specified during the design stage of user requirements specification. In that stage of the design process, various system requirements are specified, and the usability requirements should be specified in just as much detail as any other aspect of the intended system. Then, later in the design process, the emerging design can be evaluated against these usability criteria.

Usability evaluation — criteria and procedures

This section is only intended, as is the rest of this paper, to present a brief introduction. It reviews and gives references for some of the salient topics.

Evaluation is an important topic. Chapanis *(SHA15,SHA16)* has reviewed the needs and basic procedures. Hirsch *(SHA17)* has described the work and procedures of the IBM San José human factors centre, which does many evaluation studies. Neal and Simons *(SHA18)* have described a very useful recording and playback facility used at that same centre. Grudin and MacLean *(SHA19)* have described various methods for measuring performance and preference and Helmreich *(SHA20)* has presented the results of user acceptance research.

There are three general types of measurement available for evaluation: dimension, performance and attitude (see Figure 6). *Dimensional criteria* are the most familiar and simplest, relying on physical measurement; the same procedures are involved for human usability, but primarily in relation to human body size. The problem with analytic dimensional criteria is that they do not enable judgement that something is more useful simply because it is two inches higher, etc; ultimately dimensions must be related to other criteria based upon human performance or attitude if any scale is to be derived. In summary, dimensional criteria only allow pass/fail judgements; satisfying them may be a necessary but not a sufficient measure of usability.

Performance criteria involve an objective statement of some achievement, often in terms of time and errors, against which human performance can then be measured. Although the interpretation of performance criteria for evaluation purposes is often also in terms of pass or fail, the measurements obtained for comparison with the criterion give some indication of the degree of usability achieved.

Attitude criteria can be defined with the same precision and operational form as performance criteria. There has been much research in psychology on controlled methods of gathering subjective data from humans, and various forms of scaling technique are now well developed and proven.

It must be emphasised that these three types of criteria and measurement should not be regarded as alternatives, but as complementary, with regard to the assessment of usability. This is perhaps evident from the fact that different types of measurement are involved, which clearly will assess different characteristics of the tool, along with the task and environment, in relation to the user.

PROPOSED QUANTIFIABLE DEFINITION OF USABILITY

Usability can be specified and measured by means of the quantifiable criteria defined below. The terms should be given numerical values when the usability goals are set during the design stage of 'requirements specification'.

For a system to be usable the following must be achieved. The required range of tasks must be accomplished:

Effectiveness

— at better than some required level of performance (eg in terms of speed and errors)

— by some required percentage of the specified target range of users

— within some required proportion of the range of usage environments

Learnability

— within some specified time from commissioning and start of user training

— based upon some specified amount of training and user support

— within some specified relearning time each time for intermittent users

Flexibility

— with flexibility allowing adaptation to some specified percentage variation in tasks and/or environments beyond those first specified

Attitude

— within acceptable levels of human cost in terms of tiredness, discomfort, frustration and personal effort

— so that satisfaction causes continued and enhanced usage of the system.

Figure 5: Definition of usability proposed in terms of goals and quantified criteria which can have numerical values specified and measured

Criteria	Types of measurement
Dimension (analytic)	Physical, anthropometric
Performance ('objective')	Physiological, operational, experimental, functional
Attitude ('Subjective')	Psychological, eg by controlled scaling techniques

Figure 6: The general types of criteria and measurement available for evaluation

Dimensions will be primarily relevant to the size, shape and other characteristics of the tool in relation to human size and related requirements. *Performance* will assess the operational capability which can be achieved by the human user, but of course will not assess the cost or difficulty for the user. The *attitude* measures assess the user's view of the cost and relative difficulty in achieving the performance. We should note that attitude criteria are no less valid than any other; indeed in many respects they are more valid with regard to usability, because ultimately it is the human user who must express the judgement of this characteristic.

Performance measures cannot be the sole criterion, because the human may readily achieve a given performance but still not prefer to do the task or use the tool because it is very inconvenient and awkward. So he may well prefer (that is find more usable) another similar tool which gives less speed or more errors, but is easier or more convenient.

The above discussion attempts to provide a simple analytical framework for the issues of criteria and measurement in relation to usability. The procedures involved in system evaluations during design and after installation both include and reorient the above into appropriate operational and time-scheduled processes. In many respects, the processes used for the human factors evaluation of system usability are similar to those used for engineering evaluation of system utility. Some brief comments only will be made on a few points of relevance.

There are three principal evaluation procedures used in human factors:

1 *Expert review:* appraisals by human factors specialists, using the measures of dimensions (and other analytic comparison data) and of attitude (by 'expert opinion').

2 *Simulation trials:* experiments with mock-ups and prototypes, with a limited number of subjects but essentially equivalent to ultimate users, using measures of performance and attitude.

3 *User performance tests:* full experimental studies of final equipment with samples of actual users, using measures of dimensions, performance and attitude.

(SHA15,SHA21-SHA23) give guidance on principles and procedures. While these are invaluable reference sources, we should note that on the one hand they expound basic methodology, which is very necessary, but on the other their applications frame of reference mainly relates to larger military systems; there is still much to be done in modifying, developing and testing usability evaluation procedures for human/computer interaction in non-military systems. For the present, we shall recommend only one precept, which is well founded on considerable experience: attitude assessments are most reliable when users have actual 'hands-on' experience in the situation concerned, so that adequate experience (often accompanied by appropriate performance tests) is the essential prerequisite for valid attitude measurement.

Why are usability and good interface design important?

There is now no doubt about the importance of usability human factors in the eyes of the computer industry in the US, where there is greater development of human factors in industry than in Europe.

This is particularly evident in the large numbers of human factors professionals and others from industry at the regular ACM Computer Human Interaction (CHI) conferences; the total attendances in 1983, 1985, 1986 and 1987 have been 1000, 1200, 1300 and 1400, and the percentage from industry has been 70 to 80 per cent each time. Ironically, this rapid growth in attention to human factors in the US industry is attributable, at least in part, to a European ergonomic standard, namely the German DIN standard for keyboard height to be not more than 30 mm. The realisation that an ergonomic standard could override all other aspects in the marketplace came as a big surprise and had a powerful effect on quite a number of US companies.

To illustrate this changed situation one has merely to note the marked change of emphasis upon human factors in IBM which was handed down from the very top *(SHA24)*. As a result, special conferences have been held, a worldwide programme of short courses for IBM engineers has been instituted and usability has become of equal importance with functionality.

The following excerpt is typical of the writings of quite a number of the ergonomists in this field some years ago, but it is taken directly from a lecture by the IBM Vice President and Chief Scientist *(SHA25)*.

> *All that has changed. No longer the exclusive tool of specialists, computers have become both commonplace and indispensible. Yet they remain harder to use than they should be. It should be more necessary to read a 300-page book of instructions before using a computer than before driving an unfamiliar automobile. But much more research in both cognitive and computer science will be required to learn how to build computers that are that easy to use. That is why our industry is paying increasing attention to the field of applied psychology called human factors, or ergonomics.... Equally neglected has been human factors at the level of systems design. We know that system architecture has significant and widespread implications for user friendliness, but we know next to nothing about how to make fundamental architectural decisions differently, in the interest of good human factors....*
>
> *... Thus the effort to design for ease of use could benefit enormously from basic research, not only in adaptive systems and computational linguistics, but above all in terms of controlled experiments involving actual use by representative end users — for you can't evaluate ease of use without use.*

Finally, in Britain the case has been presented in an authoritative and well-illustrated report by the National Electronics Council *(SHA6)*, in which several case studies are described to emphasise the need to design for people and build in usability from the start.

What are the benefits of human factors and usability in system design?

The philosophy of ergonomics is concerned with ensuring a good match of the equipment, workplace, environment and organisation to the people therein so as to promote comfort, convenience, efficiency, health and job satisfaction; it does not have productivity as its principal goal. However, one must always recognise that managers and designers often need to see a potential advantage in productivity or economy to be persuaded to use ergonomics; therefore, the importance of this work can best be shown by examples of direct benefits, converted into cash terms if possible.

The following paragraphs will mention and give references to a number of examples to illustrate the range and type of benefits to be expected from applying human factors knowledge and methods appropriately in the design, implementation and usage of IT.

In the early days we could only point to problems and failures which badly needed ergonomics ministration; some recent examples of such failures have been given, for example, in Section 2 of the National Electronics Council Report *(SHA6)* — of the Navy's navigators reverting to pens and paper and of doctors rejecting software — and by Chapanis *(SHA26)* — of some user problems with a recent IBM software system. Instead of this negative approach which had to be taken in the past, it is pleasing to be able to give a whole range of examples, all of which are successful case studies of human factors implemented and paid for by the organisations concerned. The examples have been chosen to represent many other successful applications at the *equipment level*, the *workplace level*, the *organisation level* and the *larger system* and *national level*.

At the *equipment level* four examples will be given here. The first comes from within an IT company and the other three examples are work done by ergonomists as external consultants. Bewley *et al (SHA27)* described the human factors testing which they report as 'integral to the design process of the Xerox 8010 "Star" workstation'. Moore and Dartnall *(SHA28)* analysed for British Gas the ergonomic issues of central heating timer/programmer units and produced a number of designs leading to a final version. Galer and Yap *(SHA29)* assisted a hospital with the design of a monitoring unit for use in an intensive care ward; a new interface design was produced and tested, and the new device was found to be better than the original and was preferred by the users to manually completed charts. Finally, Davies *(SHA30)* organised the total ergonomic design of a portable billing machine for the Plessey Company which went into regular production (see fuller description below).

Because so much human factors work has been done at the *workplace level*, only one case study will be mentioned. In Section 6 of the National Electronics Council Report *(SHA6)* the case study is presented of the Merseyside Police Control Room, in which the design was led by the ergonomists. Many other examples of human factors work for workplace design are given in Grandjean *(SHA31)* and in the special issue of 'Behaviour and Information Technology' *(SHA32)* containing the papers of the Ergodesign '84 Conference.

At the *organisational level*, quite a number of case studies are presented in the symposium proceedings edited by Hendrick and Brown *(SHA33)* and by Brown and Hendrick *(SHA34)*. For example, Bowman *(SHA35)* describes the successful procedures at Honeywell for setting up cross-functional design teams, with representatives of both worker/users and managers/users, to search jointly for solutions in developing their own internal computer systems. The case study by Shackel and Eason *(SHA36)* describes the use of pilot system prototyping to develop the specification for an on-line distributed system for a company with 32 branches. Finally, some of the ongoing work at HUSAT concerned with user acceptability and user support in a large national organisation is summarised by Douglas and Marquis *(SHA37)* and Marquis and Douglas *(SHA38)*.

At the *large system* and *national level* the Olympic Message System *(SHA39)* is another good example of the human factors team taking the lead in the development of a major system where the user interface is the critical feature for success or failure; there is no doubt about the success of this system at the Los Angeles Olympic Games. In Britain the Government's Department of Health and Social Security (DHSS) has embarked upon a 10-year computerisation programme which will link all the many social security benefit offices in cities and towns throughout the country into a large on-line computer network and database system. HUSAT *(SHA40)* was asked to produce a human factors strategy plan as a contribution to this programme, and one of the major projects ongoing in HUSAT is the implementation of the human factors strategy in cooperation with the many users and design staff in the DHSS.

Conclusion

These examples help to show the growing maturity of the human factors contribution as an essential partner in the design and development process of interactive computing systems and IT. There are still many organisations which need to hear and absorb this message, but the more there are successful contributions like those referenced the more wisely will the message be heard.

From the discussion in this paper it is evident that neither the specification of usability nor its evaluation nor the application of human factors knowledge are sufficient on their own; all must be done thoroughly and skillfully if good design for usability is to be achieved. Only in that way will the end-user interfaces become not bottlenecks but gateways through which the computer and IT system successfully interact with and serve the user.

9: Integrating human factors with system development

P Walsh, K Y Lim and J B Long

Ergonomics Unit
University College London
London
UK

M K Carver

Michael Jackson Systems Ltd
London
UK

Human factors engineers complain that their contribution to interactive system design is typically sought late, that is following system implementation. Software engineers, in contrast, complain that the human factors contributions to system design are neither timely, appropriate nor implementable. One solution to this problem is for human factors contributions to be integrated with those of software engineering, that is presented at a time and in a form that contributes directly to system development, and in particular to the design of the user interface. This paper proposed how structured methods, in the form of Jackson System Development (JSD), might be used to integrate human factors generally into system development.

© P Walsh, K Y Lim, J B Long and M K Carver 1988

P Walsh
Paul Walsh graduated in Psychology from University College Galway, Ireland in 1981. He obtained an MSc in Social Psychology from the London School of Economics in 1982. He worked as a Research Assistant at the City of London Polytechnic for three years, during which time he obtained a PhD in Cognitive Psychology on the subject of metaphor comprehension. In 1985 he became a Research Fellow with a multidisciplinary Computer Science and Psychology group at the University of York, looking at the formal specification of user interfaces. He has worked at the Ergonomics Unit since October 1987, where he manages a project aimed at incorporating human factors knowledge into the Jackson System Development (JSD) method.

J Long
John Long is Professor of Ergonomics and Director of the Ergonomics Unit, University College London. He worked initially as a manager for Shell International in Africa and the Far East. Subsequently, he became a senior scientist at the Medical Research Council's Applied Psychology Unit in Cambridge. His main research interests lie in the area of Human/Computer Interaction (HCI), although he has also published papers on divided attention, typing, second language use and interpreter training.

K Y Lim
In 1982, Kee Yong Lim graduated from University College London with a BSc (Engng) in Biochemical and Chemical Engineering. Following this he took up Biochemical Engineering research at the University of Toronto (Canada); he then worked as a Process Engineer with ESSO (Singapore) Petroleum Refinery. He returned to University College to undertake an MSc in Ergonomics in 1985. He is presently working as an Associate Research Assistant at the Ergonomics Unit, University of London.

M Carver
After a varied career in Science and Information Technology, Mary Carver changed to Psychology in which she graduated from Bedford College London. Following a Postgraduate Certificate in Education at King's College London and a period in teaching, she returned to University College London and obtained an MSC in Ergonomics in 1982. After three and a half years as a Research Officer at Birkbeck and University College London working on Ministry of Defence projects, she joined Michael Jackson Systems Ltd where she is involved with developing, teaching and consulting in the Jackson System Development (JSD) method.

Integrating human factors with system development

Introduction

A well-designed interactive system provides appropriate functionality to its users and exhibits graceful evolution when modified by designers. Graceful evolution is facilitated when the system embodies a complete and coherent model that can be offered to users and communicated to other designers. Appropriate functionality enables users to satisfy their goals and to feel that using the system is worthwhile. To be effective, interactive systems need to be usable, and users need to be able to understand how the system operates without undue mental effort. Users must also be capable of remembering information about the system for future use. In general, then, the goal of human factors has been to ensure that the system, as expressed in the user interface, is both usable and useful.

Although it is generally accepted that usability is an important criterion of good design, there is less agreement as to how to organise system development projects so that the human factors element contributes optimally. Indeed, there is considerable confusion regarding the *process* of human factors contributions, that is how and when they should occur, and the *product* of human factors contributions, that is in what form they should be expressed. To be effective, human factors engineers need to be involved not only in the content of design decisions, but also in the timing of such decisions. They need to know about how project decisions are made and how to express design decisions so that they can be easily used by other members of the design team.

In this paper, the authors propose an approach to the problem of integrating human factors into system development and suggest a solution. They begin by considering the traditional methods for integrating human factors with system development and their associated problems of timing and format. In particular, they examine the use of:
- Rapid prototyping
- Structured Analysis and Design Methods (SADMs), as exemplified by Jackson System Development (JSD).

They then propose a model of the activities that would be required by JSD were it to be extended to include human factors activities. Finally, they propose a solution to the problems of timing and format by suggesting how some current human factors activities might be integrated with system development using JSD.

Human factors and current system development practice

System development attempts to apply knowledge about current systems to the satisfaction of *user needs/requirements* for new systems. These needs/requirements precede *design*, which re-expresses them in a form suitable for programming. *Implementation* describes the program that results from design and *evaluation* enables the implementation to be compared to the initial set of requirements, as expressed in the design of the new or modified system.

Two different perspectives towards system development are offered by human factors and software engineers, namely *rapid prototyping* and *SADMs*. Each approach is considered separately and its consequences for human factors integration described.

Rapid prototyping supposes that effective development results from the iterative testing of prototypes which provides feedback for design. Rapid prototyping allows the demonstration of the proposed system to the user and facilitates user suggestions on improvements and modifications. Prototyping helps solve the problem that users cannot imagine what type of system could better support their work. Rapid prototyping serves to match the design with the user requirements. Human factors may contribute by supplementing feedback, provided directly by users, with behavioural data derived from testing users on the prototype. Finally, human factors methods may be used to evaluate the implementation. However, though a description of users' errors and difficulties may give designers a better analysis of the problem of usability, it does not by itself constitute a solution.

Another problem with the prototyping approach is that it may reduce the role of human factors to the evaluation of designs rather than design development. This is because prototyping is not a substitute for design. One can design a prototype, but this is different from prototyping a design which may have received little 'design' attention. Prototyping needs a start-point, a 'first-best-guess' by the designer, before the cycle of evaluation and user involvement can begin. Prototyping may also give a misleading impression that human factors is providing a contribution to design when it is not. The illusion disappears when examined in the light of the implicit design process that generates the prototype. In short, although prototyping may contribute to the solution of some human factors problems, a number remain, in particular the absence of a direct human factors contribution to design.

The design and management of the software life-cycle represents a different approach to software development. SADMs typically recommend that system development should undergo specific stages from specification through to implementation and maintenance. SADMs make explicit the decisions which are to be made, how to make them and the order in which they are to be made. The development process is organised more strictly with the aim of getting the design right first time. JSD is an example of a widely used SADM. The authors consider JSD to have much in common with other SADMs, but it is not possible to explore this complex issue here.

The role for human factors in the process of developing a system using an SADM is often restricted to evaluation and occurs after implementation. We term this the 'too little, too late' problem of integrating human factors. Delayed involvement results in a contribution that may be little more than advice, that is 'too little'. In addition the contribution may be 'too late', since the human factors activity does not constitute a basic part of system specification. Software is delivered to the human factors engineer at a late stage in the development process, and the lateness of evaluation frequently ensures that the advice cannot be acted upon. As a result, attempts to 'put it right' are thwarted by the difficulty and expense of modifications. SADMs, then, as used at present pose a problem of *timing* for the integration of human factors with system development. An additional problem is that, even if human factors contributions are made early in the development process, software engineers find them difficult to incorporate into the design, because their expression or *format* is insufficiently structured and incompatible with their own. Human factors contributions to system development need to be expressed in a format that is usable by software engineers.

Human factors activities, then, are poorly integrated into current system development practices such as rapid prototyping and SADMs. Typically, the human factors element fails to contribute directly to the specification of the system. Any solution to the problem of integration needs to address the issues of timing and format of the human factors contributions to the system development process.

Extending JSD to integrate human factors

How might human factors be better incorporated within the system development process to resolve these problems of timing and format and to ensure that it contributes directly to the design? Carver *(WAL1)* suggests that JSD offers a solution. She argues for its promise in providing a common language for software and human factors engineers, since it can be used both to describe tasks and to specify the user interface. This 'common format' potential of JSD will be explored further in the next section. A necessary prerequisite for the exploration, however, is to identify those human factors contributions which might be incorporated into the SADM. What is needed is a model of the human factors activities that might be associated with JSD activities, were it to be extended to include them. The model should exploit existing practices since the aim of this paper is primarily to synthesise the contributions from human factors and software engineering rather than propose novel techniques. Such a model is proposed in Figure 1. The model shows human factors and software engineering activities relative to the real world from which the requirements for the system have originated and to which the system is destined. Arrows indicate the activities, that is the processes of design and the boxes indicate the products of the design process. The products of human factors processes are shaded, for example 'Task analysis'; those of software engineering are unshaded, for example 'JSD model'. Joint products are lightly shaded for example, 'User interface specification'. Products involving more than joint human factors and software engineering activities are heavily shaded, for example 'User needs/requirements'. Requirements analysis is neither exclusive to these two sets of activities nor is it a joint activity in the same way as user interface specification. Business and organisational analysis, for example, has a contribution to make to requirements identification, and human factors and software engineering contributions to user interface specification need to be integrated completely in a way not necessitated by the identification of user needs/requirements.

The model allows us to posit questions of 'who', 'what' and 'when' that pertain to system development and, in particular, to user interface design. It illustrates the 'who' by showing that some design activities are particular to human factors engineers and some to software engineers. It also shows how the user interface might be the product of combined human factors and software engineering activities. Further, some products, such as user needs/requirements may involve other types of activity. The 'what' is exemplified by the processes and products that result. The 'when' is illustrated by the timing of the human factors contribution. It occurs early in the system development process both at and prior to the specification of the user interface.

In the remainder of the paper, we describe some of the activities that offer potential as human factors contributions to the system development process. To reiterate the requirements for such contributions identified earlier, they need to be relevant, that is to contribute directly to the system specification. In addition, the format in which they are expressed should be compatible with that used by the software engineer. Further, the timing of human factors contributions should be appropriate, which means it must be integrated with the SADM practised. The next section considers the activities in Figure 1 that are carried out by the human factors engineer and how these might be integrated in the case of JSD.

Integrating human factors activities

Task analysis

Observing and analysing how users perform tasks in the real world are human factors activities which typically contribute to the prototyping and simulation of new systems. Although many different methods of task analysis exist, some common features can be identified. Task analysis typically describes actions in terms of verbs, objects and predicates. The description may also include the consequences of performing actions, often expressed as states, as well as system feedback to the user.

Before suggesting how task analysis might be integrated into JSD, it is necessary to establish the difference between task analysis and JSD modelling (see Figure 1). The subject matter for task analysis is that of users' tasks and roles, whereas JSD is concerned with the subject matter of the proposed system which may or may not include users' tasks. Some similarities can be shown to exist between JSD modelling and task analysis. In particular, the prerequisites for *entities* are similar in both. In JSD, entities must exist as part of the real world outside the system, must perform or suffer a number of time-ordered *actions* (events) and must be atomic and capable of being uniquely named. In a study of a library, for example, task analysis would be expected to describe the tasks and roles of the librarians and ancillary staff in terms of reception, administration, auditing, etc, whereas JSD would typically model such entities as 'book', which is on loan, and a 'member', whose subscription has been paid.

The problem with task analysis methods at present is the difficulty of integrating their descriptions into the specification of a proposed computer system. The notations used by individual task analysis methods are particular to the methods and are not common to software engineering methods. Another reason is that the separation of design responsibilities between human factors and software engineers is not clearly established.

Figure 1: Proposed model of system development process illustrating the integration of human factors and software engineering activities

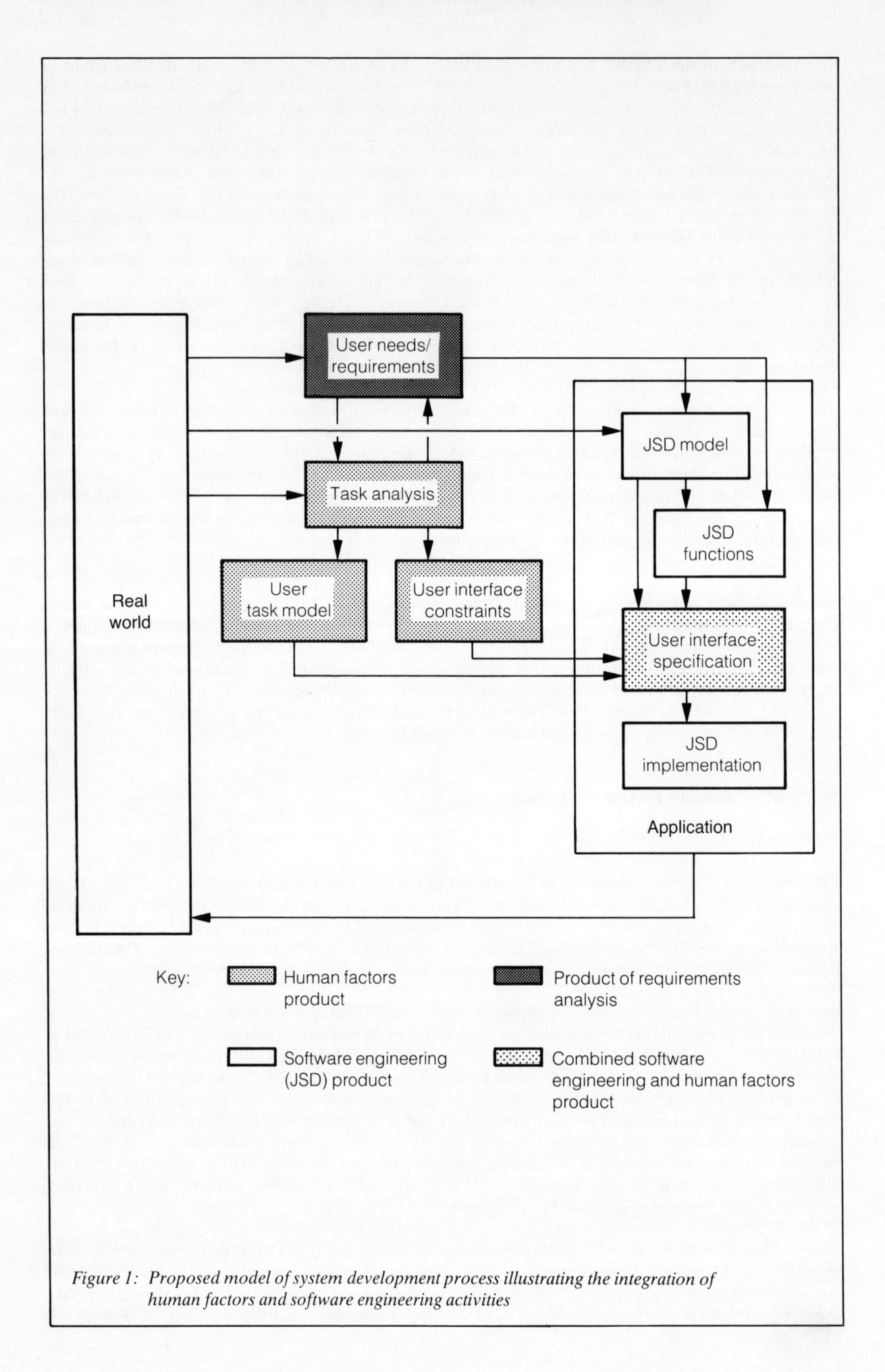

For human factors and software engineering activities to be integrated we propose, following Carver *(WAL1)*, that JSD notation be used as a means of describing tasks. A common description is likely to obviate the potential communication problems between human factors and software engineers that were described earlier. Task analysis methods already rely on techniques such as flowcharts, hierarchical tree structures, Petri nets and so on for the purposes of task description. The notational features of JSD structure diagrams, which utilise the constructs of *sequence*, *selection* and *iteration*, augmented with *backtracking*, are likely to be an effective means of representing the same information. JSD notation is also able to describe concurrency and common threads in the lives of entities. Readers should consult *(WAL2)* for further details about the use of the JSD description language.

The model shown in Figure 1 illustrates how task analysis, or, to be precise, its product, can be incorporated into the design process if it is presented as a set of JSD structure diagrams. The JSD task diagrams would form the basis for the user task model and the user interface constraint. These in turn would contribute directly to the joint human factors and software engineering activity of specifying the user interface. Since task analysis would occur early enough for the human factors activities to contribute to the interface specification, its contribution can be considered timely.

In summary then, we have shown how task analysis as currently practised by human factors might be integrated with system development. The proposed integration is based on:

1. Its contribution to interface design.

2. Its occurrence early in system development, that is prior to interface specification.

3. Its use of a notation — JSD structure diagrams — which is also used by software engineers to express the system specification.

Users' task model

As illustrated in Figure 1, the product of task analysis serves as input for the process of task abstraction, synthesis and logical design, from which the user task model is derived. This process involves characterising the user's underlying model of the extant task (or its metaphorical equivalent) and combining the model with the new system requirements to generate a design that is consistent with this model. The design would relate the task to be performed to the interface features that would support that task. In relating the interface to the task in this manner, decisions can be made about what aspects of the task (as revealed by task analysis) should be introduced into the user interface. Based on the task analysis, which is expressed in JSD structure diagrams, the user task model would also be in a format that is appropriate for use by software engineers.

The consideration of metaphors to convey system functionality to the user can serve as an instantiation of the activities carried out during this stage. The problem in choosing appropriate metaphors is to ensure that the metaphor is consistent with the intention it wishes to convey. Carroll and Mack *(WAL3)* describe a case of a learner who tried to 'tear off' a sheet of paper from a paper pad icon by sweeping the cursor across it in a tearing motion. Such errors arise because there is a lack of consistency between the off-line form of a task and its on-line equivalent. By exploring the knowledge and actions of users that are associated with a particular device, modelling user's tasks could be used in the identification of particular metaphors which might be used to constrain the specification of the interface. In the above example, the user behaviour elicited by a real-world paper pad should have been related to the projected user behaviour on the new paper pad icon. Modelling users tasks, then, would be a relevant activity to integrate into JSD because it would contribute to the design of the user interface.

At present, human factors typically discovers inappropriate user task models in systems only during the evaluation of the system. Discovery at this late stage makes it not only difficult and expensive to modify the user interface, but also requires an appropriate user task model to be created. Constructing a task model which contributes directly to the specification of the user interface at a time and in a format appropriate for the design constitutes an integration of human factors and software engineering activities.

Although analytic techniques such as task modelling may be useful in user interface specification, it would be wrong to suggest that it is either usual or useful to specify the user interface completely anew with every application. The user task model, then, needs to be developed in parallel with a consideration of existing constraints on the user interface. Such constraints are discussed in the next section.

User interface constraints

As illustrated in Figure 1, the user interface constraints (which may originally have been based on a task analysis description) are used to constrain the transformation of the user task model into the user interface specification. An example of a user interface constraint would be a generic interface style, such as a desktop metaphor. 'Generic styles' are evident in applications building tools, or in general in-house styles or standards. These would serve to constrain the user interface specification by reducing the choices available to the designer. The *consistency* that user interface standards or User Interface Management Systems (UIMSs) bring to the user interface specification process is regarded as an aid to usability. The constraints should, however, be the province of human factors. As such, they present another means of integrating human factors with system development.

Although SADMs and UIMSs are compatible, it is worth stressing that UIMSs alone do not provide the best guarantee that task-specific knowledge possessed by users will be reflected in the proposed system. This is particularly true in the case of bespoke applications, which involve specialist task knowledge. A particular problem with generic solutions is ensuring that the solution is an appropriate one.

The inappropriateness can be identified by comparing the users' task model with the user interface model. The human factors engineer can explore such issues by comparing the JSD structure diagrams representing the user task model with those describing the behaviour suggested by the user interface constraints. Since both are described in the same format, similarities and differences between them can be identified. Further, the common JSD format facilitates subsequent contributions to the user interface specification. For example, consider the off-line use of pen on paper with the on-line positioning of a cursor in many current word processing systems. It is common to observe users committing errors which can be traced to a mismatch between their existing task knowledge and the conventions of the proposed system. The users' task model may be used to decide between the acceptance, rejection or modification of conflicting generic user interface model features. In addition, the common JSD format facilitates subsequent direct contributions to the user interface specification and is timely since it precedes specification.

User interface specification

We have argued earlier that cooperation between human factors and software engineers at critical stages of the system development process will lead to important improvements in the design of the user interface. Other design decisions made by software engineers using the JSD method will also have implications for the end user, particularly in terms of the system functionality, but these are not explored in the present paper. For the sake of completeness, they have been included in the model illustrated in Figure 1 (for example JSD model, JSD functions, etc). However, currently the JSD method does not convey to the designer any conception concerning the appearance of the interface at the function specification stage. Design decisions about the sensory, motor and perceptual characteristics of the user interface, for example, are not within the scope of the current JSD method. Some may never be within the scope of an extended method. The choice of colours for information display, for example, may at best be accommodated as a set of guidelines for constraining design, but may never be the product of (extended JSD) design.

JSD notation, because it has the potential of a communication medium between human factors and software engineers, might be an important determinant of the physical appearance of the user interface. Human factors knowledge about the important characteristics of a user interface and its behaviour can be captured using the JSD notation. This knowledge can be integrated with other information, for example user task model, user interface constraints (see above and Figure 1). It can then be conveyed to software engineers in an appropriate common format for maximising its usefulness or shown to end users for their feedback. The human factors contribution is timely since it precedes system implementation.

Although the user interface specification is identified as a joint activity in Figure 1, this does not preclude differences in the emphasis that human factors and software engineers will bring to the specification. The JSD contribution (which is a product of the JSD modelling and the JSD functions activities) can be expected to provide an understanding of *what* information is passed across the user interface. Determining *how* information should pass across is an additional concern of human factors which needs to be included in the user interface specification.

Consider now the use of JSD notation for user interface specification. Let us take as an example the specification of the behaviour of *windows* in a graphics-based interface. It is apparent that the use of a multiwindowing user interface depends to a large extent on the target system's hardware. It is, therefore, primarily a matter for the implementation phase of design, since hardware is assumed to be given and would typically not be considered in a JSD specification. The separation of interface design from the remainder of the application, however, does allow for this important feature of the user interface to be considered earlier. As soon as it is recognised, following consideration of the user task model and the user interface constraints (see above and Figure 1), that implementation using a multiwindowing interface is appropriate, the JSD notation can be used in the specification of the multiwindowing interface in at least the following ways:

1 The behaviour of windows, for example, could be easily captured in a simple JSD structure diagram, in which windows are a sequence of opening, activity and closing.

2 Window opening may itself be part of a larger JSD structure, for example occurring in response to an inappropriate user action.

3 Complex window behaviour can be specified; for example a two-page edit function can be supported by the fact that the use of the same data means they are using the same aspect of the underlying JSD model.

4 Arbitration between windows can be supported by the JSD specification, that is it is possible to determine which window the user ought to be working in, or the most recently active window.

5 Multitasking using multiple windows is facilitated by the capability of JSD to model independent parallel threads.

6 Transient window presentation can be specified using JSD.

The essential point here is that while features of user interface design may not be as relevant to the software engineer as other features of the system, the human factors engineer using JSD notation can effectively direct attention to these features. Not only do important features of the user interface receive consideration early in the design process, that is are timed appropriately with respect to other activities, but the human factors contribution to design can be presented to the system implementor in a format that is rigorous and compatible with inputs from other members of the design team. In addition, the specification of the user interface is in principle directly executable, which may be an aid to user testing.

Summary and conclusions

In this paper we have suggested how user interfaces might be specified. The model proposed differs from other methods of user interface specification in that it is integrated with the development of the computer system as a whole. We have also argued that JSD can support the integration of human factors with system development and can promote useful cooperation between human factors and software engineers. Finally, we consider that JSD can help to clarify the consequences of design decisions. Such clarification is necessary to control the complexity of system development generally (and user interface design in particular), to monitor the effects of design on usability and functionality, and to evaluate the appropriateness of design.

Software engineers in the past have been presented with recommendations by human factors engineers in a manner that cannot easily be used, because the recommendations do not satisfy the conditions of timing and format identified earlier. To remedy this problem, we conclude that human factors recommendations should be made as early in the design process as is appropriate and presented in a common format, with those of software engineers, as part of a model for user interface design activities operating within an overall system development method.

Acknowledgements

The research associated with this paper is being carried out for the Ministry of Defence (Royal Armaments Research and Development Establishment) under Contract No 2047/130 (RARDE). The views expressed in the paper are those of the authors and should not necessarily be attributed to the Ministry of Defence. Particular acknowledgement is made to D Clenshaw and M Carver who originally initiated the work and who have contributed significantly to its progress.

10: Communicating with the user

P Wright

MRC Applied Psychology Unit
Cambridge
UK

This paper considers the variety of information that computer users need and examines in detail tutorial, reference and feedback information. It is shown that the advantages of alternative communication media, screen or paper, vary across these three categories of information. Although research indicates problems to avoid when designing communications, there is no single correct way of presenting information. Nor is it realistic to seek guidelines which can guarantee communication success. Therefore feedback is as important to writers and information designers as it is to computer users.

© P Wright 1988

P Wright
Patricia Wright is a member of the Medical Research Council's scientific staff and works at the Applied Psychology Unit in Cambridge. Her own research studies have explored design factors relating to many kinds of technical information (for example forms, instructions, tables, graphs) both on paper and on computer screens. She has published more than 100 papers and chapters on various aspects of written/visual communication.

Communicating with the user

What information do users need?

After considering the categories of information that users want, this paper will discuss how such information should be made available and what design characteristics it should have. There is considerable evidence that users prefer learning about a new system by interacting with it, rather than by reading about it *(WRI1)*. This has strong implications for the design of tutorial information, but other kinds of information are also needed. Users appreciate informative feedback when errors have been made. Queries arise which lead users to refer to information that is somewhere other than currently on the screen. While the preference might be for asking someone, when this is not possible users will turn to reference sources on screen or paper. The relative advantages of different presentation media will be discussed later in this paper.

The three main categories of information that users need are *tutorial information*, *reference information* and on-line *feedback*. There are other information needs, but these three categories are shared by users working with mainframes and with microcomputers. This paper will focus on the information needs of those using the computer as a tool to accomplish some task, rather than the needs of those whose task is maintaining the computer system. However, many of the general principles discussed will be relevant to both groups of users.

One information category which rates as 'minor' in terms of frequency of use, but not in terms of importance to the user, is that of upgrades. Letting registered users know when bugs have been fixed and enhancements are available is something which requires *administrative* procedures of particular kinds. In contrast, the emphasis in this paper will be on information that requires appropriate *design* procedures. Nevertheless, good design often depends on adequate administrative provision, for example time and resources for checking the accuracy and comprehensibility of the information being given. Such checking is essential. Sometimes errors slip through the proof-reading stage. The presence or absence of a space in a command string can be easily overlooked by the proof-reader but can make the difference between success and failure for the user. The documentation may refer users to facilities that have not been implemented, or may illustrate screens which have been redesigned. This happens because manufacturers try to dovetail the development of the software and its documentation so that both are finished together. So the documentation is based on a description of what the product will most probably be like. The only way writers can be sure that the information is accurate is to take the time to check it against the finished product. This paper will therefore conclude with a brief discussion of the need to empirically evaluate all categories of communication with the user. However, let us first consider the three main categories of communication between software and its users — tutorial, reference and feedback information.

Tutorial information

Price *(WRI2)* has cautioned against the assumption that users start by knowing what the software is supposed to do. In many organisations the person making the purchasing decision is not the ultimate user. So when the product arrives, the user may have little idea of its intended purpose. Another mistake is to think that 'tutorial' information applies only to communications with raw beginners. Many sophisticated packages are mastered in stages. Users learn 'enough for the present', but later return wishing to learn more. One way of meeting these differing information needs is to create modules of information among which users can self-select. Carroll *et al (WRI3)* adopted this approach and provided users with 'Guided exploration' cards, where each card dealt with a familiar task. They found that this was nearly three times as efficient as normal training manuals.

With an increase in users' skill level there is a greater willingness to consider explanations for why the system behaves the way it does. Novices tend to be highly task oriented. They want to know what steps to take to achieve their objectives. If detailed examples are offered, these are likely to be followed and the information in the accompanying explanatory text may be ignored *(WRI4)*. With experience, users develop 'mental models' which represent their view of how the system works and enable them to predict how it will behave in new circumstances. Writers may need to refine or correct such models if users are to be helped to exploit advanced facilities *(WRI5)*.

Two of the major design problems when presenting tutorial information are deciding how much information to give and in what sequence to give it. To illustrate the product's functionality the writer must choose some task, but that particular task may be unfamiliar or irrelevant to a particular user. For example, an explanation of how a spreadsheet can be used for accountancy will leave a research student with many inferences to make about using the software for data analysis. Users are likely to skip over information if they think they are not interested in those functions. There is seldom an ideal sequence for all users. Take the example of word processing software. A secretary dealing with business correspondence may have little need for footnotes, whereas these may be among the most important features for someone writing reports, where the title itself may be linked to a footnote. Such diversity in the task requirements of those using the same application argues for modularity in writing style. It also argues against maintaining a particular 'illustrative task' throughout a tutorial. Another advantage of varying the task is that this variation may help users grasp what are the critical and what the accidental features of any particular example.

Examples need not only to be read by users but also to be interactively worked through. People learn a great deal by 'doing'. In particular they learn the bounds of generality of their own knowledge, that is they learn that procedures which work on context A may not produce the same results in context B (for example closing a file and quitting an application are usually different kinds of 'Goodbye'). Learning by doing becomes more effective if users are provided with tutorial environments in which they are protected from the full functionality of the system while they are at the earlier stages of learning *(WRI6)*. This limits the mistakes that they have the opportunity of making. Carroll and Carrithers *(WRI7)* have shown that their 'training wheels' system, which was based on this approach, resulted in users getting started faster, making fewer errors and producing better work than people learning in non-protective environments.

Recognising that users select what they wish to learn means that writers must provide easy access to the sections of interest. Contents lists and indexes are therefore as crucial to tutorial materials as they are to reference information. Because users often page through looking for information, rather than using the access structures provided, summaries at the ends of modules provide an additional access route. In addition to the usual indexes, summaries of the functionality available within the product may help users realise that an 'advanced' feature exists (for example a macro facility such as a global search and replace).

Reference information

The queries users ask range from those that are well specified, such as 'How do I print this document?' to those that are ill formed 'Why is the screen flashing?'. Adequate indexing may be all that is necessary for dealing with the well-formed queries. One characteristic of this adequacy is that index entries include both the technical jargon of the product (for example 'clone') and the various synonyms which might be more familiar to users (for example duplicate, copy). This may seem repetitious but in indexing most economies are false economies. It can also be helpful if the index entries are subcategorised so that related functions are close together (for example grouping the varieties of print commands). One risk of subcategorisation is that the syntax of the entries may become convoluted. This should be strenuously avoided (for example not 'Ribbons, in daisywheel printers, the changing of' but 'Changing ribbons in daisywheel printers'. Similarly, the visual display needs to be vertically aligned so that it can be easily scanned (that is with each subentry on its own line, rather than having subentries run together like pseudo-paragraphs).

There are three commonly used organising principles for reference (alphabetic, structural and functional) and these differ considerably in their ease of use. Probably the most common is to arrange the information in an alphabetic sequence *(WRI8)*. Although this is a familiar and easily understood principle it does not correspond to the way many users will have phrased the questions that have led them to turn to the reference material. For example, listing commands in alphabetic order of the keys to be pressed would help users who were asking 'What does Command X do?', but usually they want to know how some goal can be accomplished, so the sequencing of reference materials needs to respond to the kind of questions that users will ask. Grouping the material into related topics which reflect a functional principle of organisation will be more helpful to users. Therefore *multiple* indexes are needed to cope with different kinds of question. For example, a trouble-shooting index may list as entries the symptoms which are manifested when something has gone wrong and under these headings there can be suggestions as to how to get round the problem. Another common way of organising reference information, particularly in software offering on-screen menu options, is to mimic on the printed page the display shown on the screen. This is essentially a structural organisation and can have the same limitations as an alphabetic listing, in that it seldom corresponds to the questions users ask. However, when keyboard commands can be coupled with menu items, or on-screen tools to change the functionality of those items, a reference listing in the form of a table showing the change in functionality for various key menu combinations can be helpful. However, reference information is generally easier to use when it matches the questions that users ask.

Having on-screen help which mimics the structure of a printed document is another variation of the structural organising principle and one that can be very unhelpful. Few users enjoy reading extended prose on a computer screen. Such an approach ignores the power of computer-controlled displays to respond with some degree of awareness of what the user is trying to do. Without careful design, an electronic book which slavishly copies the printed model makes it harder for users to select the information they require than when they are using print on paper *(WRI9)*.

Feedback information

If users attempt to issue illegal commands, well-behaved software will trap these commands and inform the user. Such communications can range from detailed verbal messages about the nature of the error, to a minimalist bleep indicating non-compliance by the program when an illegal move is attempted. Succinct error messages that consist of alphanumeric codes for which the user must consult another reference list are far from ideal. To be useful feedback must be informative, and also non-technical, but what counts as non-technical is not always apparent to the writer. Even the verbal message 'Referencing before first message' may be too terse to mean much to inexperienced users.

Feedback to users can also include warnings of the consequence of 'dangerous' actions by the user (for example file deletion). Such warnings give users the opportunity to change their minds if this was not their intention. Unfortunately, with increased familiarity such feedback tends to be anticipated, and the response to it prepared, so that it loses its 'warning' status. Nevertheless, reminders to users who are about to quit an application that they have not saved all their files is happily becoming a courtesy that more software developers are realising is appreciated.

A different kind of feedback is to indicate the permitted options within the current context. Menu systems can be tailored so that they present users with only those options which are currently legitimate. Also when users must switch between modes of operation (say between modes allowing text/data insertion and modes which allow control operations such as moving through the file) feedback which signifies the current mode of operation can be helpful. While working with the software, users generally know which mode they are in, but if resuming after an interruption (for example a telephone call) it is not always easy to tell which is the current mode. This concept of feedback might be extended to 'system level' information that users may want while working within an application. For example, users may wish to know about the amount of free memory available, or about the queue length for laser printers. Anticipating such information requirements can be difficult. They are not task specific and so may not become visible in any normal task analysis techniques. Nevertheless, they are part of the information needs that users have when working with computers.

Feedback must necessarily be presented on-line to users. Several display options are available, and their appropriateness varies with the kind of feedback being given. Portions of the screen can be set aside for messages to and from the system, or pop-up messages and dialogue boxes can be used to demand a response from the user before work can continue. The choice among these display options is governed in part by the need for consistency with the dialogue style chosen for the application itself. For tutorial and reference information the choice of *how* to present the information is much wider, concerning both the communication medium (screen/paper) and the display characteristics within that medium.

Reference materials, if topically or functionally organised, need a contents list. In this list the entries should be short enough to be easily scanned, while still being informative enough for users to match them against their current information needs *(WRI2)*. Sections with cryptic titles such as 'The beginning' and 'Advanced uses' are very little help as reference tools.

Choosing the presentation medium

The relevant media for tutorial and reference information are mainly the computer screen and print on paper. Media such as Compact Disk Read Only Memory (CD-ROM) may be important elsewhere for reference, and possibly for organisations who do a lot of training, but they are not as yet a practicable alternative for communicating with users of microcomputers. Auditory feedback is attention getting and some tutorials combine audio cassettes with interactive displays. Although tape-recorded information has the potential advantage of allowing the learner to concentrate fully on the screen and keyboard, in practice users often have to turn the tape on and off while they practice doing various things. Audio material also has the disadvantage that users cannot turn easily to the sections of interest. So the learner is forced into a more passive role of accepting the information sequence chosen by the writer. The memory demands on the learner can be more arduous as they are now determined by the information giver, who decides where to pause. Recapping tends to be more cumbersome for users who forget some of the steps in a sequence. Perhaps when the speech capabilities of computers allow them, rather than audio tapes, to be used these difficulties may be less. But even then, a coarse 'play it again' request will be easier to implement for audit instructions, whereas written information allows an easier check as to whether step 3 was this or that. Of course, when speech recognition is a practical reality (that is affordable), the trade-offs among modalities (sound/vision) may well change again.

For reference material, decisions must be made about whether to make information available to users on-line or to provide printed documentation, and whether to duplicate or subdivide the content across media. A valuable and extensive summary of the research done in relation to on-line help has been provided by Shriver *et al (WRI10)*. On-line help can be made sensitive to the user's current context. This has two advantages — it restricts the information to the relevant subset and it also lets users access help through a single command (such as '?') which gives different answers on different occasions. Such solutions are more appropriate for the simpler applications. For powerful packages, which allow users a wide range of operations in almost all contexts, exploiting the advantages of on-line help will be easier for users with sufficient experience to formulate questions in system terms (for example 'How do I change directories?') rather than beginners ('How can I send this file to Jim?') *(WRI11)*. Another advantage of on-line documentation is that it is easier to keep to to date, particularly for mainframe systems.

Although the 'space' requirements may be less constraining in an electronic medium than on paper, the designers of on-line help are often short of space for visually displaying information. The screen resolution may limit the size of legible text and this, in turn, reduces the amount of information that can be shown at any one time. The size of the screen may force users to alternate between seeing their problem and seeing the documentation. Many of these problems have been documented by Rubens and Krull *(WRI12)*.

Rather than displaying large amounts of text on screen the information can allow users to select the most relevant portions. In hierarchical structures, accessing information can become unacceptably slow as users move down through the tree. Moreover, if a mistake is made at any choice point, users may have to start again. Hypertext systems, which allow users to jump directly from one portion of the text to another (and back again if required), may offer solutions *(WRI13)*. As yet little is known about how readers cope with navigating inside a hypertext. These seldom offer views of the overall structure of the information, which would make the material easier for browsing. Compromise solutions between the linear and non-linear approaches, such as fish-eye structures, have been proposed *(WRI14)*. In these electronic documents the focal text is viewed in full detail, but the text preceding and following is viewed more schematically (for example just subheadings). This could help readers to decide if they are in the right section, but the ability to move around in electronic texts remains a critical factor. Readers already have many techniques for moving around in printed materials.

Paper as a medium conveys many of the characteristics of the information structure which readers rely on. Alternatives need to be found in an electronic medium. For example, knowing how long a tutorial session will last, how far away the end is and how to quit before reaching that end point is information that is very readily available to those reading print on paper.

Another limitation of on-line documentation concerns the range of typographic options which can be denoted. Larger, bit-mapped screens are becoming more common and our understanding is growing concerning why reading has often been found to be slower from computer screens than from paper *(WRI15,WRI16)*. So some of these problems may be overcome in the longer term. Nevertheless, while many people still work with 80-column by 24-line raster displays, these limitations must be borne in mind when considering how much and what kinds of on-line support to provide for users.

Although the printed medium has the disadvantage of being bulky, of going missing and of sometimes being out of date, it also has a number of advantages that will not be influenced by developments in screen technology. It can be much easier for users to customise a printed manual to their own task requirements. This customisation can take many forms such as leaving a bookmark in the section most often wanted, or writing notes in the margin summarising the most relevant portions of a section. Print on paper is also much more *browsable* than electronic information and so is better at coping with poorly formed questions (for example 'I wonder if there is some other way that I could do this to speed things up?') where the visible structure of printed material may suggest where to look. Readers can simultaneously refer to two sections of a document with only mildly cumbersome page turning. On a large screen this *could* be much easier electronically, but the control needed by the user to create and manipulate such displays may restrict their use to more advanced users. In time these techniques may become standard and most computer users will be familiar with them, but we have not reached that point yet.

Selecting among visual design options

Most of the material presented to computer users is visual, so information providers need to know about good and bad design features. Often there is more than one 'right way', but unfortunately communication styles that work well in one context may be less successful in another *(WRI17)*. Certainly information providers need to avoid design features known to cause user difficulties. Several summaries of research on designing technical information are available *(WRI18,WRI19)*. For convenience the following brief review will separately consider the use of language and the characteristics of the graphic display, but in practice these may not be independent design choices. For example, decisions about window size may result in the use of an abbreviated language style, and decisions about the words used to label operations may have implications for the graphic portrayal of these items (for example the Macintosh 'trash can') and vice versa.

Language choices

Communication can succeed or fail at many levels ranging from words and phrases through the sentence structures used, to the structures for paragraphs and larger textual units. Let us consider some of the pitfalls at each of these levels. More detailed summaries are available elsewhere *(WRI20)*.

The most obvious problem with words is that their meaning may be unfamiliar to the user. The terms themselves may be technical words, or abbreviations, outside the user's experience (for example modem, SCSI) or they may be previously familiar words (for example memory, handshake) now used in a specialised technical sense. It is these previously familiar words which can be particularly troublesome because readers may not at first realise that they are misunderstanding the writer's intended message. Such communication problems can be hard for writers to spot in their own documents because of their familiarity with the subject matter *(WRI21)*. Computer-based writing tools such as Writers' Workbench™ *(WRI22)* can help to detect some difficult terminology because long words are more likely to be unfamiliar than short ones, although there are numerous exceptions. Nouns created from existing verbs (for example *reduction* from *reduce*) are usually longer than the verb forms and tend to make the comprehension process more cumbersome for readers. It is also more difficult for readers when writers string together several adjectives to create a highly modified noun phrase (for example 'The previously formatted, soft-sectored, single-sided, double-density floppy disk') rather than using a slightly longer clause (for example 'The floppy disk which you have previously formatted should be single sided and have double density with soft sectors').

Shortness and familiarity are no guarantee that communication will succeed. Short, familiar phrases, such as 'on top of' are ambiguous but many writers see only their intended meaning. For example, the instruction 'Put A on top of B' may have meant to the writer 'Overlay B with A' but to the reader it may have signified 'Vertically align A and B with A at the top'. Analogies can run into similar problems since readers may not know which are the intended points of similarity and which are the incidental features of the image that was chosen *(WRI23)*. The image of a desktop may be helpful for introducing the concepts of files and folders, but Macintosh users who take the metaphor too literally may be very surprised to find that files moved to the 'desktop' outside the open window will disappear when the disk holding these files is ejected from the drive. The inherent difficulty of spotting ambiguities contributes to the writer's need for feedback about the reader's interpretation of the material.

Words involving negation either explicitly (not, un-, dis-) or implicitly (decrease, reduce) can cause readers more difficulties than their antonyms. For example, when comparisons between quantities are being made there is evidence that people find it easier to decide whether A is *more* than B rather than whether B is *less* than A *(WRI24)*. There is a logical equivalence between these two expressions but not a psychological equivalence. In general, increases are easier for readers to cope with than decreases. This applies to a number of comparative terms with *longer* being easier than *shorter*, *higher* easier than *lower*, etc *(WRI25)*. Once aware of this asymmetry, writers can choose the order of mentioning the items being compared so that the easier comparative term is used.

Although shortness is often seen as a desirable characteristic of sentences, it is sentence structure rather than length which causes readers difficulty. Of course, longer sentences are more likely to have complicated structures than short ones and it is advisable to split sentences with more than two clauses into separate sentences. If the sentences are giving procedural instructions then the order in which information is mentioned within them can be important. Sequences of steps need to be mentioned in the order in which these steps will be carried out by the user. 'Do this, then do that' is a safer communication than the logically equivalent 'Do that after doing this' *(WRI26)*. The display of a sequence of steps as a visible list of numbered stages is preferred by readers *(WRI27)*.

Expressing contingent relationships ('If this then that, otherwise something else') can become convoluted if several dependencies are involved. One way out of such difficulties can be to abandon prose for some other representational form such as a table or diagram, although these too can be sources of ambiguity and misunderstanding. Changing the representational form of the information does not guarantee success, but the point to bear in mind is that clear communication does not necessarily mean writing flowing prose.

When thinking about textual units larger than the sentence, the potential contribution of overviews and summaries must be considered. These are not substitutes for each other. The function of an overview is to provide a framework within which readers can interpret the text. Dixon *(WRI28)* showed that when instructions were given in two sentences, people read faster if the overview information came first rather than second. A heading may be sufficient for creating an interpretative framework, but often an articulation of the relation among the following sections of text will be needed. The detail given in a summary will tend to reflect the information density within the text. If summaries are given before the text, readers may mistakenly think that they have enough information to proceed and may begin interacting with the system before reading the text *(WRI3)*. Therefore summaries belong at the ends of sections/chapters. Here they can help readers assess how well the text has been understood and also provide a supplementary reference tool for users hunting through the documentation.

Display choices

The physical appearance of visual information is important and can affect both the legibility and the interpretation of the material displayed. Readers make use of the outline shape of a word when reading, so ascenders and descenders (the strokes above and below the line) contribute to the distinctiveness of a word's shape, when it is written in lower case letters. Text of any length written entirely in capital letters is read more slowly, whether on screen or on paper. This is obviously less critical for small segments of text, such as headings. Word shape also becomes more distinctive if thin characters (i, l, f) are allotted less space than wide characters (m, w). That is why professionally printed material is usually easier to read than typescript. For a review of typographic research see *(WRI29)*.

Research has shown that space needs to be used to give a visual grouping of functionally related elements *(WRI30)*. Appropriate use of space contributes to the legibility of information. There needs to be adequate spacing between lines of text and between text and any contours (for example boxes) that surround it. Longer lines of text require more spacing to maintain equivalent legibility, but always there needs to be a clear separation of the descenders from the line above and the ascenders on the line below. The spacing between words should be uniform, which means that a ragged right-hand margin will be better than one vertically aligned unless sophisticated 'justification' facilities are available which can distribute the extra space within as well as between words.

Design features, such as space, are not good or bad in themselves; much depends on the way they are used. A common bad use of space is in contents lists with unnecessarily wide gaps between the words and the page numbers. The position on the page or screen may lead readers to suppose that the information is of a particular kind. For example, text under an illustration may be thought of as a caption and perhaps ignored for that reason. With on-line displays it can be helpful to allow users to position the information for their own convenience.

Feedback to writers

Writers need feedback that can tell them how successfully they are communicating with the intended audience. Fortunately the availability of in-house 'desktop publishing' systems make it increasingly realistic for writers to experiment with draft versions in various styles and collect feedback about the strengths and weaknesses of alternatives.

There are many techniques for collecting feedback, each with its own strengths *(WRI31)*. Feedback can be achieved informally, simply by showing the draft to colleagues. It may also undergo more formal assessment, for example the stylistic critiques offered by software such as the Writers' Workbench^{TM} *(WRI22)*. The formal and informal techniques focus on different aspects of the text. Factual mistakes and ambiguities are more likely to be noticed by humans, whereas grammatical and spelling errors are more likely to be picked up by the software *(WRI32)*. Several kinds of performance testing can also be carried out. For example, the writer, or a substitute, can run through the information and check that what the user is told will happen and does actually happen *(WRI33)*. This is the safest way of ensuring the information being given is accurate. Other kinds of performance test involve having users carrying out tasks on the computer using the manual. For all evaluation techniques, as soon as communication difficulties are found the material must be revised, and the revisions themselves must be evaluated because not all revisions are improvements *(WRI34)*. In this way, the content and presentation of the final communication is achieved iteratively.

Conclusions

This paper has briefly considered the variety of information that computer users need, particularly tutorial, reference and feedback information. The advantages of alternative communication media, screen or paper, vary across these three categories. Research has shown some of the problems to avoid when designing visual information. However, there is no single correct way of communicating, nor do guidelines exist which can guarantee communicative success. Feedback is therefore as important to writers and information designers as it is to computer users.

Invited Paper references

CLE1
Johnston R
'Taking issue with the domain experts'
Expert System User
(Jan 1987)

CLE2
Cleal D M
'Teaching computers by example'
CCTA News
(Jan 1984)

CLE3
Clancy W J
'The epistemology of a rule-based system: a framework for explanation'
Artificial Intelligence
vol 20 (1983)

DOW1
Long J B
'People and computers: designing for usability'
In 'Proc of 2nd Conf of the BCS HCI SG'
M D Harrison and A F Monk (eds)
Cambridge Univ Press
(1986)

DOW2
van Gisch J P and Pipino L L
'In search of a paradigm for the discipline of information systems'
Future Computing Systems
vol 1 no 1 pp 71-89
(1986)

DOW3
Dowell J and Long J B
'Towards a paradigm for human computer interaction engineering'
In 'Contemporary ergonomics'
E Megaw (ed)
Taylor and Francis
(1988)

DOW4
Long J B
'Cognitive ergonomics and human-computer interaction'
In 'Psychology at work'
P Warr (ed)
Penguin
(1987)

DOW5
Rouse W B
'Systems engineering models of human machine interaction'
Elsevier/North-Holland
(1980)

DOW6
Norman D A and Draper S W
'User-centered system design'
Lawrence Erlbaum Associates
(1986)

DOW7
Card S K, Moran T and Newell A
'The psychology of human computer interaction'
Lawrence Erlbaum Associates
(1983)

DOW8
Ross Ashby W
'An introduction to cybernetics'
Methuen
(1956)

DOW9
Meister D
'Human factors testing and evaluation'
Elsevier
(1986)

DOW10
Gregg L W and Simon H A
'Process models and stochastic theories of simple concept formation'
J of Math Psychol
vol 4 pp 246-276
(1967)

DOW11
Carroll J M and Campbell R L
'Softening up hard science: reply to Newell and Card'
Human Computer Interaction
vol 2 pp 227-249
(1986)

DOW12
Norris M T, Shields M W and Ganeri J
'A theoretical basis for the construction of interactive systems'
British Telecom Technology J
vol 5 no 2 pp 5-11
(1987)

DOW13
Dowell J
'An investigation of the influence of CAD graphical representation on design performance'
Unpublished MSc Thesis
Univ of London
(1986)

EAS1
Emery F E and Trist E L
'Sociotechnical systems'
In 'Management science, models and techniques'
C W Churchman and M Verhulst (eds)
vol 2
Pergamon Press
(1960)

EAS2
Mumford E
'Designing human systems'
Manchester Business School Publications
(1983)

EAS3
Pava C
'Managing new office technology: an organisational strategy'
New York Free Press
(1983)

EAS4
Eason K D
'Information technology and organisational change'
Taylor and Francis
(1988)

EAS5
Trist E L et al
'Organisational choice'
Tavistock
(1962)

EAS6
Rice A K
'Productivity and social organisation: the Ahmedabad experiment'
Tavistock
(1958)

EAS7
Singleton W T
'Man-machine systems'
Penguin
(1974)

EAS8
Eason K D, Damodaran L and Stewart T F M
'Evaluating the impact of a computer-based system in a hospital'
In 'The application of information technology'
S D P Harker and K D Eason (eds)
Taylor and Francis
(1988)

EAS9
Björn-Anderson N, Eason K D and Robey D
'Managing computer impact'
Ablex (1986)

EAS10
Grudin J
'Social evaluation of the user interface: who does the work and who gets the benefit?'
In 'Human-computer interaction — INTERACT '87'
H J Bullinger and B Shackel (eds)
North-Holland
(1987)

EAS11
Gower J A and Eason K D
'Implementing office automation in a city firm'
In 'The application of information technology'
S D P Harker and K D Eason (eds)
Taylor and Francis
(1988)

EAS12
Hannigan S and Kerswell B

'Towards user friendly terminals'
Proc of ISSLS '86 Conf
Tokyo Japan
(1986)

EAS13
Checkland P
'Systems thinking, systems practice'
John Wiley & Sons Ltd
(1981)

EAS14
Mumford E and Weir M
'Computer system in work design: the ETHICS method'
Associated Business Press
(1979)

EAS15
Eason K D and Harker S D P
'An open systems approach to task analysis'
Internal Rep
HUSAT Research Centre
(1980)

EAS16
Eason K D, Gower J A and Harker S D P
'Task analysis in the specification of systems for electricity supply distribution'
In 'The application of information technology'
S D P Harker and K D Eason (eds)
Taylor and Francis
(1988)

EAS17
Cherns A B
'The principles of sociotechnical design'
Human Relations
pp 781-792
(1976)

EAS18
Harker S D P et al
'Classifying the target for human factors output'
Alvey Conf
UMIST
(14-16 July 1987)

GAR1
Gardner A and McKenzie J
'Human factors guidelines for the design of computer-based systems'
Parts 1-6 Issue 1
Ministry of Defence (PE) and Department of Trade and Industry
(1988)

GAR2
McKenzie J
'Guidelines and principles of interface design'
In 'Designing end-user interfaces'
State of the Art Rep
series 15 no 8
Pergamon Infotech Ltd
(1988)

GAR3
'Software tools for application to large real-time systems'
STARTS Guide
National Computing Centre
(1987)

GAR4
Smith S L and Mosier J N
'Design guidelines for user-system interface software'
Rep MTR-9420 by The Mitre Corporation
Bedford MA for USAF
(1984)

GAR5
Parrish R N et al
'Development of design guidelines and criteria for user/operator transaction with battlefield automated systems'
Rep WF-82-AD-00
Synectics Corporation of US Army Research Institute for the Behavioural and Social Sciences
Alexandria VA
(1983)

GAR6
Benz C, Grob R and Haubner P
'Designing VDU workplaces'
Verlag TUV Reinland
(1983)

GAR7
Grandjean E
'Ergonomics in computerised offices'
Taylor and Francis
(1987)

GAR8
Schneiderman B
'Designing the user interface: strategies for effective human-computer interaction'
Addison-Wesley
(1987)

GAR9
Galitz W O
'Handbook of screen format design'
North-Holland
(1985)

GAR10
DEF STAN 00-25
'Human factors for designers of equipment'

Parts 1-12
Directorate of Standardisation
Ministry of Defence
(1987)

GAR11
Boff K R, Kaufman L and Thomas J P
'Handbook of perception and human performance'
vols I and II
John Wiley & Sons Ltd
(1986)

GAR12
Salvendy G (editor)
'Handbook of human factors'
John Wiley & Sons Ltd
(1987)

GAR13
Damodaran L, Ip K and Beck M
'Integrating human factors principles into structured design methodology'
In 'Proc of Eurinfo '88'
North-Holland
(1988)

GAR14
Kloster G V and Zellweger A
'Engineering the man-machine interface for air traffic control'
Computer
vol 20 no 2
pp 47-62
(Feb 1987)

GAR15
Phillips M D et al
'Operations concept for the advanced automation system man-machine interface'
DOT/FAA/AP-84/16
Computer Technology Associates for US Federal Aviation Authority
Washington DC
(1984)

GAR16
'Quality systems'
BS 5750 Parts 0-6
British Standards Institution
(1987)

GAR17
Tainsh M A
'Job process charts and man-computer interaction within naval command systems'
Ergonomics
vol 28 no 3
pp 555-565
(1985)

GAR18
Jarsch V and Muller K G
'Handbook on man-machine interfaces for CCIS'
Tech Memo STC TM-649
SHAPE Technical Centre
The Hague
(1982)

GAR19
'Information processing systems interconnection — Basic Reference Model'
ISO 7498
International Standards Organisation
(1982)
(Also available from British Standards Institution as BS 6568)

GAR20
Bird D F
'International standards in military communications'
In 'Advances in command, control and communication systems'
C J Harris and I White (eds)
Peter Peregrinus Ltd
(1987)

GAR21
Nielson J
'A virtual protocol model for computer-human interaction'
DAIMI PB-178
Computer Science Department
Aarhus Univ Denmark
(1984)

MAG1
Martin A
'A new keyboard layout'
Applied Ergonomics
vol 3 p 1 (1972)

MAG2
Grandjean E
'Ergonomics in computerized offices'
Taylor and Francis
(1987)

MAG3
'Draft British Standard recommendations for ergonomics requirements for design and use of Visual Display Terminals (VDTs) in offices'
Technical Committee PSM/39 Applied Ergonomics
British Standards Institution
(1987)

MAG4
Kroemer K H E
'Human engineering — the keyboard'

Human Factors
vol 14 no 1 pp 51-63
(1972)

MAG5
Ilg R
'Ergonomic keyboard design'
Behaviour and Information Technology
vol 6 no 3 pp 303-309
(1987)

MAG6
Ring T
'Faith, hope and an ergonomic keyboard'
Computing
pp 24-25 (28 Apr 1988)

MAG7
Koffler R P
'Office systems ergonomics report'
Koffler Group
(1986)

MAG8
Conrad R and Hull A J
'The preferred layout for numerical data entry keysets'
Ergonomics
vol 11 no 2 pp 165-174
(1968)

MAG9
Haller R, Mutschler H and Voss M
'Comparison of input devices for correction of typing errors in office systems'
INTERACT '84
vol 2 pp 218-223
(1984)

MAG10
Bewley W K et al
'Human factors testing in the design of Xerox's 8010 "Star" office workstation'
Proc CHI '83 on 'Human factors in computer systems'
pp 72-77 (Dec 1983)

MAG11
Card S K, English W K and Burr B J
'Evaluation of mouse, rate-controlled isometric joystick, step-keys and text keys for text selection on a CRT'
Ergonomics
vol 21 pp 601-613
(1987)

MAG12
Roberts T
'A comparison of a mouse and cursor keys in an editing task'
BSc Ergonomics Final Year Project
Department of Human Sciences
Loughborough Univ of Technology
(June 1984)

MAG13
Malone S
'Canon IX-12: learning to read'
Practical Computing
vol 10 no 5 pp 54-55
(May 1987)

MAG14
Dubash M
'Kurzweil Discover 7320: intelligent scanner'
Practical Computing
vol 10 no 10 pp 60-61
(Oct 1987)

MAG15
Coler C R
'In-flight testing of automatic speech recognition systems'
Proc of Speech Technology Conf
Prentice-Hall
(1984)

MAG16
Murray J, van Praag J and Gilfoil D
'Voice versus keyboard control of cursor motion'
Proc Human Factors Society 27th Annual Meeting
p 103
(1983)

MAG17
Morrison D L et al
'Speech-controlled text editing: effects of input modality and of command structure'
Intl J of Man-Machine Studies
vol 21 no 1 pp 49-63
(1984)

MAG18
Talbot M
'Speech technology: is it working?'
Proc of Conf on 'People and computers'
BSI Human Computer Interaction
Specialist Interest Group
Univ of East Anglia
pp 345-358
(Sep 1985)

MAG19
Mariani J
'Speech technologies in Western Europe — a review'
Speech Technology
vol 3 no 2 pp 26-38
(1986)

MAG20
Joost G J, James F G and Moody T
'Ergonomics research in speech I/O'
Speech Technology
vol 3 no 2 pp 42-47
(1986)

MAG21
Cooper M
'Human factors aspects of voice input/output'
Speech Technology
vol 3 no 4 pp 82-86
(1987)

MAG22
Schmandt C and Hulteen E
'The intelligent voice-interactive interface'
Proc 'Human factors in computer systems'
Gaithersburg MA
pp 363-365
Washington DC Chapter Association for
Computing Machinery
(Mar 1982)

MAG23
Zimmerman T G et al
'A hand gesture interface device'
Proc 'CHI + GI '87' Conf on 'Human factors in computing systems and graphics interfaces'
Toronto
ACM/SIGCHI pp 189-192
(1987)

MAG24
Weber G
'Gestures as a means for the blind to interact with a computer'
Proc INTERACT '87 on 'Human-computer interaction'
pp 593-595
North-Holland
(1987)

MAG25
Bolt R A
'Eyes at the interface'
Proc 'Human factors in computer systems'
Gaithersburg MA
Washington DC Chapter Association for
Computing Machinery
pp 360-362
(Mar 1982)

MAG26
Fletcher D
Letter in Computer Guardian
p 27 (7 Apr 1968)

MAG27
'Ergonomic principles in office automation'
Ericcson Information Systems AB
(1983)

MAG28
Hammond C
'The big screen: monitors for DTP'
Practical Computing
vol 10 no 10 pp 50-52
(Oct 1987)

MAG29
Kemp M
'Map reading car tells its driver where to go'
Daily Mail
p 17
(14 Apr 1988)

MAG30
Stobie I
'NEC P-2200 & Epson LQ-500: 24-pin matrix printers'
Practical Computing
vol 11 no 3 pp 36-37
(Mar 1988)

MAG31
Stobie I
'Three ink jet printers: the sound of silence'
Practical Computing
vol 10 no 5
pp 42-43
(May 1987)

MAG32
Stobie I
'Data products SI-480: leapfrogging the laser'
Practical Computing
vol 11 no 1 pp 32-34
(Jan 1988)

MAG33
Lennox J
'Take a letter: budget daisywheel printers'
What Micro
(Mar 1986)

MAG34
Green Armytage J
'Huskies boost Monarch's income'
The Observer
p 78
(10 Apr 1988)

MAG35
Financial Times
(27 Apr 1988)

MAG36
Times Educational Supplement
(25 Mar 1988)

MAG37
Hampshire N
'Memory media'
Personal Computer World
vol 10 no 9 pp 118-122
(Sep 1987)

MAG38
Hammond C
'The integrated office: Discus 1000'
Practical Computing
vol 10 no 9 pp 94-96
(Sep 1987)

MAG39
Moody G
'Getting it together: the integrated office'
Practical Computing
vol 10 no 9 pp 85-96
(Sep 1987)

MAG40
Gardner A and McKenzie J
'Human factors guidelines for the design of computer-based systems'
Parts 1-6 Issue 1
Ministry of Defence (PE) and Department of Trade and Industry
(1988)

MAG41
Schneiderman B
'Designing the user interface: strategies for effective human-computer interaction'
Addison-Wesley
(1987)

MCK1
Gardner A and McKenzie J
'Human factors guidelines for the design of computer-based systems'
Parts 1-6 Issue 1
Ministry of Defence (PE) and Department of Trade and Industry
(1988)

MCK2
Gardner A
'Methodologies for designing User/Computer Interfaces (UCIs)'
In 'Designing end-user interfaces'
State of the Art Rep
series 15 no 8
Pergamon Infotech Ltd
(1988)

MCK3
Bennett J
Unpublished briefing papers prepared for the NATO Advanced Research Workshop Loughborough
(9-14 Sep 1984)

MCK4
Marshall C, Nelson C and Gardiner M M
'Design guidelines'
In 'Applying cognitive psychology to user-interface design'
M M Gardiner and B Christie (eds)
John Wiley & Sons Ltd
(1987)

MCK5
Smith S L and Mosier J N
'Design guidelines for user-system interface software'
Rep MTR-9420 by the Mitre Corporation for the USAF
(1984)

MCK6
Parrish R N et al
'Development of design guidelines and criteria for user/operator transaction with battlefield automated systems'
Rep WF-82-AD 00 Synectics Corporation for US Army Research Institute for the Behavioural and Social Sciences
(1983)

MCK7
Galitz W O
'Handbook of screen format design'
North-Holland
(1985)

MCK8
Schneiderman B
'Designing the user interface: strategies for effective human-computer interaction'
Addison-Wesley
(1987)

MCK9
Coutaz J
Tutorial 1, presented at 1st European Software Engineering Conf
(1987)

MCK10
Sperandio J C
'Software ergonomics of interface design'
Behaviour and Information Technology
vol 6 no 3 pp 271-278
(1987)

MCK11
Cleal D M and Heaton N O
'Knowledge-based systems: implications for human-computer interfaces'

Ellis Horwood Ltd
(1988)

MCK12
Maguire M
'Dialogue design'
HUSAT memo
HUSAT Research Centre
(1988)

MCK13
Hopgood F R A et al
'Methodology of window management'
Springer-Verlag
(1986)

MCK14
Thimbleby H
'User interface design: generative user engineering principles'
In 'Fundamentals of human-computer interaction'
A Monk (ed)
Academic Press
(1984)

MCK15
Hammond N et al
'The role of cognitive psychology in user-interface design'
In 'Applying cognitive psychology to user-interface design'
M M Gardiner and B Christie (eds)
John Wiley & Sons Ltd
(1987)

MCK16
DEF STAN 00-25
'Human factors for designers of equipment'
Parts 1-12
Directorate of Standardisation
Ministry of Defence
(1987)

MCK17
'Draft British Standard recommendations for ergonomics requirements for design and use of Visual Display Terminals (VDTs) in offices'
British Standards Institution
(1987)

MCK18
Cohill L F
'A taxonomy of user-computer interface functions'
In 'Human-computer interaction'
G Salvendy (ed)
Elsevier
(1984)

MCK19
Dysart A et al
'Hewlett-Packard Personal Software Division user interface guidelines'
Hewlett-Packard
(1984)

MCK20
Walton J
'ICL human factors in design: introduction to dialogue design'
International Computers Ltd
(1986)

MCK21
Rose C et al
'The Macintosh user interface guidelines'
In 'Inside Macintosh' vol 1
Apple Computers Inc
(1985)

MCK22
'Panel design and user interaction'
IBM systems application architecture — common user access
IBM Corporation
(1987)

NOR1
Bide A
'Information technology — a plan for concerted action'
Rep of the IT '86 Committee
(1986)

NOR2
Fitts P M
'The information capacity of the human motor system in controlling amplitude of movement'
J of Exp Psychol
vol 47
(1954)

NOR3
Card S K, Moran T P and Newell A
'The keystroke-level model for user performance time with interactive systems'
Communications of the ACM
vol 23 no 7 pp 396-410
(1980)

NOR4
Smith S L and Mosier J M
'Design guidelines for user-system interface software'
Tech Rep ESD-TR-84-190
Hanscom Airforce Base MA USAF Electronic Systems Division
NTIS no AD A154 907
(1984)

NOR5
Maguire M
'An evaluation of published recommendations on the design of man-computer dialogues'
Intl J of Man-Machine Studies
vol 16 no 3 pp 237-261
(1982)

NOR6
Pfaff G E (editor)
'User interface management systems'
Springer-Verlag
(1985)

NOR7
Wasserman A I and Shewmake D T
'Rapid prototyping of interactive information systems'
ACM Software Engineering Notes
vol 7 no 5 pp 171-180
(Dec 1982)

NOR8
Lipke D E et al
'Star graphics: an object-oriented implementation'
Computer Graphics
vol 16 no 3 pp 115-124
(1982)

NOR9
Morgan D G, Shorter D G and Tainsh M A
'Towards systems engineering'
Information Engineering Directorate Rep
Department of Trade and Industry
(1988)

NOR10
Meeks B N
'An overview of conferencing systems'
Byte
vol 10 no 13 pp 169-184
(1985)

NOR11
Halasz F G, Moran T P and Trigg R H
'NoteCards in a nutshell'
CHI/GI Conf Proc Toronto Canada Apr 1987
Association of Computing Machinery
(1987)

NOR12
Goodman D
'The complete HyperCard handbook'
Bantam Books (1987)

NOR13
Shafer B
'HyperTalk programming'
Hayden (1988)

NOR14
Adobe Systems Incorporated
'PostScript language reference manual'
Addison-Wesley
(1986)

NOR15
Suchman L
'Plans and situated actions: the problem of human-computer communication'
Cambridge Univ Press
(1987)

NOR16
Young R M and Barnard P
'The use of scenarios in human-computer interaction: turbocharging the tortoise of cumulative science'
CHI/GI Conf Proc
Toronto Canada Apr 1987
Association of Computing Machinery
(1987)

NOR17
Trevellyan R and Browne D
'A self-regulating adaptive system'
CHI/GI Conf Proc
Toronto Canada Apr 1987
Association of Computing Machinery
(1987)

NOR18
Baecker R M and Buxton W A S
'Readings in human-computer interaction: a multidisciplinary approach'
Morgan Kaufmann
(1987)

SHA1
OTA
'Automation of America's offices'
US Congress
Office of Technology Assessment
Rep OTA-CIT-287
Library of Congress No 85-600623
US Government Printing Office
(1985)

SHA2
McConnell M
'The workplace — investment or overhead'
Mind Your Own Business
pp 24-26
(July/Aug 1986)

SHA3
Nicholls J E
'Programming by the end user'
In 'Man/computer communication'
B Shackel (ed)

State of the Art Rep
vol 2 pp 263-272
Infotech International
(1979)

SHA4
Pearce B G (editor)
'Health hazards of VDUs?'
John Wiley & Sons Ltd
(1984)

SHA5
Nickerson R S
'Why interactive computer systems are sometimes not used by those who might benefit from them'
Intl J of Man-Machine Systems
vol 15 pp 469-483
(1981)

SHA6
National Electronics Council
'Human factors in information technology'
John Wiley & Sons Ltd
(1983)

SHA7
Shackel B
'Human factors for usability engineering'
In 'ESPRIT '87 — achievements and impact'
Proc 4th Annual ESPRIT Conf Brussels 28-30 Sep 1987
vol 2 pp 1019-1040
North-Holland
(1987)

SHA8
Shackel B
'The concept of usability'
Proc IBM Software and Information Usability Symposium
Poughkeepsie NY 15-18 Sep 1981 pp 1-30
(1981)

and

In 'Visual display terminals: usability issues and health concerns'
J L Bennett et al (eds)
pp 45-88
Prentice-Hall
(1981)

SHA9
Ramsey H R and Atwood M E
'Human factors in computer systems: a review of the literature'
Tech Rep SAI-79-111-DEN
(NTIS No ADA075679)
Science Applications Inc (1979)

SHA10
Eason K D, Damodaran L and Stewart T F M
'The MICA survey: a report of a survey of man-computer interaction in commercial applications'
SSRC Project Rep on Grant HR 1844/1
(1974)

SHA11
Bennett J L
'The commercial impact of usability in interactive systems'
In 'Man-computer communication'
B Shackel (ed)
State of the Art Rep
vol 2 pp 1-17
Infotech International
(1979)

SHA12
Miller R B
'Human ease of use criteria and their tradeoffs'
IBM Rep TR 00.2185 12 April
IBM Corporation
(1971)

SHA13
Bennett J L
'Managing to meet usability requirements'
In 'Visual display terminals: usability issues and health concerns'
J L Bennett et al (eds)
pp 161-184
Prentice-Hall
(1984)

SHA14
Shackel B
'Ergonomics in design for usability'
In 'People and computers: designing for usability'
M D Harrison and A F Monk (eds)
Cambridge Univ Press
(1968)

SHA15
Chapanis A
'Evaluating ease of use'
Proc IBM Software and Information Usability Symposium
Poughkeepsie NY 15-18 Sep 1981
pp 105-120
(1981)

SHA16
Chapanis A
'Evaluating usability'
In 'Human factors for informatics usability'
B Shackel and S Richardson (eds)

Proc of SERC/CREST Advanced Course
Cambridge Univ Press
(1988)

SHA17
Hirsch R S
'Procedures of the human factors center at San José'
IBM Systems J
vol 20 pp 123-171
(1981)

SHA18
Neal A S and Simons R M
'Playback: a method for evaluating the usability of software and its documentation'
Proc ACM CHI '83 Conf on 'Human factors in computer systems'
pp 78-82
Association of Computing Machinery
(1983)

SHA19
Grudin J and MacLean A
'Adapting a psychophysical method to measure performance and preference tradeoffs in human-computer interaction'
In Proc INTERACT '84 Conf
B Shackel (ed)
pp 737-742
(1985)

SHA20
Helmreich R
'Human aspects of office systems — user acceptance research results'
In Proc INTERACT '84 Conf
B Shackel (ed)
pp 715-718
(1985)

SHA21
Chapanis A
'Research techniques in human engineering'
John Hopkins Press
(1959)

SHA22
Meister D and Rabideau G F
'Human factors evaluation in system development'
John Wiley & Sons Ltd
(1965)

SHA23
Parsons H M
'Man-machine system experiments'
John Hopkins Press
(1972)

SHA24
Shackel B
'IBM makes usability as important as functionality'
The Computer J
vol 29 pp 475-476
(1968)

SHA25
Branscomb L M
'The computer's debt to science'
Perspectives in Computing
vol 3 no 3 pp 4-19
(1983)

SHA26
Chapanis A
'Training and civilizing computers'
Annals of the New York Academy of Sciences
vol 426 pp 202-219
(1985)

SHA27
Bewley W L et al
'Human factors testing in the design of the Xerox's 8010 "Star" office workstation'
Proc ACM CHI '83 Conf on 'Human factors in computer systems'
pp 72-77
Association of Computing Machinery
(1983)

SHA28
Moore T G and Dartnall A
'Human factors of a microelectronic product: the central heating timer/programmer'
Applied Ergonomics
vol 13 no 1 pp 15-23
(1982)

SHA29
Galer I A R and Yap B L
'Ergonomics in intensive care: applying human factors data to the design and evaluation of patient monitoring systems'
Ergonomics
vol 23 no 8 pp 763-779
(1980)

SHA30
Davies D G
'Case study of a system for remote users'
In 'User-friendly systems'
State of the Art Rep
series 9 no 4
Pergamon Infotech Ltd
(1981)

SHA31
Grandjean E (editor)

'Ergonomic and health aspects in modern offices'
Taylor and Francis
(1984)

SHA32
'Ergonomics and design in the electronic office'
Ergodesign '84 Conf
Behaviour and Information Technology
vol 3 no 4
(Dec 1984)

SHA33
Hendrick H W and Brown O (editors)
'Human factors in organisational design
and management'
North-Holland
(1984)

SHA34
Brown O and Hendrick H W (editors)
'Human factors in organisational design
and management II'
North-Holland
(1986)

SHA35
Bowman B L
'Cross-functional collaboration: teaming for
technological change'
In 'Human factors in organisational design and
management II'
O Brown and H W Hendrick (eds)
pp 511-515
North-Holland
(1986)

SHA36
Shackel B and Eason K D
'Organisational prototyping — a case study
in matching the computer system to the
organisation'
Paper to 2nd Intl Symposium on 'Human factors
in organisational design and management'
Vancouver
(19-21 Aug 1986)

SHA37
Douglas D M and Marquis F A
'Supporting computer user staff in an automated
office — a case study assessment'
In 'Ergonomics International '85'
I D Brown et al (eds)
pp 325-327
Taylor and Francis
(1985)

SHA38
Marquis F A and Douglas D M
'User acceptability of a computer system —
a case study'
In 'Ergonomics International '85'
I D Brown et al (eds)
pp 76-78
Taylor and Francis
(1985)

SHA39
Boies S J et al
'The 1984 Olympic Message System — a case
study in system design'
IBM Research Rep RC-11138
IBM T J Watson Research Center
(1985)

SHA40
HUSAT Research Centre
'Social security human factors strategy'
Loughborough Univ of Technology
(1983)

WAL1
Carver M K
'Practical experience of specifying the human-
computer interface using JSD'
In 'Contemporary ergonomics: Proceedings of
the ES Conference'
D Osborne (ed)
Manchester
(11-15 Apr 1988)

WAL2
Cameron J R
'An overview of JSD'
IEEE Transactions on Software Engineering
vol SE-12 no 2
pp 222-240
(1986)

WAL3
Carroll J M and Mack R L
'Metaphor, computing systems and
active learning'
Intl J of Man-Machine Studies
vol 22
pp 39-57
(1985)

WRI1
Carroll J M et al
'Exploring a word processor'
Human Computer Interaction
vol 1 pp 283-307
(1985)

WRI2
Price J
'How to write a computer manual: a handbook
of software documentation'
Benjamin/Cummings Publishing Company
(1984)

WRI3
Carroll J M et al
'The minimal manual'
IBM Res Rep RC 11637 (52295)
(1986)

WRI4
Lefevre J and Dixon P
'Do written instructions need examples?'
(In preparation)

WRI5
Kieras D E and Bovair S
'The role of a mental model in learning to operate a device'
Cognitive Science
vol 8 pp 255-273
(1984)

WRI6
Carroll J M
'Presentation and form in user interface architecture'
Byte
vol 8 pp 31-62
(1983)

WRI7
Carroll J M and Carrithers C
'Training wheels in a user interface'
Communications of the ACM
vol 27 pp 800-806
(1984)

WRI8
Rosson M B
'The role of experience in editing'
In 'INTERACT '84'
Proc 1st IFIP Conf on 'Human-computer interaction'
B Shackel (ed)
North-Holland
(1984)

WRI9
Wright P
'Reading and writing for electronic journals'
In 'Executive control processes in reading'
B K Briton and S J Glynn (eds)
pp 23-55
Lawrence Erlbaum Associates
(1987)

WRI10
Schriver K A et al
'Designing computer documentation: a review of the relevant literature'
Communications Design Center
Carnegie-Mellon Univ
(1986)

WRI11
Duffy T M and Langston M D
'On-line help: design issues for authoring systems'
Technical Rep 18
Communications Design Center
Carnegie-Mellon Univ
(1985)

WRI12
Rubens P and Krull R
'Application of research on document design to online displays'
Technical Communication
vol 32 pp 29-34
(1985)

WRI13
Stone D et al'
'Hypertext as a component in a computer-based technical information system'
Paper presented at the Association for the Design of Computer Instructional Systems
Denver CO
(1983)

WRI14
Furnas G W
'Generalized fisheye views'
In Proc of Conf on 'Human factors in computing systems'
M Mantei and P Orbeton (eds)
Association of Computing Machinery
pp 16-23
(1986)

WRI15
Haas C and Hayes J R
'Reading on the computer: a comparison of standard and advanced computer display and hard copy'
Technical Rep 7
Communications Design Center
Carnegie-Mellon Univ
(1985)

WRI16
Gould J D et al
'Reading is slower from CRT displays than from paper: attempts to isolate a single-variable explanation'
Human Factors
vol 29 pp 269-299
(1987)

WRI17
Wright P and Reid F
'Written information: some alternatives to prose for expressing the outcomes of complex contingencies'
J of Appl Psychol

vol 57 pp 160-166
(1973)

WRI18
Wright P
'Manual dexterity: a user-oriented approach to computer documentation'
In Proc of Conf on 'Human factors in computing systems'
A Janda (ed)
Association of Computing Machinery
pp 11-18
(1983)

WRI19
Wright P
'Issues of content and presentation in document design'
In 'Handbook of human-computer interaction'
M Helander (ed)
North-Holland
(1987)

WRI20
Kieras D E and Dechert C
'Rules for comprehensible technical prose: a survey of the psycholinguistic literature'
Technical Rep 21
Univ of Michigan
(1985)

WRI21
Hayes J R
'Is this text clear? — How knowledge makes it difficult to judge'
Paper presented at the American Educational Research Association (AERA) convention
San Francisco CA
(1986)

WRI22
Cherry L L and Macdonald N H
'The UNIX writer's workbench software'
Byte
vol 8 pp 241-248
(1983)

WRI23
Halasz F and Moran T P
'Analogy considered harmful'
Proc of Conf on 'Human factors in computer systems'
pp 383-386
(1982)

WRI24
Wright P and Barnard P
'Effects of "more than" and "less than" decisions on the use of numerical tables'
J of Appl Psychol

vol 60 pp 606-611
(1975)

WRI25
Flores d'Arcais G B
'Linguistic structure and focus of comparison in processing of comparative sentences'
In 'Advances in psycholinguistics'
G B Flores d'Arcais and W J M Levelt (eds)
pp 307-321
North-Holland
(1970)

WRI26
Clark H H and Clark E V
'Semantic distinctions and memory for complex sentences'
Quart J Exp Psychol
vol 20 pp 129-138
(1968)

WRI27
Frase L T
'Writing text and the reader'
In 'Writing: vol 2 — Process, development and communication'
Lawrence Erlbaum Associates
pp 209-221
(1981)

WRI28
Dixon P
'The processing of organizational and component step information in written directions'
J Memory and Language
vol 26 pp 24-35
(1987)

WRI29
Watts L and Nisbet J
'Legibility in children's books: a review of research'
National Foundation of Educational Research
(1974)

WRI30
Hartley J
'Designing instructional text'
2nd ed
Kogan Page
(1985)

WRI31
Wright P
'Is evaluation a myth? Assessing text assessment procedures'
In 'The technology of text: vol 2'
D H Jonassen (ed)
pp 418-435
Educational Technology Publications (1985)

WR132
Hartley J
'The role of colleagues and text-editing programs in improving text'
IEEE Trans on Professional Communication
vol 27 pp 42-44
(1984)

WR133
Sullivan M A and Chapanis A
'Human factoring: a text editor manual'
Behaviour and Information Technology
vol 2 pp 113-125
(1983)

WR134
Duffy T M, Currant T E and Sass D
'Document design for technical job tasks: an evaluation'
Human Factors
vol 25 pp 143-160
(1983)

146

Analysis

1: Definition of the problem

The design of end-user interfaces encompasses more than just the interface between the user and the technology. The issues range from the relatively well-defined problems associated with the design of the appropriate hardware through to the complex and ill-understood issues associated with the user and the computer in a sociotechnical system. Attempts are being made to formalise the problem and to produce guidelines to help designers avoid costly mistakes and increase the speed with which interfaces are produced. This Section defines the problem, introduces some of the terminology and looks at the failure of IT systems and the costs associated with poor interfaces. It also considers some of the diverse reasons why systems fail.

Definition of the problem

Introduction

The need to adopt a user-centred design approach and to consider the user interfce has been increasingly recognised by suppliers *(001,002)* and by users *(003)*. Shackel describes the general aim of user-centred design as being:

Shackel (004):
... to produce well integrated human-machine and human-environment combinations, the ergonomic approach has three definite sections, some or all of which are implemented according to the type and complexity of the task, machine or system being considered, system analysis, workstation analysis and evaluation.

Norman states:

Norman:
Other pressures exist for the designer to take more conscious and positive steps to design the user interface — the increasing number and range of end users, the increasing proportion of code that has to be devoted to handling the user system interaction and the improved display resolution that is now commonly available. The designer cannot leave to chance or intuition the design of the user interface.

The problems that are involved here have been very neatly encapsulated by Thimbleby:

Thimbleby (005):
Conventional interface design is not constrained — rather it is bottom-up. User interfaces typically grow by adding unrelated features and no method is used to specify coherent sets of user interface techniques. Features are added because they are locally powerful, and no orthogonal 'neat' design theme ever emerges, or if one does, the USER cannot rely on its being uniformly applicable.

This unfortunate situation is the result of a number of influences on the DESIGNER. One strong influence comes from the USER. Presented even with a manifestly bad system, USERs invest a lot of themselves in learning how to handle it just in order to use it at all. They, then, justifiably, resent any so-called improvements. On the other hand, if there are no precedents there is a 'chicken-and-egg' problem. Neither DESIGNER nor USER has a clear idea of what is required until they have a working system, and only then do they really know....

Another problem is the confusion between functionality and ease of use. A system becomes easier to use for a DESIGNER as more capability is added. However, the DESIGNER has a higher threshold for complexity than the USER, especially when the USER is learning. A system

> *becomes harder to use for the USER the more that needs to be learned and, indeed, the more that can be done accidentally....*
>
> *What we know ... is that without specific guidance USERs will construct their own models of the system and methods to achieve goals using them. There is no reason for these models to have any rational, let alone axiomatic basis: such models will be, at best, ritual 'magical' systems. When USERs are not computer experts, their models will be over-complex, difficult to generalise and, most likely, of a wildly superstitious nature.... And, because USERs may lack appropriate training, there is no reason whatsoever to assume that their self-established models are entirely conscious or provide any foundation for reasoning about the interface issues which confront them. This last point is important as under these circumstances it is highly likely that a computer-naive USER will react very differently, in a emotional way, than a DESIGNER would. The DESIGNER (often a computer scientist, of course) interprets unexpected behaviour in a computer system as an intellectual challenge; the non-expert, who has possibly struggled against all odds to acquire what skill that he has, will see unexpected behaviour as a personal threat, because he is unable to differentiate a partially subliminal (eg, pre-verbal) model from his Self. When his user model is wrong, his perception is that HE is wrong.*

The aim of this Report is to define the key areas of human factors research and to identify how designers can improve the overall system by taking into account the relevant human factors issues. As Eason states:

> *Eason:*
> *Most of the work undertaken on human/computer interaction has so far concentrated on individual users. An implicit assumption has been that users have individual tasks which they can undertake with the support of computer systems and that successful human/computer interaction will result in the effective performance of these tasks. While this has led to significant advances in ease of use and ease of learning of computer systems, it leaves other critical issues out of the equation. There is considerable evidence to suggest that these other issues create major problems of implementation and acceptability, and they need to be more formally addressed if these problems are to be avoided.*

The need to involve current designers in the human factors process has been well recognised. Christie and Gardiner discuss the need to influence designers of interactive systems:

> *Christie and Gardiner (006):*
> *However firmly human factors recommendations might be based on the theoretical rocks of psychology (and however sound or shaky these rocks), they will be useless if they fall on deaf ears: the products of human computer interaction research must not only be relevant and true, but also 'user-friendly' to the designer.*

However, Norman notes:

> *Norman:*
> *One approach that has been advocated is the provision of a specialist, someone well versed in UID, to serve alongside the members of the design team. It seems to the author that the practical difficulties of achieving this end make it unlikely that it will be accepted. Besides considerations of 'cultural' differences, there is an implicit assumption that it will, in any case, be acceptable to have a person monitoring and reviewing the work of others, a situation which will only be exacerbated when the inevitable pressures of meeting deadlines arise. Further, there just are not enough interface design specialists presently trained or available to fulfil such roles.*

The theme of involving more than just the deep specialist in the design of human factors and ensuring that information is available to the designers who are responsible for end-user interfaces is echoed by Gardner and McKenzie, who distinguish between human factors specialists and human factors general practitioners:

> *Gardner and McKenzie (003):*
> *Typically, the HF Practitioner will have a background in physical science or engineering but will have been trained in human factors by such means as these Guidelines and the associated training.*

Compared with:

> *Gardner and McKenzie (003):*
> *Human Factors 'consultants' who have a deep specialisation in the human sciences.*

In the Invited Papers Gardner states:

> *Gardner:*
> *Most handbooks are written for specialists in human factors (for example people with a training in psychology, ergonomics or human engineering). By analogy with the medical profession, these deep specialists are 'consultants' of human factors. In contrast, most of the decision making in design teams will be made by people without this deep specialisation.*
>
> *... many of the most valuable sources of human factors advice for the 'consultant' are too technical for the non-specialist with a background in physical sciences, programming or engineering. By analogy, what is needed is a set of methods suited to the 'general practitioner of human factors'. The conclusion is that equipping the general practitioner is the priority target for handbooks and training courses.*

Terminology

Shackel describes the end-user interface thus:

> *Shackel:*
> *It is evident that the end-user interface must comprise any feature with which the users may interact during their work. So the interface consists not only of hardware aspects but also of any relevant software and documentation.*

Any developing discipline typically uses jargon to cover certain issues. Designing end-user interfaces is no exception. The Alvey Programme in 1982 identified the Man/Machine Interface (MMI) as one of the four main themes. Subsequently other terms have been used to define the broader areas. Man/Machine Interaction (also MMI) attempted to capture issues which were broader than merely the interface. The term 'man/machine system' has been used by Grandjean *(007)*, who defined it as the reciprocal relationship between the man and the machine, comprising perception of all information and manual operation.

The term 'Human/Computer Interaction (HCI)' is preferred by the UK and US communities, though recent developments in the UK have used the term 'User/System Interaction (USI)'. The term 'User/Computer Interface (UCI)' is usually taken to refer to just the hardware and software aspects of the interface, leaving out the wider associated areas. For the purposes of this Analysis the abbreviation HCI is used. Shackel makes the following important point:

> *Shackel:*
> *It is important to remember the total context within which the interface and terminal reside. In essence there are two contexts, one organisational and the other operational. The organisational context involves the task/job/organisation dimension and the operational context involves the terminal/workspace/environment dimension with which we are primarily concerned in this Report. While the organisational aspects are not dealt with in depth in this Report, it is essential for designers to recognise that no system design can escape that context; these aspects have to be the starting point for the contribution of the human factors designers, from which they then move on to provide their direct contribution to the technology design.*

The term 'Human/Computer Interaction' is taken to cover the relationship between the user and the computer as well as sociotechnical and environmental issues associated with the system within which the HCI lies.

Failures of IT systems

The failure of computer systems is well documented. The reasons for the failures have been less obvious. A vice-president and chief scientist at IBM in a private communication stated:

IBM (008):
We know that system architecture has significant and widespread implications for user friendliness, but we know next to nothing about how to make fundamental architectural decisions differently, in the interest of good human factors.

One of the main reasons for IBM's change in policy was probably associated with the expensive failure of its PC junior 'chiclet' keyboard. The standard PC junior keyboard used small keys which were awkward to use, so awkward that IBM, in July 1984, announced that they would replace all existing chiclet keyboards with a standard keyboard, at no extra cost to the owner. The original keyboard was produced as a result of a marketing decision and directly against advice from human factors engineers. While IBM did not announce the cost of this replacement policy, it is estimated to have cost the company approximately 5 000 000 US dollars. The basic principles of good keyboard design were well understood when the chiclet was marketed, yet the company's failure to observe good human factors practice proved costly, both in money terms and in the user's perception of the company. As Shackel points out:

Shackel:
Some of the consequences of poor interface design have become common knowledge in the community at large. Only too often VDU terminals are just dumped on the existing user's desk, and the resulting aches, pains and complaints from awkward posture and bad interaction with local lighting conditions are obvious and easily predictable.

Mowshowitz *(009)* studied a number of information systems and assessed their success rate. The systems which were accounted a complete success represented 20 per cent of the sample. Forty per cent of the systems studied were partial successes and 40 per cent failed.

More recently, the DTI sponsored a number of IT pilot schemes. In 1985 analysis of the results of the pilot showed that the failure rates of IT systems had changed little in 10 years (37 per cent of the systems were complete successes and 33 per cent were failures). Hirschheim *(010)* gives many reasons why IT systems may fail. Few are to do with the technology (though the failure of technology to deliver its promised solution is still a problem). The main items which Hirschheim identifies as reasons why IT systems fail are:

1 Organisational issues.
2 Individual differences.
3 Inadequate technology.
4 Inadequacies of the systems profession.
5 Poor process for the implementation of the technology.
6 The nature of managerial work and the poor understanding of this work.
7 The myths of the systems professionals.

Despite the wealth of experience in how to design good systems, bad systems are still being designed. However, good human factors can produce better systems. For example, Plessey invested very heavily in human factors in the design and production of a Portable Billing Machine (PBM) for meter readers. This PBM was designed to allow meter readers to take their reading, input it to the PBM and produce the bill straight away. Human factors consultants were involved in the project from its inception, through prototype design and testing in both the laboratory and the field to final production and training. The final product was so successful that Plessey spun off a company to market it worldwide.

Understanding the user

The key to good interface design is to understand the complex relationship between the user, the system and the task which the user is required to perform. To aid this understanding it is important to have a clear idea of the user's physical and physiological capabilities. Unfortunately this cannot be a static view. The user's physical characteristics will change with time, for example changes in eyesight, manual dexterity, etc. This occurs over a relatively long timescale and is less important than the user's cognitive capabilities. For example few users will remain naive for long if they are required to use a system on anything other than an occasional basis. The same population of users is likely to yield individuals with markedly different skills and capabilities with respect to use of a computer-based system and familiarity with technology. Attempts have been made to categorise user types and to construct interfaces to adapt to the user's changing needs. These are all covered within the main body of the Analysis.

Specific tasks and different user abilities are not covered in detail. However, the main thrust of the Report is on the design of end-user interfaces to computer-based systems, specifically office-based systems, though other types of environment are also discussed. The issues change with the environment. For example, errors and system failures have a different significance when applied to the design of a nuclear power plant control room rather than a word processing pool. Similarly, designers building systems which are for use by the general public must consider a different range of problems from designers of business systems. Public systems tend to adopt a lowest common denominator approach, making few assumptions about typing skills and computer knowledge.

Hardware problems

The ergonomic design of hardware has been a well-studied problem over the last 10 years. A variety of 'cookbooks' and guides are available to help the designer check that specific requirements are met. The problems with such guidelines is that, with the rapid change in technology, information becomes either redundant or out of date. For example, no standards yet exist for the design of a mouse and the number of buttons it should use (though a maximum of three has been widely agreed). Similarly, recommendations which apply to the design of characters on dot-matrix screens (such as matrix size) are not as relevant to bit-mapped screens where special screen fonts can be defined and used. It should be noted, however, that there is a draft British Standard which attempts to overcome some of the technology-dependent factors by adopting an approach of setting performance standards for equipment. There is also considerable work internationally with the same aims, for instance as pursued in the International Standards Organisation (ISO) Committee TC154.

The main aim of the designer should be to build a system which is hardware independent and then to identify the most appropriate hardware to match the user's requirements and tasks. For example, if the system is required for a user in a hands-busy operation and reasonably high error rates can be tolerated and the number of system operations are small, then speech might represent the best input/output hardware. On the other hand, speech would be most inappropriate in an open-plan office for driving a word processing system, even if the hardware was up to it.

The designer must aim to maximise the user's performance by ensuring that the best match is made between the user and the hardware. While it is neither possible nor desirable to prescribe hardware solutions for all possible tasks, the designer should ensure that hardware solutions are not arrived at too early in the design stage and that the interface is designed around the characteristics and capabilities of the hardware rather than the user.

Software problems

In 1980 Schneiderman *(011)* considered the problems of software with respect to the user. He scoped the problem thus:

> *Schneiderman (011):*
> *Software psychologists focus on human concerns such as:*
> - *Ease of use*
> - *Simplicity in learning*
> - *Improved reliability*
> - *Reduced error frequency*
> - *Enhanced user satisfaction*
>
> *while maintaining an awareness of:*
> - *Machine efficiency*
> - *Storage capacity*
> - *Hardware constraints.*
>
> *The key software issues are much the same as the hardware problems — don't let the software drive the interaction and define the interface. One of the main problems facing many users (especially naive users) is that of power. Powerful tools are being developed which allow an experienced user to perform many operations. Unfortunately providing users with power*

without an adequate interface severely impairs performance and can cause the user to reject the system.

Conclusions

The problem of designing end-user interfaces is not simple. There are many interacting variables which contribute to the success or failure of a system. The theme of the book is that the likelihood of success will be maximised and the risk of failure minimised if the design of a system is user centred.

Failures of modern, complex IT systems are expensive. The cost/benefit of considering human factors is thus high. A review of the key issues highlights the main areas where human factors can contribute and what HCI methods are available for improving current practice. Carey states:

> *Carey (012):*
> *Effective design of the working interface between humans and computers cannot merely depend upon catalogues of previous 'characteristics' of each of these two entities, nor on optimising individual functions in the interactions ... the entire task, including its goals, is therefore the proper reference for design.*

The Report aims to set the design of end-user interfaces into a system context and to explore those specific aspects of the system which will influence the design of the interface.

2: Psychological and social factors

This Section explores the psychological and social characteristics of the user, considering those factors which will significantly impact the design of the interface. The type of user is considered, together with the need to adopt a flexible rather than a static view. The cognitive capabilities of the user which influence interface design are discussed. The wider problems associated with new technology and the design and implementation of computer systems are discussed, including issues relating to the resistance to change. Strategies for the design of computer-based systems which involve the user to a greater or lesser extent are discussed, as are the reasons for the failure of IT systems which have neglected the human component.

Psychological and social factors

Introduction

Smith and Collins (013):
In attempting to incorporate a better model of people into computer systems, researchers have not only incorporated knowledge about typical users ... but also sought principles that characterize human information-processing capacities so that these principles could be considered in the design of the system. The search for these principles has made use of several different strategies.

This Section will examine aspects of the user which influence the design of end-user interfaces.

Eason:
Conventional forms of systems analysis concentrate upon functional specification. Inasmuch as they examine the tasks undertaken in user organisations, they are concerned with the identification of the information being manipulated and stored and the information flows. These features require quantification in order to specify and size the technical system. Such an analysis says very little about the human agents who need and process this information, or about the relations that exist between them. Where the roles of users are described and associated with information requirements, the basis of the description may be suspect. It may, for example, reflect the formal or prescriptive view of the organisation rather than the complex reality which may include role conflict and ambiguity, and a continual redefinition of work role boundaries. Alternatively, systems designers may attempt to redefine the social structure by presuming the roles of the people who will operate or use the system. In this case they may produce new social structures which are neither feasible or acceptable within the user community.

Specifically it will consider different types of user, their characteristics and how these interact with user tasks.

Shackel:
Successful system design for usability requires much attention to various aspects of the user. However, the user must not be considered in isolation from other aspects of the situation; that would only be perpetuating in reverse the all too common fault in the past of considering the technological tool in isolation from the user.

It will discuss the user's cognitive capabilities and examine how these capabilities should be best utilised by the designer. The human will be placed in the context of a complex sociotechnical system, where issues to do with resistance to change, the roles users play in the design process and the impact of user teams influence the success not only of the interface but of the whole system.

Dowell and Long:
It is no longer sufficient for systems simply to work — they must also contribute to the success of the organisations which exploit them. In particular, there is a need to optimise the interactions of

users with the computers they operate in the course of their work — an interaction which determines fundamentally the effectiveness of these systems. The importance of this interaction has gone largely unrecognised and its design has been ad hoc and unprincipled.

The aim of this Section is to emphasise the central role which the user must assume in the design process and to ensure that the interaction between the user's psychological and social characteristics and the system are adequately considered.

Types of user

When describing the types of user for any particular system it is rarely sufficient to employ one simple classification, for example only naive users. Shackel *(014)* made some attempt to describe the vast range of user types. Typically this includes new users (who are computer experts), naive users, casual users, etc.

> *Shackel (014):*
> *In talking about the user, in the singular, it is very easy to forget that there are many different types and levels of user. So there is not just one man/computer communication gap to be bridged but many.*

The most useful way to describe the user is to consider the user as located somewhere on a multidimensional graph whose axes include:
- Frequency (frequent versus infrequent users)
- Expertise (computer versus non-computer users)
- Knowledge (knowledgeable about the task versus naive about the task)
- Training (trained users versus untrained)
- Understanding (wide knowledge about the system's functionality versus narrow understanding of the system).

A designer who considers only one type of user is likely to be designing for the wrong person. Not only are the user's characteristics multidimensional, they also change with time. Naive users become experts, users gain knowledge about the task or application and the more frequently the system is used the more its limitations are likely to be revealed.

If no other information is available, the most practical approach to designing interfaces for particular types of user is to assume that at least some of the users will be both naive about computers and about the task, that these users will want to learn rapidly both about the system and about the task, and that users will be experts in both the system and the task and may also see both the system and the task in a different, wider perspective. At any point during this process of learning to use the system people might stop using it for some time. When they return, their knowledge about the system may have deteriorated to a greater or lesser extent. The designer should try to allow the user to return to the system with the minimum deterioration in their performance.

The other important feature of user skills is that they are unequal. Within any system users will have varying abilities.

> *Draper (015):*
> *A frequently encountered commonsense view holds that in a computer system such as UNIX there are experts and novices ... this apparently commonsense notion of an 'expert' does not provide an adequate analysis of the nature of expertise in systems like UNIX, and hence does not provide a sound basis for designing help facilities.*

Cognitive capabilities of the user

The cognitive capabilities of users will significantly influence their abilities to use a system. The book by Christie and Gardiner *(006)* contains four chapters detailing the following psychological principles which influence user/interface design:

1 Thinking and mental models.

2 Memory.
3 Skill acquisition.
4 Language.

Brocks *et al (016)* also detail four areas:

1 Psychological factors.
2 Transfer of skills.
3 Medium of communication.
4 Problem solving representation.

The basic theme of these texts is that cognitive and psychological characteristics will play an important role in producing a usable interface. A typical system will require a user to learn new skills, remember information, solve problems and communicate with the system. Generally the user will behave in a goal-directed manner. The system will be used to solve a particular problem or fulfil some requirement. The user will have a set of constructs about how the system works and how the system can be utilised to meet the user's goals. Once he is using the system (depending on his training and experience), actions will be remembered and instances will be drawn from other similar systems with which he is familiar (though the similarities might be more imagined than real). Similarly, the characteristics of the task and the domain of application will also significantly affect the way in which the user is able to utilise the system.

It is important that the design attempt to exploit the user's existing information or stereotypes. Indeed, failure to conform with a stereotype can produce excessive errors. For example, many systems allow users to print the item they are seeing in exactly the form they are seeing it in (WYSIWYG — What You See Is What You Get). If the document which is printed is markedly different, for no apparent reason, users become confused, frustrated and more prone to other errors. Similarly, if users have expectations as to how a task should be undertaken, the interface should support, rather than ignore or contradict these expectations.

Another critical user characteristic, which needs to be understood and designed for, is the memory. There are different types of memory, utilised at different times, depending upon the circumstances. The present view is that there are primarily three types of memory — iconic, working and long term. It is the latter two which are particularly important in interface design, particularly working memory. The key problem with working memory is its limited capacity. Card *et al* describe some of the issues which are associated with memory:

> *Card, Moran and Newell (017):*
> *The original view of working memory, following Miller [(018)], was that it had a capacity of 7 ± 2 items, coinciding with the immediate memory span. Gradually, much of the support for the existence of an independent Working Memory came from the recency effect in free recall (the fading ability to remember the last few items heard ... various ways of calculating Working Memory size from the recency effect all give answers in the range $2.5 \simeq 4.1$ items for capacity. This implies that the immediate memory is a compound effect of more than one process.... At the opposite end of the spectrum from the sizes $2.5 \simeq 4.1$ versus 7 ± 2 is the notion of Working Memory as an activation of Long Term Memory, hence, of essentially unlimited instantaneous extent, but of limited access.*

The important message is that, because the working memory is of limited capacity, it is likely to be fully occupied in performing the task, leaving little room to be devoted to the system's operation. The well-established rule is that unless the system is well understood and frequently used, one should make minimal demands on the user's short-term/working memory. One should not require users to memorise complicated, one-off, commands or page numbers (for example with Prestel, where rapid access to a particular page requires the user to input the page number).

Another important role for designers is to promote consistency and the transfer of skills between different tasks (and preferably between systems). As noted previously, users will expect the interface to conform to certain stereotypes. Inconsistent interfaces or ones which conflict with user stereotypes will take longer to learn, will be forgotten more quickly, will lead users into producing more errors and will decrease the performance of users on other machines, as the different interface styles and commands come into conflict. As stated by Norman:

> *Norman (019):*
> *Be consistent. A fundamental set of principles ought to be evolved and followed consistently throughout all phases of the design.*

To promote problem solving, the system must represent a problem in a way which the user perceives to be 'natural'. Users should be allowed to manipulate the interface and data easily and 'comfortably' to facilitate the production of a satisfactory solution. For example, a graph package should allow the user to input data as raw information and then choose a scale and a style to display the information (while allowing him an easy way to change both scale and type of presentation). The representation on the interface should reflect both the data and the output (for example it should not distort the sizes or inaccurately reflect what the user will get once the graph has been printed).

The user in the sociotechnical system

> *Eason:*
> *The development of interfaces that are easy to use and easy to learn has made rapid strides in recent years. However, these interfaces are primarily designed as though the world were organised into a series of discrete human/computer connections. What are the implications for the interface of recognising that the user is in various kinds of cooperative and conflicting relations with other users who may also have access to the same computer system?*

Designing interfaces is not just a matter of matching the computer, the user and the task. There are external factors which will influence the success of an interface. These are associated with the environment which the system is being put into — the issues of how the system will interact with, and impact on, a user's job as well as how it will fit into the existing work environment. The wider issues related to the introduction of new technology into an existing work environment will significantly affect the success of a system. As Machiavelli said in 1514:

> *There is nothing more difficult to arrange, more doubtful of success and more dangerous to carry through than initiating change.*

Leavitt *(020)* relates the task, the technology, the organisational structure and the people with a stake in the process in the 'Leavitt Diamond', illustrated in Figure (2)1. A deliberate change in one of the four factors will produce changes in the others, often of an unanticipated and sometimes undesirable nature. The main message from Leavitt is that change will not only affect the factor which is being changed. There will be a series of knock-on effects which will influence each component within the overall system.

There are many adverse responses to change and often change is resisted because it is bad *per se*. Such resistance to change is the most typical response to the introduction of new technology into an existing work environment. People have many fears associated with change and the designer must attempt to understand these fears and to either anticipate and overcome them, or to prevent them.

Fears associated with change might be specific or more general. There might be fears about coping with new demands and the threat to a valued aspect of life. There might be problems associated with deskilling or change in the social and job hierarchies (for example, it is often felt that young people cope better with the new technology than old, hence older and more senior employees might have their status threatened). A user might have specific fears associated with the company's past history, his past experience of change, job loss and other adverse affects on his job.

A common response to change is to attempt to reject it. The user might feel resentment, frustration, anxiety, fear, insecurity and dissatisfaction. The demands which the job places on him might suddenly dramatically increase and he will perceive no benefits from this increased demand.

An aggravating factor in introducing change is the speed with which it happens. The more rapid the change, the more pronounced and extreme the reaction to it. It is a common assumption that resistance is a normal response to change and that the faster it is carried out, the sooner the adverse affects will be dealt with and the faster they will go away. It is also common to assume that change will always be accompanied by uncertainty, which will produce a number of unsatisfactory consequences, either in the

```
              Task
             /|\
            / | \
           /  |  \
          /   |   \
   People-----+-----Technology
          \   |   /
           \  |  /
            \ | /
             \|/
           Structure
```

Change in one, changes others

Figure (2)1: The Leavitt Diamond

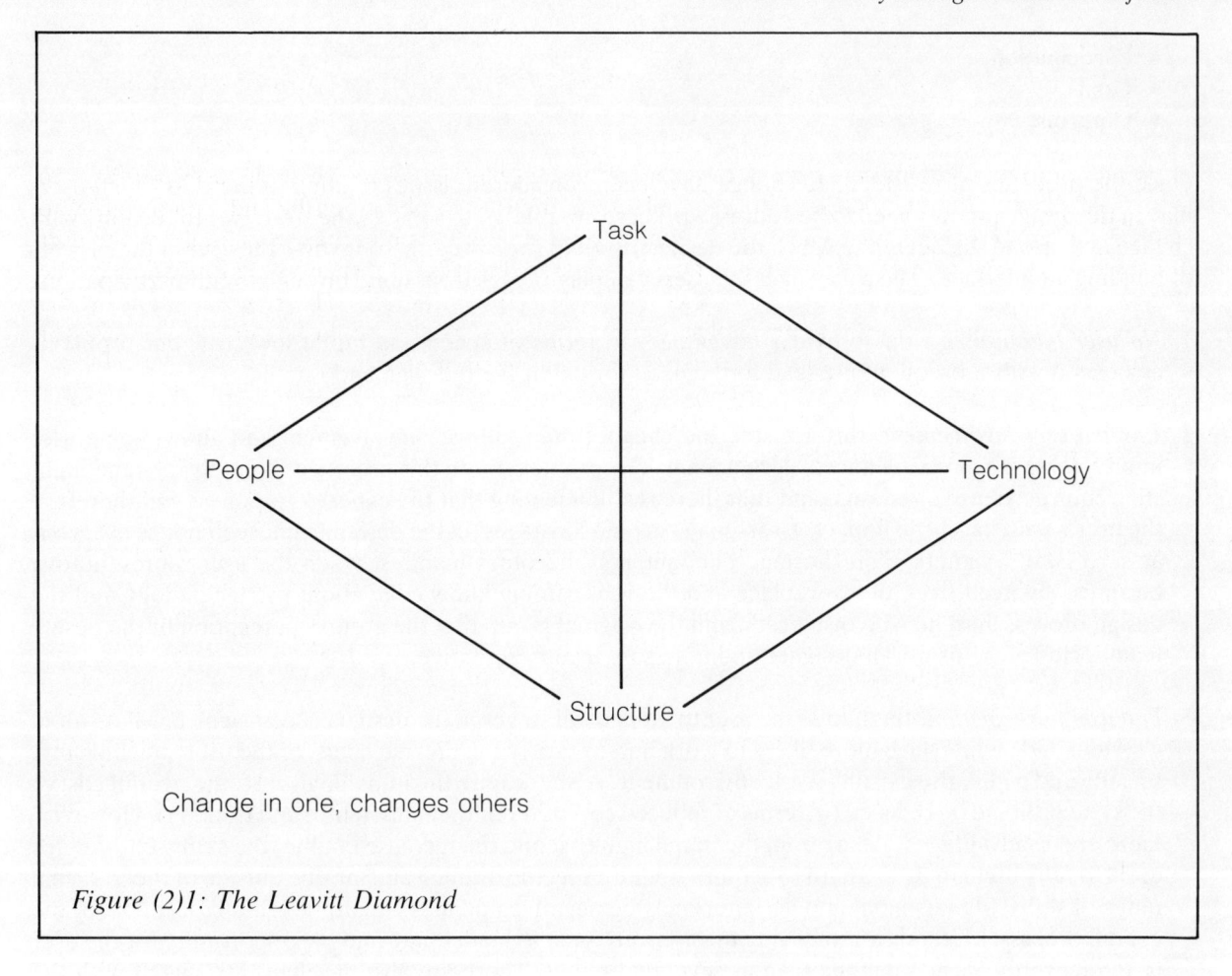

form of overt resistance, for example strikes, 'go slows' or long, drawnout negotiations, or more covert resistance, for example subtle sabotage through 'misunderstanding', in-fighting between different stakeholders or the 'it will never work' syndrome. To overcome these effects change must be planned. It need not be a *fait accompli*, nor need it be left to chance. System designers need to consider alternative forms of work organisation and how individuals or groups are likely to be affected. Likely reactions to change should be explored and shifts in influence amongst individuals examined. Finally, realistic timescales should be put on the introduction of the new system and serious steps taken to avoid the shock of the new.

The most important facet of monitoring the effects of change is to obtain data on performance and to review it. Too often systems are introduced with vague goals about increasing speed and efficiency without any reference to measures of performance. Thus the true cost of the system is poorly understood when evaluated *post hoc*.

There are many strategies to overcome or prevent resistance to change. These include the following:

1 *Overcome strategies:*
   - Persuasion — demonstration that the change is beneficial
   - Training — implementation of training regimes. Ensuring that the training is adequate and giving support at a high level
   - Group methods — use of group dynamics to gain support for change. Strengthening of lateral links within the group, performing analysis of the needs and discussing new goals and consequences
   - Other 'social' methods — use of social surveys, feedback and discussions to explain the plans and explore the options.

2 *Prevention strategies:* use of a model for introducing change which takes full account of the many sources of problems and which particularly addresses issues such as:
   - Leadership
   - Communication
   - Decision making

- Participation
- Goals
- Controls.

Once the problems of resistance to change have been considered, issues relating to the role which users play in the design process need to be addressed. These are related to some of the strategies for dealing with change and also to the degree to which the designer should (or is willing to) involve the user in the process of building an interface. The role which the users can play ranges from none through to full participation:

1. *No user involvement:* this provides advantages in terms of speed and initial low cost, but problems associated with subsequent use lead to the need for extensive redesign and rebuild.

2. *Limited user involvement:* this is faster and cheaper than full user involvement and allows some user input, creating a more 'balanced' design team. The problems with this process are that the system might still require extensive redesign and that there is still a feeling that the expert knows best and therefore the user's voice has little impact. Users may become 'hostages' in the design team, seen not as users but as surrogate designers. This 'hostage phenomenon' becomes manifest when the user representative becomes divorced from the workplace and the job, gaining knowledge about the technology and the design process until he is so distanced from the original group that the group's perception of the design team includes the user as a designer and not as their representative.

3. *Full user participation:* this allows the user to input at all stages in the design process, which will result in a system and an interface more likely to work and to satisfy the diverse needs of the users, technically, socially and within the existing work environment. Also, despite the initial high cost, the overall cost of the system should be reduced (in terms of reduced cost of rebuild, maintenance and training). However, there are disadvantages. Apart from the initial high cost and the increase in time, the skills required for users to fully participate are hard to acquire, require specific training and may be outside of their normal range of skills. Management and designers may be negative and users might be initially sceptical of the overall process. Methods for involving the users are seen as inadequate and the opportunity for the user to influence the design may be seen as severely limited. There are also problems associated with the changing roles of the people involved in the design team. The designer may feel threatened and confused as to what are the roles of those involved. This, in turn, may lead to conflict which the members of the team will be unused to and will fail to handle effectively. Despite all these drawbacks, because of the expense of modern IT systems and their tendency to fail, it is a participative approach which is most likely to meet with success.

Studies on the success of IT systems by Mowshowitz *(009)* and in the Department of Trade and Industry's Office Automation Project (1986) show success rates of between 60 and 70 per cent. Hirschheim *(010)* has proposed many reasons why IT systems fail, particularly problems associated with:
- The organisation
- Individual differences
- Inadequate technology
- A poor implementation process
- Poor understanding of the nature of managerial work
- Inadequacies of the systems profession.

The basic conclusion seems to be that design is a complex process which should involve many people. Short cuts in time and money will produce results which are expensive to live with and systems which will ultimately fail.

The design team should optimise user involvement and ensure that risks are minimised. The basic model for this approach is to allow the users to fully participate in the design process. There are other issues concerned with the need to solve problems and not simply to produce solutions. The design process is iterative and designers must be prepared to discard ideas which do not work. There must be a mechanism whereby ideas which occur later on in the design process can be included in the design. This is especially important in circumstances where the nature of the problem is initially ill understood. One such approach is outlined in *(021)*. In a case study, the design and implementation of an expert system is described, through a number of incremental phases, from feasibility study, demonstration system, pilot system to enhanced pilot. At all stages of the design both users and designers were heavily involved. The study concludes:

Central Computer and Telecommunication Agency (021):
This project illustrates a phased approach, which has been adopted by one Government Department, to an investigation into the use of expert systems. It has thus far shown that there is the potential for such a system to be developed, tested and maintained with the user in the lead, supported by the Data Processing Department, where the system needs to interact with existing or conventional systems or software. This offers scope for fundamental changes in the manner in which applications are managed.

3: Principles of interface design

This Section examines the key issues in relation to the interface between the user and the system. It examines the relevancy of some of the hardware debates and the need to match technology to the user and the task. The match between particular hardware and software is discussed and the complexity of the problem examined in relation to user characteristics. A brief summary of hardware is given. Dialogue design is considered, both in terms of low-level rules and higher-level rules which are more related to the user's cognitive capabilities. Adaptive interfaces and the role of mental modelling in the design process are considered. Bespoke, as opposed to general, interfaces and the special demands which specific tasks place on interfaces are briefly considered. Finally, issues of user support, particularly error messages, are examined.

Principles of interface design

Introduction

This Section will examine issues relating to the interface between the user and the system. It will consider the role that hardware plays in determining the type of interface which is produced. It will also consider the design of dialogues between the user and the system, as well as the building of systems which adapt as the user's needs and capabilities change. Bespoke versus general interfaces will be examined and the implications for designing an interface for a specific individual or group will be considered. Finally, this Section will discuss how best to support the user.

> *Card, Moran and Newell (017):*
> *The human-computer interface is easy to find in a gross way — just follow a data path outward from the computer's central processor until you stumble across a human being. Identifying its boundaries is a little more subtle.*

Interface design has been dominated by the capabilities of the computer and the hardware available to communicate with it. Little consideration has been given to the user and for the user's preferred modes of communication. The technology has not been capable of taking advantage of more 'natural' ways of communicating.

> *McKenzie:*
> *It is important that suitable combinations of UCI devices with the chosen UCI dynamics and imagery are made. The choice of dynamics and imagery will place requirements on the UCI devices (for example screen resolution or need for, and properties of, a pointing device). It is important to note that this is the most appropriate way to make decisions concerning the UCI protocol, as opposed to the initial choice of UCI hardware influencing the dynamics and imagery. For more details on the choice of UCI devices and their main features for the chosen UCI dynamics and UCI imagery there are several useful sources.*

More recently, increasing emphasis is being placed on the design of interfaces which are tailored to the requirements of the user, rather than the capabilities of the technology. A more diverse range of input/output options are available to the interface designer, who is able to choose the appropriate technology for the task rather than having to alter the user's method of interaction.

The focus of the hardware debate is now which particular method of interaction is best suited for each task or system. This is epitomised by the debate over mouse versus joystick versus keyboard. Card *et al* (022) conclude that for the task investigated there is a significant advantage in using a mouse:

> *Card, English and Burr (022):*
> *Of the four devices tested the mouse is clearly the superior device for text selection on a CRT:*

1 The positioning time of the mouse is significantly faster than that of the other devices. This is true overall and at every distance and size combination save for single character targets.

2 The error rate of the mouse is significantly lower than that of the other devices.

3 The rate of movement of the mouse is nearly maximal with respect to the information processing capabilities of the eye-hand guidance system.

As a group the continuous movement devices are superior in both speed and error-rate. For continuous movement devices, positioning time is given by Fitt's Law. For the key devices it is proportional to the number of keystrokes.

This result has been challenged by Karat *et al (023)*. The thrust of this paper is that while a specific input device might be superior for one task, if a different task were chosen the results might be very different. The paper concludes:

Karat, McDonald and Anderson (023):
At the very least we must conclude that 'unnatural' devices, such as a keyboard, can in some circumstances both be preferred and lead to better performance than 'natural' pointing devices such as a mouse.

The fact that performance will be influenced by task and that no one device is likely to offer all the answers should be apparent to any interface designer. It is evident that the interface design and user performance is only partially affected by the choice of hardware. The design of the task and the capabilities of the user (as well as the user's preference) plays a crucial role in the production of an acceptable, usable system.

The interface designer must begin by analysing the user's requirements and defining the task in such a way that an optimum interface, irrespective of any particular device, can be determined.

Texts such as *(024)* lay down simple guidelines on the human as an information processor and discuss methods of stimulus to ensure that appropriate alarms and attention grabbers are used in different situations. It is important that the interface designer be aware of these fundamental characteristics of users and avoid situations such as the user having to deal with many tens of alarms and stimuli (such as happened in the control room at Three Mile Island).

More recent work by Gardner and McKenzie *(003)* has documented techniques for determining user requirements and analysing tasks. It presents a comprehensive and systematic approach to the problem of matching the user and the task. Damodaran *et al (025)* endeavour to place the user centrally in the design process and include chapters on the user aspects of systems analysis and system design, as well as equipment design, workplace design and user support.

Only when the designer has a clear understanding of the user's requirements should interface decisions be taken. Interfaces which are designed too early can produce costly system failures. The constant theme of the interface designer should be to ensure the best possible match between the user and the system. The designer must also take account of the way in which the user will develop and tasks will change over time. Furthermore, systems are rarely designed for a single individual and there will be a need to consider the general characteristics of users.

The hardware options have to be linked to other design decisions, for example how best to facilitate the dialogue between the user and the computer, how best to support the user, etc.

Hardware

The most common choice for a computer interface is a keyboard and a screen. The arrangement of keycaps was determined by Sholes in the last century and is reputedly based on the need to prevent the clash of keys and their subsequent jamming in mechanical systems. The screen was of low resolution based on the Cathode Ray Tube (CRT), with the individual characters generated by a matrix of green or white dots on a black background. Simple guidelines on the physical aspects of such an arrangement —

the keycaps, minimimum size of the dot matrix, etc — will produce a system which is efficient to use and cost effective for simple word processing tasks. However, the arrangement does not begin to recognise the requirements of more complex tasks or to exploit the interaction potential of most systems. Simple keyboard/screen-based systems should only be used when a minimum number of functions are required or when excessive time and errors cause no problems. Choosing hardware which better matches the user and the task will help reduce errors and provide additional benefits such as ease of learning, ease of use and increased performance.

For example, the use of a pointing device such as a mouse will produce a significant improvement in the performance of inexperienced users who are required to choose between a limited number of options. On the other hand, a mouse will not be as effective when an experienced typist can perform the task using the keyboard without having to move the fingers away from the main body of the keyboard.

A touch-sensitive screen is very useful if users are required to make limited choices over a short period of time and are likely to be unfamiliar with keyboards and mice or if space is at a premium. However, this too loses its advantages over keyboards and mice as users become more experienced or when they are expected to use the system for more than a few minutes. A finger generally makes a poor pointing device, is subject to fatigue and potential inaccuracy, and is fairly stubby and grubby. Screen-based light pens offer few advantages over fingers as pointing devices, but are useful when combined with bitpads and tablets, allowing users to perform complex motions which can be reproduced on a screen or interpreted as strings of complicated commands.

The use of combinations of high-resolution screens, well-designed graphics, windows, icons, menus and mice produce systems which are flexible and can be made usable. It must be noted that Windows, Icons, Mice and Pull-down menus (WIMP) are not *per se* a good thing.

> *McKenzie:*
> *One common representation that is gaining place in office automation is that of the visual metaphor of the 'desktop'. In trying to match the language of the interface to the user's cognitive model of office work, icons of symbolic telephones, documents, wastepaper baskets, etc, appear on an office desk. Such models and metaphors are highly task specific. In office automation the desktop has proved to be a successful metaphor to the extent that users already possess an effective cognitive model of an office desk and the objects/activities which it presumes. These can improve if different applications consistently reinforce the cognitive model. However, these standard metaphors are not likely to carry successfully to other environments — other metaphors will be needed, such as map displays in a military environment or mimic diagrams in process control.*

The device which is most suitable for the system is not merely that one which will perform best in hardware terms. Marshall *et al* note that:

> *Marshall, Christie and Gardiner (026):*
> *The complexity of the problem posed for device choice by all these interacting variables is great and is further compounded by social, political and economic constraints. In a recent study [(027)] it was found that integrated circuit designers using a computer-aided design system preferred a puck to a mouse. This seemed to be principally motivated by the fact that all the designers had considerable past experience of design systems which provided a puck. Thus there was a resistance to change and not just a technical objection. The puck and the mouse are very similar in most respects.*

McKenzie states:

> *McKenzie:*
> *The inconsistent use of a visual metaphor, or the use of an inappropriate visual metaphor, is likely to decrease the usability of the application.*

In terms of the social and organisational impact of specific hardware, the devices which are likely to have the most impact are speech I/O mechanisms. Apart from the many technical difficulties associated with the construction of speech recognisers and synthesisers there are organisational issues which indicate that speech might be precluded as an I/O method. Open-plan offices and individual expertise in dictating are likely to cause problems, as are the psychological barriers associated with talking to machines. Undoubtedly speech technology has improved but there are few studies which have looked at the myriad problems associated with the introduction of such technology into the workplace. The studies which have been carried out indicate that while speech is very good in some environments (typically the hands-busy/eyes-busy areas) it will have significant social and psychological barriers to overcome. Speech recognition and synthesis as interface mechanisms are still the subject of research and their use is still not clear.

The following list presents a summary of the hardware options:

1 *Input devices:*
   - Voice
     — restricted vocabulary versus large vocabulary
     — problems are technical (user dependency, continuous or discrete speech, etc) and sociotechnical (the quiet office, speak to a machine, etc)
   - Keyboards
     — QWERTY
     — chord
     — membrane
     — advantages in speed and familiarity but inflexible and difficult to use for naive subjects
   - Pointing
     — touch screens
     — wands
     — light pens
     — good for naive users, becoming less useful with experience
   - Direct (mouse)
   - Cursor (thumb wheels)
   - Controls
     — tracking balls
     — joystick (rate controlled and positional)
     — buttons
     — can offer significant advantages especially when matched to the task
   - Indirect
     — bitpad/puck
     — bitpad/membrane
     — good for macro input and complex motions
   - Specials
     — robot arms (industrial)
     — spade grips (MoD)
     — building bricks (industrial)
     — eye movements/head movements
     — limb positions
     — holographic displays
     — voice.

2 *Output devices:*
   - Visual
     — CRT (TV-type, projections, flat screens)
     — liquid crystal matrices
     — plasma
     — CCD
   - Specials
     — head-up
     — false colour
   - Aural (synthesis).

There are other developments in I/O technology — for example the production of handwriting recognition, such as the work carried out at the National Physical Laboratory, the vast improvement in hardcopy output with the widespread use of laser printers and the trends toward higher resolution and colour displays.

Devices which are oriented toward non-conventional office-type tasks and environments are most likely to develop in the next few years. Most technology is two-dimensionally based, but the problems are moving beyond these domains into the area of design and manufacture which traditionally has required a three-dimensional approach. This has made the problem of interacting with a computer more complex and the demand for three-dimensional representation and interaction will significantly increase. Work carried out as part of the Alvey Design-To-Product development and at the Loughborough University of Technology Computer Human Interface Research Centre (LUTCHI) on the problem of three-dimensional interaction indicates that only now is the technology becoming sufficiently sophisticated to deal with the problem adequately.

Whitefield concludes that:

> *Whitefield (028):*
> *It is obvious that devices can vary in their capabilities. However, no single device is suited to all of the input functions, due partly to the difference between information input tasks and selection tasks. Pointing is a technique well suited to the latter, and the need for this is likely to increase as graphic displays capable of supporting multi-tasking processing become more common. Users will increasingly select among displayed tasks rather than input commands to change tasks. The use of sets of complementary input devices will increase in new systems, and pointing devices will be an important member of this set. The selection of the most appropriate subset in any instance will of course be heavily dependent on the nature of the tasks to be performed.*

In this section issues associated with the choice of appropriate hardware have been examined. However, the relationship between the system and the user is not merely dependent upon the selection of 'the right kit', the design of the dialogue is equally important, to complement the hardware and support the user.

Dialogue design

The design of a system's dialogue should be determined by an understanding of the user's needs and requirements and a fundamental understanding of the task. The designer should aim to explicitly determine the user's goals and expectations. While this Section will explore some of the guidelines for dialogue design, the need to determine the characteristics of the user and the task must be the first step in the construction of a successful dialogue. For example, issues such as the experience of the user population and frequency of use will fundamentally effect dialogue style.

Schneiderman offers eight golden rules for the design of dialogues:

> *Schneiderman (029):*
> *1 Strive for consistency.*
> *2 Enable frequent users to use shortcuts.*
> *3 Offer informative feedback.*
> *4 Design dialogues to yield closure (that is ensure that the dialogues have a beginning, middle and an end).*
> *5 Offer simple error handling.*
> *6 Permit the easy reversal of actions.*
> *7 Support internal locus of control (that is encourage actions rather than reactions).*
> *8 Reduce short term memory load.*

The rules do not examine how to determine the basic tasks which the system is undertaking, nor how this relates to the user's expectations of the system. Schneiderman's rules should be followed once the designer is confident that the fundamental issues associated with the production of the dialogue have been understood and their implications for the design of the dialogue acted upon.

Prior to producing a dialogue the designer should ascertain that the dialogue will:

1 Ensure that the functions which the system is performing and the way in which a task is carried out matches the user's perception of how the system is performing. While users are very flexible in their perceptions and will use investigation as a powerful tool for exploring the system and adapting their models, problems will occur when there is a mismatch. For example, studies on the use of calculators by

Young *(030)* illustrated the difficulties of a user's model not matching that of the system. The mismatch (that is cognitive dissonance) caused severe problems.

2 Ensure that there is a match between the user and the task. It is not enough to ensure that the user understands how the system works, it is necessary to make sure that the system's functions are useful and usable. It is only then that the system's true potential can be realised.

3 Assume that the user will change. The user's characteristics and skills will evolve with use of the system. A system which is easy to learn is not necessarily easy to use once the user becomes an expert. This is one of the hardest features of designing an end-user interface and will be discussed in detail later.

4 Assume that the dialogue will not be perfect first time and allow for some iteration in the design to achieve a closer match between the system and the user.

Hammond and Barnard note:

> *Hammond and Barnard (031):*
> *Ease of use of a system must take into account not only the nature of the interface dialogue itself, but also the detailed cognitive context in which a particular exchange occurs. The cognitive context of an interaction includes the general cognitive demands imposed by the system, information extracted from the wider task environment, the specific question or problem motivating the exchange and the cognitive strategies mobilised in the course of learning and use.*

Once the fundamental characteristics of the task and dialogue have been determined it is possible to utilise the sort of rules described by Schneiderman and listed earlier. In applying such principles, other guidelines in the choice of a particular style of interaction should be followed. The current status and range of dialogue styles are included in the following list:

1 *Menu selection:*
   - Types
     — fixed: good for displaying only available options
     — pull down/up: current vogue. Use of highlighting, grey-out, keying equivalents (for example control character alternatives). Not always the best option for inexperienced users
     — pop-up: useful but the user needs to know about them. Best kept for functions which are independent of specific task, for example window controls, etc
     — walking: quick way to get depth, can also be used for command sequence. Not good for naive computer users
   - Issues
     — breadth versus depth: how deep should a menu be? Broad and shallow menus offer advantages over narrow and deep menus
     — consistency: menus should be consistent, for example quit should always appear at the bottom of the list and as option 0
     — grouping and display features: make good use of conceptual grouping, colour coding (where available) etc.

2 *Command languages:*
   - Types
     — natural: based on abbreviations of existing words. Can be useful if the word is apparent to the user, for example 'cat' for concatenate
     — random: a group of letters which have no apparent meaning to the user, for example 'cat' to print (as in concatenate a file to the printer)
   - Issues
     — experience: do not expect naive or inexperienced users to master the system
     — consistency: wherever possible be consistent, both in choice of commands and in the methods used to choose them
     — support the user: command-driven systems will have higher error rates and the user will need to be supported throughout the use of the system.

3 *Direct manipulation:*
   - Types

— icon based: the most popular direct manipulation method. This has caused problems with non-obvious icons and their interpretation
— object oriented: manipulating not only icons but any screen-based object. Can provide the user with a powerful method for carrying out complex operations
- Issues
  — tools: direct manipulation interfaces need to be created and maintained by special tools
  — power: the user is able to carry out main operations which are potentially very damaging to the system or the task. Irretrievable operations will require confirmation and undo should be a viable option
  — identification: there can be problems in identifying screen objects or groups of objects. Determining boundaries and individual items can cause problems.

4 *Form filling:*
- Types
  — system driven: user inputs data in highly structured, system-driven way
  — spreadsheet: user is presented with a blank shell which can be filled with many types of data and options
- Issues
  — control: the locus of control of form filling dialogues tend to be very much based with the computer. The user might feel constrained and frustrated. Provide shortcuts where possible
  — navigation: allow the user to move freely within the form but prevent the user from getting lost through the use of 'home' or 'where am I' options
  — redundancy: do not require the user to input information more than once or to provide information which is not necessary for the problem.

In conclusion the dialogue should be designed to complement the task and the user.

> *McKenzie:*
> *Where possible the provision of several types of dialogue should be provided in order to account for such variances among users as skill levels, experience levels or simply personal preferences. What appears to be an easy-to-use system to an infrequent user may appear to be slow and cumbersome to a more experienced person who does not require the same level of guidance or feedback on his actions.*

One should allow both the user and the system to evolve within the dialogue structure and ensure that the dialogue supports not only the functionality of the system but also its usability.

The next section considers methods of designing a more flexible system, where the dialogue is required to support a changing view of the user and the task.

Adaptive systems

The design of systems which adapt to the user's needs and capabilities has been a major research theme in recent years. Advances in the understanding of the user and the construction of user models, coupled with the processing power to translate these models into computer-based systems, have provided the impetus to design an adaptive system. The major premise behind such systems is that they include an embedded model of the user which alters the style or nature of the interaction between that system and any one user. As well as adapting to each user individually, adaptive systems will alter their interaction with a single user over time. The aim of such systems is to match the internal model of the user with the user's internal model of the system and the task. The need to consider the user's perceived needs and expectations becomes paramount and the possibilities of cognitive dissonance causing problems increase.

The first major problem with an adaptive system is determining a user model on which to base it. Norman notes:

> *Norman (032):*
> *1 Mental models are incomplete.*
>
> *2 People's abilities to 'run' their models are severely limited.*

> *3 Mental models are unstable: people forget the details of the system they are using, especially when the details (or the whole system) have not been used for some period.*
>
> *4 Mental models do not have firm boundaries: similar devices and operations get confused one with another.*
>
> *5 Mental models are 'unscientific': people maintain 'superstitious' behaviour patterns even when they know they are unneeded, because they cost little in physical effort and save mental effort.*
>
> *6 Mental models are parsimonious: often people do extra physical operations rather than the mental planning that would allow them to avoid those actions: they are willing to trade-off extra physical action for reduced mental complexity. This is especially true where the extra actions allow one simplified role to apply to a variety of devices, thus minimizing the chance of confusion.*

Hamill states:

> *Hamill (033):*
> *Decision makers will develop their own mental models of what they understand to be going on in both the decision-aiding system and the design environment, and they will be using such systems to help them improve their understanding of the interaction at hand…. For this reason it is most important to determine what those users are doing, how they are thinking, what knowledge they are using and how and why they are using it to make their decisions and solve their problems.*

The best adaptive interfaces are based on an understanding and a model of the user which the user is clearly able to perceive. The model adapts in an obvious way such that the user does not become confused when similar actions produce markedly different results. Adaptive interfaces should not neglect the rules of good interface design described throughout. One adaptive interface responded to a request for help by providing increasingly more information in an 'adaptive way'; thus, the naive and confused user was provided with several screenfulls of information.

Methods of achieving adaptive interfaces rely on providing the computer with increasingly complex and variable models of the user. These range from simple interfaces which allow the user to select an experience level through to systems which are continually adapting across a spectrum of performance criteria to consistently provide the user with an interface which is appropriate to the task demands and the user's skills. In general, adaptive interfaces should be used with caution. Their potential to confuse and alienate the user must be addressed and the rules for the design of good interfaces (irrespective of whether the interface is adaptive) should be followed.

Bespoke versus general interfaces

Ideally most interfaces should be general. Unless the designer is specifically able to determine the precise nature of the user population, the interface should cater for all possible tasks, performed by all possible users. However, there are occasions when the general interface is not required. An analysis of the potential users is able to highlight characteristics which are unique to one group and these characteristics, either of the task or of the users, will lead the interface to take on a different form. For example, an interface might be designed for the Armed Forces, for one of the large utility organisations or for a disabled user or group of users. In these situations, the user population and the tasks can be very precisely defined. Designers will be required to maximise performance given these constraints and issues such as learning time, ease of use, number of errors made, etc will become tightly constrained by the task and the user population. The general rules outlined in this section on the design of the interface might not apply. When designing control rooms, for example, safety precautions might dictate that specific information is so important that it overrides all other considerations. Certain information will need to be displayed, irrespective of the operator's current task. In this environment, it is essential to look at critical information and system failure to determine what information must always be available to the user and to ensure that in certain circumstances the user's performance is as near 100 per cent error free as possible.

Bespoke interfaces offer a method of exploiting more unusual, novel interfaces. Speech might be useful in areas where users are constrained and need to use their hands and eyes for other purposes, for example parcel sorting. Similarly, speech could be used as an input mechanism for a user who is able to produce consistent sounds, even if this is not speech. Sounds can be defined to represent inputs which the computer will recognise and translate into commands. As with all interfaces, the user's potential will only be fully realised if it is matched to the task. The optimum matching might not only significantly improve performances, it might also allow users who are not normally capable of using a computer the freedom to do so.

User support

A key to the design of good interfaces is the provision of adequate support to users. Whether this is in the form of manuals, help messages, a local expert or a help hot-line, no system will operate without some form of support. If the aim of the designer is to create an error-free system, which is totally self-explanatory, the system will still require help and explanation. Users will invariably fail to use a system correctly and unless the designer has assumed and catered for every possible user response, some form of error will occur.

One of the most notable features of some systems is the unhelpful nature of their error messages. These can range from the obscure (but frequently occurring):

> Syntax error

to the disturbing, but possibly retrievable:

> Invalid input, run aborted

to the frightening (and presumably disastrous):

> Fatal error. Unable to recover. Killed

The assumption is that the user is careless, stupid and a potential murderer. Such messages provide an interesting insight into the nature of the designers who write them; however, they are without exception unilluminating to the user. As Wright notes:

> *Wright:*
> *If users attempt to issue illegal commands, well-behaved software will trap these commands and inform the user. Such communications can range from detailed verbal messages about the nature of the error, to a minimalist bleep indicating non-compliance by the program when an illegal move is attempted. Succinct error messages that consist of alphanumeric codes for which the user must consult another reference list are far from ideal. To be useful feedback must be informative, and also non-technical, but what counts as non-technical is not always apparent to the writer. Even the verbal message 'Referencing before first message' may be too terse to mean much to inexperienced users.*

Yet the provision of well-designed error messages provides the designer with a unique opportunity to educate and help the user. The most basic rule in producing an error message is: If the message does not enable the user to act, does not suggest a course of action, is unhelpful or obscure, or requires a manual to gain further (more useful information), do not use it. Produce a better one instead!

McKenzie comments:

> *McKenzie:*
> *It is important that error messages are as informative as possible and not only indicate to the user what has caused the error, but also attempt to provide information on how to put the error right. This becomes more important for infrequent and important actions by the user rather than frequent and minor ones.*

Apart from their advantages as methods of training users, keeping a log of errors and using help screens can rapidly highlight flaws in the design of a system. Analysis of such data can allow the designer to design out areas or operations which lead the user into producing errors.

A system which is flexible and which the user perceives as safe will be more fully explored and exploited. The user will feel able to try things out in the knowledge that the system is 'forgiving'.

Similarly, to fully exploit the potential presented by help and error messages, one should ensure that they are context sensitive and problem oriented. They should address a user's particular need or goal and provide an explanation of the problem, suggesting a course of action or a potential solution. Remember that the provision of more information is not, *per se*, the solution to a user's request for more help.

Schneider *(034)* points out that users do not generally consult user manuals. Draper states:

> *Draper (015):*
> *... [the] assumption is that novices will need more help than experts and will make more use of any help facilities provided ... the view is wrong. This apparently common-sense notion of 'expert' does not provide an adequate analysis of the nature of expertise in systems like UNIX, and hence does not provide a sound basis for designing help facilities.*
>
> *The designer should be ready to meet the varying levels of expertise (say novice, intermediate, expert) when providing help, and not expect these levels to be properties of individuals across all commands, but to be, for a given individual, specific to at least a subject area and probably to particular commands.*

Thus, even within an application, a static view of an individual user's level of skill is unlikely to work. Help should also be flexible, such that even when a supposed expert has a problem, the relevant information is easily available.

It is important to note that it is not sufficient to produce user support across the interface in isolation. The use of the system must be coupled with adequate training and off-line support.

Conclusions

This Section has examined the design of interfaces. The emphasis has been on the need to design the interface around the user and the task, rather than to fit the user into an existing interface design. A good interface is one which is flexible, adaptive and transparent. The interface should not hinder communication between the user and the system, rather it should actively enhance the interaction. Once a task and user have been adequately defined, the interface options should be explored and prototyped. An iterative design approach, involving real users and rapid prototyping, provides essential feedback to the interface designer. The design of simple surface features, such as menus and icons, while they will significantly affect the user's performance, are not the whole story. The designer must consider the deeper issues and adopt a user-centred approach.

4: Computer intelligence and interface design

This Section examines the role which AI has played in the design and development of end-user interfaces. Intelligent Front End processors (IFEs) are explained and their strengths and weaknesses discussed. The potential for explanation and help and the potential for expert systems to allow the user to ask why, explain strategy and justify rules is considered. Natural Language Front Ends (NLFEs) are looked at, as well as issues associated with naturalness, user understanding and the system overhead. The problems and methods of knowledge acquisition are discussed and, finally, the interface to expert systems is briefly examined.

Computer intelligence and interface design

Introduction

This Section will examine the role of Artificial Intelligence (AI) in the design and development of end-user interfaces. Norman states:

Norman:
There has been much interest in the development of 'intelligent' systems and, although this is a much misused term, there are evident techniques and methods related to the provision of intelligent interfaces which require further exploration.

AI has been variously defined; however, one of the most accepted definitions is given by Minsky:

Minsky (035):
Artificial Intelligence is the science of making machines do things which would require intelligence if done by men.

As the field of AI has expanded various subtopics have been defined. The areas which are particularly relevant to designing end-user interfaces are Intelligent Knowledge-based Systems (IKBSs) and expert systems. This paper concentrates on expert systems, which are defined as:

(036):
Systems that process information pertaining to a particular application and perform functions in a manner similar to that of a human who is an expert in that field. They solve problems by drawing inferences from a collection of information that is based on human experience.

This definition of an expert system is slightly different from that offered by Bramer:

Bramer (037):
An expert system is a computing system which embodies organised human knowledge concerning some specific area of expertise, sufficient to perform as a skilful and cost-effective consultant.

The difference in the two definitions is that the first appears to emphasise the expert system as a problem-solving tool, while the second emphasises the expert system's performance in terms of skill and cost effectiveness. It is this second definition which is of more relevance to the interface designer. The main application of an expert system to an interface is to improve the user's performance and hence increase the cost effectiveness of the system. Cleal states:

Cleal:
In an ideal world, one interface would cater for the needs of all the different tasks that go towards

the production of an expert system. To do this, and cater for computer-based support for the elicitation task, it is necessary to design the knowledge interface accordingly.

He also says:

> *Cleal:*
> *Most computer systems require only one interface, which is designed by the system builder for the use of the system user. Many well-documented cases exist which amply serve to illustrate the confusion which the differences in experience, understanding and objectives between these two can lead to. Typically, the upshot of this confusion is a system which does not do the things the user wanted it to, but does do some other things exceedingly well.*
>
> *Expert system developments add two or three more variables into the equation, causing a correspondingly greater degree of confusion. An 'expert' is required, as is an interface to the knowledge contained within the computer system. More sources of difficulty arise and things go from bad to worse when a 'knowledge engineer' is added.*

The main thrust of research in terms of designing end-user interfaces has been the development of systems which are better able to intelligently support the user.

> *Walsh et al:*
> *A well-designed interactive system provides appropriate functionality to its users and exhibits graceful evolution when modified by designers. Graceful evolution is facilitated when the system embodies a complete and coherent model that can be offered to users and communicated to other designers. Appropriate functionality enables users to satisfy their goals and to feel that using the system is worthwhile. To be effective, interactive systems need to be usable, and users need to be able to understand how the system operates without undue mental effort. Users must also be capable of remembering information about the system for future use. In general, then, the goal of human factors has been to ensure that the system, as expressed in the user interface, is both usable and useful.*

Examples of how AI can be applied to the interface are:

1 Provision of adaptive interfaces, based on embedded models of the user.

2 Explanation systems which are context sensitive and adaptable to the user's ability and previous performance.

3 Provision of sophisticated help facilities which allow the user to explore the use of a system in a 'safe' way.

As Norman states:

> *Norman:*
> *... the principal concerns are those of the internal representation or embedding of models of the user (including thereby a sense of history into current system responses to user actions), and the provision of context-sensitive responses (intelligent help systems, etc).*

The most obvious way in which AI techniques are applied to the interface is in the provision and development of Intelligent Front End processors (IFEs).

This Section will investigate the design of IFEs and the implications for interface designs. It will discuss the issues associated with the provision of explanation and help and will look at how developments in Natural Language Front Ends (NLFEs) are allowing users to manipulate sophisticated software packages with only minimal computer training. The Section will also consider problems associated with the acquisition of knowledge from users and why users have a critical role to play in the application of AI to interface design. Finally, it concludes by examining the interfaces to expert systems.

Intelligent Front End processors (IFEs)

Cleal and Heaton state:

> *Cleal and Heaton (038):*
> *A typical IFE needs to accomplish a number of tasks. These are:*
> - *Carry out a dialogue with the user*
> - *Produce a specification of the user's task or problem*
> - *Use this specification to generate instructions for running a software package*
> - *Interpret the results of running the package in the light of the user's specified problem*
> - *Relay answers to the user as part of the continuing dialogue.*

Ramsay identifies the following four specific aims for an IFE, that is that it should:

> *Ramsay (039):*
> *1 Establish user goals.*
> *2 Obtain more information about the task from the user.*
> *3 Allow the user to browse the system's knowledge about how to achieve these goals.*
> *4 Answer user requests for an explanation of the system's actions and goals.*

The IFE is seen as sitting between the user and the software with which the user is interacting. This can have effects on the system response time and the way in which the interaction is structured. An additional layer, on top of an existing package and interface can seriously affect the speed of the system. However, the main benefits to the user, in terms of ease of use and ease of learning, are seen to outweigh the disadvantages. It is important for the designer to be aware of this speed versus ease of trade-off and not to restrict the more experienced user with the system interface. What is easy to use for a naive or occasional user can be frustrating or unusable to the more frequent and experienced one.

Wilson *et al (040)* give a description of a theoretical IFE, where the IFE is seen as sitting between the user and a number of electronic mailbox systems. The theoretical benefits of such a system are described in terms of consistency, the ability to preprocess information before the user has to deal with it (for example sorting junk mail and prioritising incoming information, etc) and the facilitation of the user's interaction with a variety of markedly different systems. The work on electronic mailboxes is being continued as the COSMOS project which is run under the Alvey initiative.

A practical example of a working IFE is ECO, which is a system to help ecologists to build FORTRAN simulations of ecological models *(041)*.

The strengths of an IFE are the ability to allow user access to complex computer software via a simple interface and the provision of a method to allow existing software packages to be used via an interface which has been designed specifically for a particular user or group of users. One of the most important applications of an IFE is to provide an interface to databases *(042)*. Another application is as an interface to complex statistical packages such as REX, the Regression Expert, developed by AT&T's Bell Laboratories.

The main weaknesses of IFEs are associated with the following problems:

1 Knowledge representation, both in the system to which the IFE is providing an interface and in the manner in which the knowledge is presented to the user.

2 Control of the overall structure of the dialogue, particularly in issues such as navigation and ensuring that the underlying structure of the package with which the IFE is interfacing does not dominate the manner in which the interface is structured to the detriment of the end user.

Bundy *(043)* distinguishes between the control of the overall structure of the dialogue and the detail of the method of interaction. He presents a process of translation, synthesis and inference, where the user interacts with the system through a dialogue handler which produces a task specification which is eventually translated to a method, then to instructions, then to a plan and finally to a package. The important point of this model (see Figure (4)1) is that the effect which the user requires and has

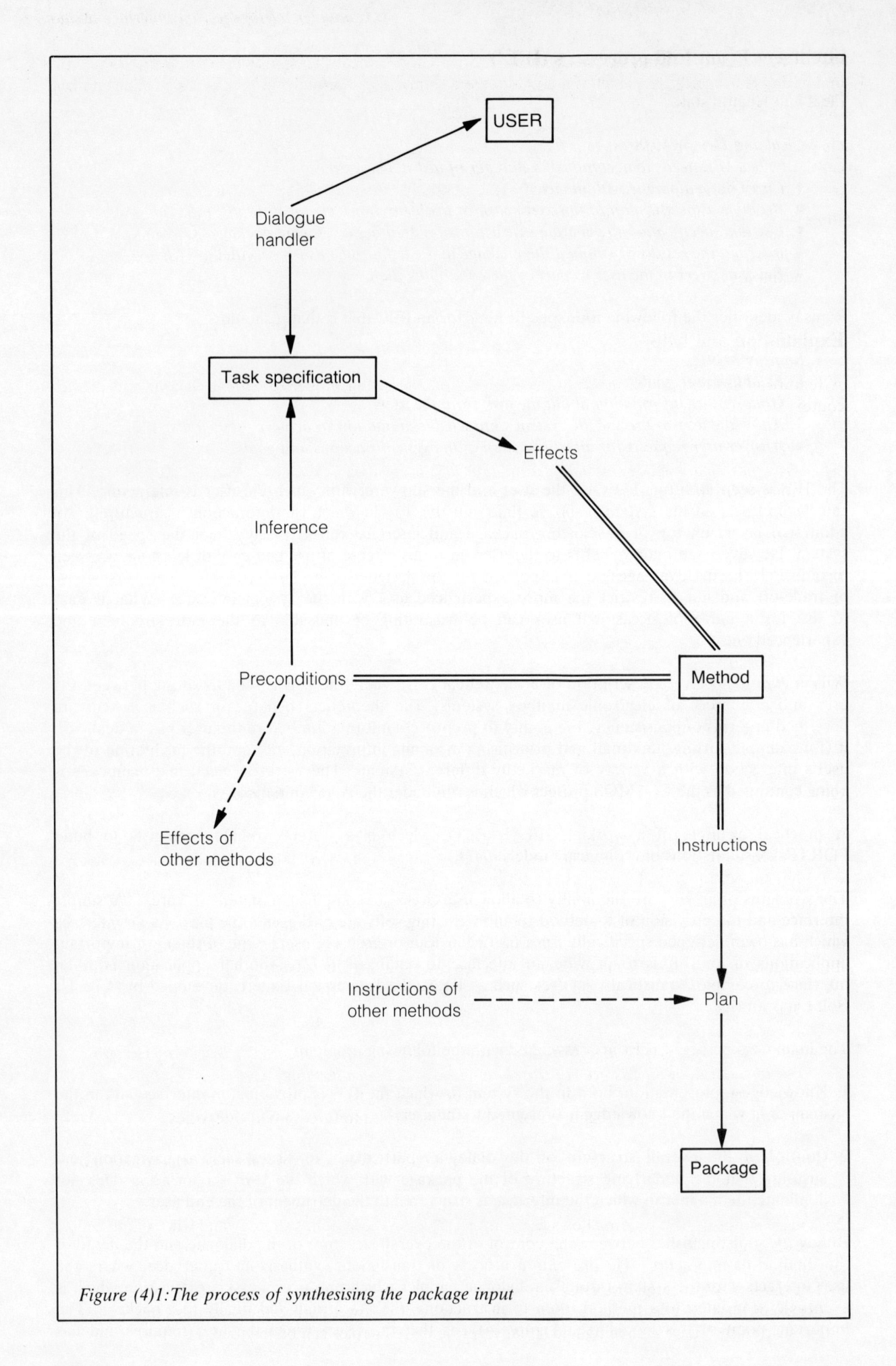

Figure (4)1: The process of synthesising the package input

attempted to achieve through task specification is matched to the instructions which the IFE passes to the underlying package. If this match is not made, the system's response to the user can be confusing and lead to many errors.

Overall, Cleal and Heaton conclude:

> *Cleal and Heaton (038):*
> *IFEs represent work at the leading edge of interface design. They amply illustrate the need to consider user requirements, user models and user limitations ... [they also] represent an area in which new technology is being used essentially to enable better use of older [or existing] technology.*

Explanation and help

A feature of systems which incorporate elements of AI is their ability to explain actions and provide context-dependent help.

> *Wright:*
> *Price has cautioned against the assumption that users start by knowing what the software is supposed to do. In many organisations the person making the purchasing decision is not the ultimate user. So when the product arrives, the user may have little idea of its intended purpose.*

McDonald has identified six query types supported by one system:

> *McDonald (044):*
> *1 Why or how a conclusion has been reached.*
> *2 How to further substantiate a conclusion.*
> *3 What must be done to prove a hypothesis.*
> *4 What information provided is contradictory.*
> *5 What information has been provided so far.*
> *6 What background information pertains to the current situation.*

Other query types which a system might have to deal with include explaining the domain. This can be critical in systems which are used for teaching/education purposes. Systems might be required to explain the structure of the knowledge, again for education and also for extending the system or for dealing with a change in circumstances, for example when the information contained in the knowledge base is changing with time and needs to be constantly readjusted.

Thus help and explanation facilities provide not only simple feedback on 'What did I do wrong?' or 'What do I do next?'. It is goal oriented — 'How do I do this?' — and it is also capable of providing complex information on reasoning, for example 'Why have you given me this advice?', as well as information on 'Why not?', for example 'Why didn't you advise me to do this?'. Wright states:

> *Wright:*
> *The queries users ask range from those that are well specified, such as 'How do I print this document?', to those that are ill formed — 'Why is the screen flashing?'.*

Systems which incorporate help and explanation facilities fall into three broad categories:

1 The simplest system allows for users to ask why and provides an explanation of why an action was recommended.

2 A more sophisticated system allows users information on the system's strategy and will explain actions at a strategic level.

3 The most sophisticated systems will deal with justification of rules. Users will be allowed an explanation of why a particular course of action was followed, what the system's strategy was in following that line of reasoning and, finally, how particular rules can be justified.

The explanations are progressively more complex and require an increasingly more comprehensive understanding of the user, the user's goals and strategies, the system and the domain in which the system is operating. Thus as the complexity increases, the demand placed on the designer increases and many of the implicit assumptions and ideas which become embedded in the system's design need to be made explicit.

Asking why

Typical of the information provided by an 'asking why' facility is a simple statement of a particular rule which the system is trying to satisfy. This will generally be the rule which is the 'top of the stack' and the system will probably provide a reply in pseudo-English, for example:

> Computer: 'Please tell me the size of your database'
> User: 'Why?'
> Computer: 'Because I am trying to satisfy Rule 2: "If the database is large, then a suitable package is dBase II"'

The user is unable to probe more deeply into the system's reasoning, though such a system might support 'Why not' queries in the form:

> User: 'Why did you not recommend dBase II?'
> Computer: 'Because Rule 2 states: "If the database is large, then a suitable package is dBase II" and your reply to the question: "Is the database large?" was NO'

The user might then be presented with the opportunity to alter the response to that particular question and rerun the system.

The interface designer is able to support this type of query fairly easily. If the knowledge is represented in an explicit rule-based form, the relevant rules can be fed back to the user. Many expert system shells have explanation and help in this form already embedded into them.

Explaining strategy

The next level of interaction allows the users to learn something of the system's rules and strategies. Whereas 'asking why' allows the users to see rules, if a system is required to explain its strategy, it is required to put those rules into the context of an overall goal. Thus, instead of an individual learning about a particular rule, rules about rules (meta-rules) can be viewed. This has two advantages. The first is that the designer is required to explicitly state strategy when building the system and will always be aware of the need for a particular rule or rule set. The second is that the user will be able to learn about the particular domain and the way in which larger problems might be solved.

In practice, the user asks for the top-level explanation ('asking why'), with a further level of explanation available to provide a more detailed account of why a particular rule happened to be top of the stack and what the system's longer term goals are in obtaining that information. The system determines these goals from the meta-level rules and explanations which the system designer has input while constructing the system.

Justifying rules

The most sophisticated and complex level of on-line user support is the provision of a justification of rules and strategy. This level of explanation requires the system to not only explain why and what the longer term goals are, but also how those longer term goals have been determined and why the system is operating in the way in which it appears to the user to be. The problem with providing users access to explanations about meta-rules and meta-explanations is that the leap between a simple rule and a complex justification can be too great. The user becomes aware of information which is not only unnecessary but also confusing. There becomes a need to determine what to explain to the user about the world in which the rule was applied, for example to determine what is commonsense and what domain knowledge a typical user might possess. There is thus the need to determine what to leave out. Justification could easily include a complex explanation of how the system works, rather than how the problem relates to it. An excellent discussion on the problems associated with justification is given by Clancy *(045)*.

The ability of systems to explain why, how, why not, and to justify rules is important. The potential for the interface to educate and allow users to explore scenarios in a safe and relatively error-free way gives such systems significant advantages over more rigid methods of interaction. However, the provision of these facilities requires the designer to be much more aware of the domain and the likely users. There are pitfalls associated with the provision of inappropriate or excessive information. If the user is overloaded or the information is not appropriate for the user's level of skill then the usability of the interface is actually reduced. Thus it is important to remember that simply having a help and explanation facility will not, *per se*, improve the usability of the system.

Natural Language Front Ends (NLFEs)

An NLFE offers a way in which a user can interact with a complex system without the need to learn a complicated programming language. It is a specific instantiation of the more general IFE discussed earlier. However, it is sufficiently important to be considered separately. An NLFE allows the users to communicate with the system through the use of normal typed speech. It is claimed that NLFEs provide users with a significant advantage when using complicated packages such as databases which normally require a user to learn a complicated logical (or quasi-logical) operating language. Cleal and Heaton *(038)* summarise some of the factors for and against the use of natural language interfaces and when they might be applied (see Figure (4)2).

Natural language interfaces are subject to a number of criticisms. These are the following:

1 *Naturalness:* to what extent is a NLFE natural? Often vocabularies are contrived and very restricted. The designer must determine a complete set of permissible words prior to exposing the user to the system. Alternatively, the user must be allowed to input words which the system does not know and define these words in terms of the system's existing vocabulary. This can be both time consuming and confusing to the user and specialised training is invariably required. Also the permissible syntaxes constrain the user to particular sentence constructions. This can be confusing and can

For	Against
A precisely defined domain	A loosely defined domain
A wide range of possible commands or system actions	When all interactions with the system are likely to follow one of a small range of options
When complex explanations are required	
When a less familiar mode of interaction is likely to be rejected	When the flexibility of natural language may lead the user into a false estimate of the system's capability
When natural language may provide useful input to a user model	When natural language may require the user to memorise many specialised words (and a menu-driven system may be better) where users are occasional or non-professional

Figure (4)2: Factors for and against the use of natural language interfaces

provide the user with incorrect information when one sentence is reinterpreted in the light of the system's syntax rules to produce an answer to a question which the user did not ask.

2 *User understanding:* an NLFE may lead the user to overestimate a system's capabilities and understanding of the domain. At best this can increase the time it takes the user to interact with the system, at worst it can cause the user to totally reject it. An example of such a system might be ELIZA. This allows the user to input information in any form. The system then spots words and responds to the user. This has not only produced some bizarre dialogues, but has also caused people to widely overestimate the sophistication of the system. The following examples are taken from *(046)*.

Frudes (046):
E Hi, I'm Eliza, what's your problem?

N I feel tired.

E Tell me more about such feelings.

N I'm not alert.

E Did you come to me because you are not alert?

N Yes.

E Are you sure?

N Maybe I have other problems too.

E You don't seem quite certain.

N Sorry.

E Please don't apologise.

[A second dialogue]

E Do you often feel sad?

N No.

E Are you saying that to be negative?

N Not at all.

E Please don't repeat yourself.

N I'm not.

E Did you come to me because you are not?

N Not what?

E Why do you ask?

N Now I'm really confused.

E How long have you been confused?

N Only since I met you.

It must be stressed that ELIZA's designer had no intention of producing either an intelligent system or a NLFE; however, the example illustrates some of the problems which users can cause if the interface is not carefully produced. It is only in the second example that some insight is given into the way the system is operating. Yet in the first example the system appears to be both rational and understanding.

3 *System overhead:* using an NLFE will have implications both in terms of the cost of the system and in its response time. Most NLFEs are expensive. The more sophisticated they become, the more they cost. Similarly, it can be very expensive to develop a bespoke interface and very time consuming to tailor a general package to a specific application. Similarly, because the package sits between the user and the rest of the system, using an NLFE can greatly increase the system's response time.

In general, NLFEs are useful if the application and the user base are well understood and the application is well understood by the user in spite of the complexity of the system. NLFEs tend to assume that the user is a reasonable typist and operates towards specific goals. Thus, an NLFE should not be considered suitable when users are inexperienced and use the system only infrequently. It is useful in circumstances where the users have a specific requirement to perform complex operations, fairly frequently and without the need to learn a complex unnatural package. It should be noted that NLFEs are generally wordy and fairly unspecific, and might not therefore be suitable for frequent expert users who have a need to ask specific questions, economically.

Knowledge acquisition

Knowledge acquisition is traditionally seen as the bottleneck in the design of expert systems. The number of individuals who have a stake in a system is generally large. Their knowledge is diverse and sometimes contradictory as are their goals. Often knowledge engineers need to become skilled in the domain in which they are attempting to elicit knowledge. They also need to become expert in conflict resolution and in distinguishing the different system stakeholders and to be able to translate the knowledge which is elicited into terms which are usable by a system and which can be easily reviewed and modified. This requires that the sources of knowledge be involved throughout the design process and that they gain familiarity with the system and the way in which it represents knowledge.

The main aim of knowledge acquisition is to get the relevant knowledge as quickly and as accurately as possible from the expert into the system and available to the user. The following four broad classes have been identified:

1 *Text analysis:* the knowledge is extracted from textbooks and manuals without recourse to the user. This speeds up the process of knowledge acquisition but reduces its accuracy and allows greater potential for mistakes. It also neglects to check on the relationship between theory, that is how a task should be done and how in fact it is done.

2 *Interview analysis:* this requires the knowledge engineer to have direct access to the experts. This is helpful in that it can provide *in vivo* examples of how tasks are carried out (provided that the experts do not alter their behaviour 'for the camera') and allows the knowledge engineer to ensure that the system is accurately reflecting their expertise by consulting the experts during development. The problem with these techniques is that they are time consuming and require knowledge engineers to analyse a wealth of data and interpret it.

3 *Behavioural analysis:* this relies on observational studies of experts carrying out tasks. Here there is even more data to analyse and often the framework for the analysis is less clear (for example why an expert carries out a task one way as opposed to another). The advantages of this approach are that the knowledge engineer is hopefully less intrusive and the experts genuinely are experts (inasmuch as they can perform the task under investigation).

4 *Machine induction:* this is the generation of general rules from sample cases (for example many past examples) based on the premise that many expert tasks come down to a classification problem. The expert's rules are induced from the examples and the knowledge engineer needs neither access to the users nor a clear understanding of the problem. The problems with such systems is that they are hard to understand. Rules are produced which fit the facts but bear no relationship to the methods employed by experts and, if the domain changes in any way, such systems become redundant and unmaintainable.

Each method of knowledge acquisition has its advantages and drawbacks and no single method seems to answer all the requirements for the production of an expert system from knowledge possessed by experts. The safest approach seems to be to adopt several methods for acquisition and to ensure that all the stakeholders in the system are fully involved at all stages of the process. The key to acquisition is to ensure that the knowledge is complete as possible; thus an iterative approach helps ensure completeness (even at the expense of time and the disregarding of prototype systems which do not work properly). Once knowledge has been gathered, interpreted and represented in the system it must be validated. The system must be maintainable and usable. This has raised issues about the representation of knowledge so that experts and users can view it and if necessary alter it. So the interface problem lies not only between the user and the application but also in the way in which the application is determined and represented within the system. This means that the expert system must have a well-designed interface between the user and the system, the knowledge engineer and the system, and the expert and the system.

Expert system interfaces

Cleal:
A prime shortcoming of most current expert system shells is the disparity between the user interface's reflection (and thus the user's understanding) of the knowledge within the system and the knowledge itself. There are three major reasons for this:

1 Much of the knowledge within many expert systems is not explicitly represented at all. For example, many rule-based systems, faced with the choice of which rule to use first (and hence of the order in which questions are posed to the user) rely upon some strategy such as 'try the rules closest to the top of the knowledge base listing'. Thus in, for example, a PROLOG program, the problem-solving strategy is implicit in the ordering of clauses within the program listing, and not available for inspection by the user.

2 The frequency of systems which possess two quite distinct interfaces — one for inputting, modifying and maintaining knowledge bases, and a separate one for actually using the system. This kind of approach permits the growth of 'cognitive dissonance', whereby the user's internalised model of the system's operation is at odds with the reality.

3 This dissonance at best means that the expert knowledge used by the system is unlikely to rub off on users. At the worst, it may cause the user to make invalid analogies, misinterpret conclusions and ultimately carry quite erroneous beliefs away from a consultation with the expert system.

Due to the wide range of facilities which expert systems can potentially offer, for example explanation, help, why, how, etc, the interface to them is critical. Often expert systems are used to provide an individual with support in a domain which is complex and may not be well understood. For example, in fault diagnosis the expert system might be required to provide information about a part of the problem of which the user has little or no knowledge, but which is essential to a full understanding of the possible fault and its location. Thus the interface must be sufficiently well designed to provide this information in a form which is accessible and understandable to the user. The aim of this Report is to provide general guidelines on the design of end-user interfaces. Expert systems provide a special example of the need for such interfaces. The wide range of users and the variations in their skills with computers and the task domain necessitate that special care be taken in the production of such interfaces. Also, the issues associated with validating and maintaining an expert system's knowledge base need to be carefully considered at the earliest stages. The power of an expert system is its embedded knowledge and this power will only be realised if it is adequately interpreted and presented to the user through the interface.

Conclusions

This Section has outlined some of the issues associated with the design of end-user interfaces and AI. It has provided the reader with an overview of key developments and explored how these developments will impact the interface. AI cuts across many boundaries and is often sold as the solution to many problems. This will only be the case if such systems are usable. The fundamental problems associated

4: Computer intelligence and interface design

with the production of usable interfaces are becoming increasingly complex. The power of the underlying system and its ability to provide the user with an ever larger and more powerful range of options means that the interface must be capable of supporting the user even more. The typeof user is changing, together with the technology, and the two can only be matched across the interface.

5: Systems aspects of the human/computer interface

This Section stresses the importance of considering the interface not as an object on its own, to be addressed on its own, but as an entity in an extremely complex, changing environment. It commences by criticising prevailing approaches to the design of interfaces by outlining a number of criticisms made by erudite, and concerned, users. The necessity of considering users as the designer's agents is outlined, followed by a discussion of the problems of specifying how the needs of these agents are to be specified. The problems of formal specification languages are covered, and the role of design guidelines is discussed. Finally, this Section takes a brief look at the current trend towards direct manipulation and object-based interfaces, as well as the move to multi-window systems.

Systems aspects of the human/computer interface

Let us consider the following forthright comment from one of the leading thinkers in the design of interfaces:

Hollan (047):
I believe, for example, that it is an egregious error to suppose that one can discuss interface design outside of the cognitive contexts of the task domain in which the interface is embedded and contend that most current investigations ... focus too exclusively on a syntactic rather than semantic level of analysis. This often myopic perspective is evident in the research literature by the myriad studies concerned with menu structures, formulation of command names, and issues of what type of pointing interface is 'best'.

Versions of this comment can be found from many other authors as well. They all reflect the view that the purpose of interface design is to enable some goal or goals to be met, by a system comprising people and computers. As stated by Shackel:

Shackel:
Computer designers are primarily, and quite rightly, concerned to improve the performance of the computer hardware and software; they often forget that what matters most is the efficiency and performance of the total human/computer system, of which their computer contributions are only a part. Efficient performance can only result from proper attention to the needs and problems of the human users as well as the hardware and software aspects. However, the complexity and sophistication of modern computer technology often results in the designer being so busy with his own technical problems that he has too little time, and often too little knowledge, to deal with the human problems adequately.

Thus people and computers jointly have tasks to perform, and the purpose of the interface is to accomplish the task, not just to ensure quick, error-free communication between the user and the computer. Furthermore, there is the added complication that the completion of tasks does not occur in a vacuum, occupied only by a single user working at a single terminal, but in a rich, social environment, where many people may be working together to solve problems — a good paradigm would be in a manufacturing organisation, where teams of designers and engineers are engaged in producing new products for the market. An illustration of these points is the following:

Schaffitzel and Kersten (048):
Experience has shown that these [specification] *activities must not be confined only to modelling the pure DP solution, but must also estimate, evaluate and incorporate the possible effects of system introduction on the organisation, work flows and structures within the company into the process of organisational adaptation. The results of the study show that, in the introduction phase, the restructuring and designing of the company organisation is a decisive factor in these CAD system introductions and that an extension of requirements analysis to include this aspect is urgently needed....*

> ... a CAD system is a qualitatively new instrument which brings with it revolutionary changes for the entire technical sphere and which, above all, has a far-reaching integrative effect. When CAD methods are available, the structural organisation and all work processes from development and design to manufacturing and technical sales are changed step by step. The traditional autonomy of the individual technical departments is greatly curtailed by the integrative effect of CAD systems....
>
> In the design sphere, CAD created new preconditions for the management of the department. It is doubtful if the prevailing, extremely hierarchical design methods whereby the (senior) department head can supervise and influence the development process at any time simply by leafing through the drawings which lie open and accessible at all times on the drawing board, will survive the introduction of CAD....
>
> While in terms of hardware he is still limited to working with relatively small screens, the individual designer can often only work on small areas of his project at one time. Only he has the overall concept in his head. Inspection by superiors during development is possible but difficult, since the superior himself must first sit down at the screen and acquire a general view.

There are a number of points in this quote that indicate the problems that are now being faced in interface design. There is the fact that with the introduction of computer systems the nature of people's tasks and responsibilities change, implying that individuals will wish to change the nature of their interactions with the computer and that these changes are not static. Taken to a logical conclusion, this implies that unless it is known what the transactions at the interface are likely to be, it will be difficult to ensure a satisfactory interface. There is also the implication that change is an ongoing process, and that the interface might therefore have to change over the lifetimes of the hardware and applications software. This is highlighted in the following quotes from a seminal paper by Rasmussen and Goodstein:

> *Rasmussen and Goodstein (049):*
> The context of this paper is automated industrial processes and the requirements they place for providing adequate and timely support to the operating staff in connection with the tasks commonly associated with the 'job' of supervisory control. The operators usually have little or no manual control activities. Thus what traditionally is called 'hands-on-process feel' cannot play any important role and reliance must therefore be placed on the information and manipulation facilities provided by the display and control interface to provide what the operators need to know and do in order to ensure that the system operates reliably, economically and safely in the face of deviations from 'normal' because of disturbances, technical faults and/or inappropriate human actions.
>
> In effect, the crew is part of a decision-making team who, in accordance with the functional allocations of the designers, play certain assigned roles in dealing with the process. Use of the word 'team' reflects the fact that the supervisory control of such complex systems is actually a co-operative effort within a team, consisting of the designers, the automatic (computer-based) control system and the operating staff. This three-way arrangement arises from the fact that the decisions of the designers are embedded in the automatic system as well as the training of the operators....
>
> Since the designer [of the system] will not be able to foresee the necessary control responses for all possible disturbances, he needs a representative on site — the operator(s) — who have to be able to take over in a competent way. The operators' supervisory control task is indeed in many respects a completion of the system design for the particular, perhaps infrequent, situation being dealt with. As a consequence, the operator will need information about the problem space underlying the design and the designer will have to communicate this kind of information to the operator....
>
> To consider an operator only as an agent for executing (system) designer's preplanned actions will be unreliable. Instead, he should be considered to be the designer's representative on site, and the role allocation to consider is that of co-operative decision making.

These quotes indicate very clearly the need to consider interface design at many levels — not just the dialogue with a given program, but the structuring of the tasks to be undertaken and of the system itself.

There is also a third problem, exemplified again from the CAD field, in the two quotes that follow. The first is from the Chief Designer of an automobile manufacturer, whose company is among the leaders internationally in the application of IT.

> *Axe (050):*
> *Designers, in my experience, have always been fascinated and excited by computers and their application to design, yet when confronted by the machine there has been a total switch-off. Let me give my reasons why I believe this is so.*
>
> *The computer is designed by engineers for engineers and as such it fits the engineering regime. It is a highly disciplined regime, working with mathematical accuracy in a way that engineers can appreciate. Designers do not operate this way; the whole process of thought and transmission of ideas relies on a much more flexible expression. The designer needs the freedom to express form and shape in terms of light and shade — he needs to draw and visualise. I have personally spent many hours with computer engineers trying to explain this basic fact.*

Very clearly, this brings out three points. Firstly, that people use computers primarily to solve tasks and that the design of the interface must reflect this fact (as stated earlier) and, secondly, that there is still a long way to go in interface design. Interfaces that are good for what are basically clerical systems are not necessarily good for more sophisticated needs. The third point, and an important discussion topic in this section, is that recognising what is required, let alone delivering it, is a difficult problem.

This third point is exemplified in the following quotation — perhaps one of the most direct and honest admissions of communications failure to be found in the open literature.

> *McPhater (051):*
> *At the early stages of development of* [a bespoke CAD package] *it became clear that the engineering team and the CAD development team were not speaking exactly the same language. Engineers and software developers define and solve problems in different ways. An engineer might build in safety factors to his design which a software developer would only consider as mathematical constants. Alternatively, the software developer might get excited about clever techniques to save computer memory and make the software process faster, which the engineer might consider abstract and inconsequential in engineering terms....*
>
> *This culture gap between engineer and software developer did not only exist at the detailed technical level. It also existed at senior management level and presented both sets of senior management with new problems which their training had not equipped them to overcome....*
>
> *First, it was essential to have an independent consultant advising senior management. On a number of occasions the* [client] *engineers and the* [supplier] *software development staff were obliged to turn to the casting vote of the independent consultant to bridge the cultural divide and give unbiased counsel.*
>
> *Secondly, at a more detailed technical level, it was found essential to have one man full-time on the* [supplier] *software team who had a knowledge both of ductwork engineering and software. His role was to bridge the culture gap between the draughtsmen and the software writers.*

While this quotation is certainly concentrating on the difficulties of ensuring that the applications software does the right things, one may be sure that the interface will reflect the same difficulties, and perhaps others. So we may summarise the problems so far as:

1. The need to specify the tasks people undertake, in order to ensure that the communication between the people and the application software is at least efficient, if not optimal.

2. The need to recognise and accommodate the fact that users change, partly because of changes within the organisation and partly because of changes within themselves.

3. Definition of what is required is a non-trivial task.

4 Reaching out to the users; basically, they are usually not interested in the inner working of computers and the constraints thereof; they want to solve the problems for which they have responsibility.

We should also consider another aspect — the team user. Here, there are two possible problems:

1 The case where one has many users at one terminal. An example is the shop-floor terminal, where a group of people responsible for, let us say, a flexible manufacturing cell may all at one time or another during the day communicate with the computer system via a single terminal onto which only one of the team has logged-on. The flow of transactions at the terminal thus reflects two extra discontinuities compared to the single-user paradigm; the 'user' may exhibit sudden changes in expertise together with sudden changes in task or he may exhibit a total lack of knowledge of what has just been happening at the terminal.

2 The multi-user multi-terminal interface. This is the more interesting case, the answers to which will probably represent the next great step forward after the WIMP interface, considered earlier. This is already being discussed:

> *Packham (052):*
> [Workgroup computing] *is used to describe peer-to-peer communications at the PC level. 'The PC was a fantastic invention from the point of view of putting computing power on someone's desk, but it actually worked against the way that most people operate in the company ... it was a stand-alone device and nobody in most organisations works alone. Everyone works as part of a team or a department or whatever, therefore you need shared resources.' This realisation ... was the start of workgroup computing.*

Clearly, networking is an important part of this distributed, multi-user interface and, together, networking and multi-users create problems that ultimately impinge on the interface, as the following two quotations indicate:

> *Packham (052):*
> *Most of the processing takes place in the server, rather than being passed to and fro for the workstation to handle, thus reducing the network traffic and boosting performance. Additionally, in setting up databases using this client-server model, where the workstation or client makes requests for the processing power of a remote server, rules about accessing files and data are held only in the server. As Alan Sloane, managing director of Ashton Tate pointed out: 'It's a nightmare if you have a workgroup and you get in a mess with corrupted data, because you are not sure who's done what and where and when'. Data integrity is particularly important in a distributed workgroup, where users are not necessarily going to communicate verbally about their use of centrally held data files.*

> *Sweet (053):*
> *... senior management are just starting to realise that they have lost control of the network, probably the company's single most valuable resource. The network manager meanwhile, who undoubtedly grasps the technical issues over matters such as security, may have little idea of what the network facilities mean for the business.*

> *Fraud, theft or the disclosure of confidential information are not the only problems facing an unprotected network. Other nightmares include poor availability, which may seriously hamper a company's ability to process orders and keep business, and lack of integrity, so that data arrives incomplete or is lost. The company network is popular and is widely used and this can make it more difficult to protect than the main CPU. 'You tend to lock up the computer in a big building with card key access. The network aims to bring facilities out to the business user via terminals which are spread around the company', Wong pointed out. 'So you can probably add links to the customer, or allow technical staff to work at home and dial in to the network for program maintenance, or maybe even have links to other countries and suddenly there are all sorts of people dialling in who you don't know about, who are taking information from the company network', Wong added.*

> *It would be possible to impose serious constraints on individual network users, while at the same time investing heavily in the latest security gadgets and providing comprehensive*

redundancy features. But to do so would be prohibitively expensive and would [probably] mean that the company would forego potential benefits, such as the ability to dial through sales orders on a portable terminal by users with a low security clearance, or the use of remote diagnostic routines, which would be too risky and too difficult to supervise.

As far as the user interface is concerned, these potential problems raise issues of retrievability and control of access, and how these are to be accomplished for users who are not interested in the inner workings of the system. But there are other, hidden, problems here as well. A characteristic of workgroups, implicit in the quotes above, is that many of the files that users will work on will be centralised, perhaps in a single network server, perhaps in a more complex arrangement. Because of the workgroup approach, it is quite likely that many of these files will be massive (sales orders, for example), will have a complicated structure and will be in a state of continuous flex. In turn, this raises the notion of needing process managers to control what is happening on the distributed interface and to protect the integrity of the system and its data.

As far as the user is concerned, then, we may characterise the problems at the interface as being the following:

1 Accreting information into massive databases.

2 Navigating through massive changing databases (for example seeking details of a part that you know was designed in this design office, perhaps by person X, maybe five years ago — everybody calls it a widget, but it has some other official name).

3 Communicating interactively with other team members (perhaps opening a window on another user's screen to show what you are currently doing).

4 Being aware of, and/or learning, what other users are doing.

5 Understanding the nature of the User Interface Management System (UIMS) and the process manager(s) involved.

Thus, in the same sense as we discuss distributed computing, we may discuss the distributed user.

Drawing the strands together, then, what seems clear is that we are faced with new, acute problems — interfaces that must accommodate undefined, changing users, perhaps carrying out very complex, long-term tasks, always subject to change, where the interface may not be at a single terminal. In the words of Donald Norman:

Norman (054):
The major points are these:

1 There really is a problem: as we expand the base of the user population, we must attend more and more to the needs and abilities of a variety of users.

2 Special skills are needed: skills in programming, psychology, and in the tasks to be accomplished.

3 Software engineering: the interface should be separated from the rest of the system — modularised so as to be functionally independent. With an interactive system, the interaction IS the system. Therefore, specification of the interface should be among the first tasks during the design of a computer system — not the last, as is now often the case.

4 Formal design tools for the human-computer interface need to be developed. Until we have better design tools, design must be iterative, with cycles of design and experimental tests frequently repeated. Rapid prototyping tools are essential.

Let us consider the first activity required, that of systems analysis. In practice, it has been accomplished by systems analysts, who have generated a well-structured process for this; one develops a requirements specification, the software is written and it is iteratively tested and developed until it matches the user's requirements. This represents the classical approach, which is well documented and formalised. Methodologies abound — examples are the Structured Systems Analysis and Design Methodology (SSADM) and the Departmental Integrated Application Development Methodology. There are even more techniques for formalising the process — entity relationship modelling, Jackson state diagrams, Controlled Requirements Expression (CORE), IDEF, etc — the list appears endless. There appear to be two detectable characteristics here. Firstly, there is the entirely laudable aim expressed by many software experts that in order to shorten development time, to minimise errors and to make best use of scarce human software skills, the correct approach is to find ways of producing rigorous, logically sound requirements specifications, from which applications software may be generated automatically, or nearly so. Norman states:

> *Norman:*
> *One response to this increasing complexity is the adoption of a more disciplined approach to the crafting process, such that the resultant artefact — the designed object — is devised in a more manageable way. Since the focus for the realisation of designs is predominantly the construction of software, the disciplined approach that is most evident is that of software engineering — an approach which calls for, among other things, a clear requirements specification, the development of demonstrable and robust code (notated and capable of validation) and the provision of code which is certainly maintainable and potentially reusable. All this so that the resultant artefact can, notwithstanding its inherent complexity, be designed, shared, maintained and used.*

As an example, Jacob *(055)* draws some lessons from such an endeavour, in generating a messaging system. He discusses the need and attributes for specification systems, and then compares Backus Normal Form (BNF) notation and state transition diagrams as means of specification generation (he favours the latter). His requirements for a specification system for human/computer interfaces is as follows:

> *Jacob (055):*
> *In selecting a technique for specifying a human-computer interface, one should seek the following properties:*
>
> *1 The specification of a user interface should be easy to understand. In particular, it must be easier to understand and take less effort to produce than the software that implements the user interface.*
>
> *2 The specification should be precise. It should leave no doubt as to the behaviour of the system for each possible input.*
>
> *3 It should be easy to check for consistency.*
>
> *4 The specification technique should be powerful enough to express nontrivial system behaviour with a minimum of complexity.*
>
> *5 It should separate what the system does (function) from how it does it (implementation). The technique should make it possible to describe the behaviour of a user interface, without constraining the way in which it will be implemented.*
>
> *6 It should be possible to construct a prototype of the system directly from the specification of the user interface.*
>
> *7 The structure of the specification should be closely related to the user's mental model of the system itself. That is, its principal constructs should represent constructs that will be meaningful to users (such as answering a message or examining a file), rather than internal constructs required by the specification language. Alternatively, the specification should directly yield a reasonable table of contents for a user manual, but not necessarily the material in the user manual.*

Other, perhaps better known, examples of formal approaches are Command Language Grammar (CLG) *(056)* and Reisner's BNF-based approach *(057)*. Unfortunately, while these approaches have received much recognition, they do not seem to have had great impact; three cogent criticisms indicate why. Firstly:

Roberts (058):
In theory, once a command language has been described by such a grammar, the result can be analysed for conciseness and consistency. Unfortunately, such grammars are cumbersome; any attempt to describe a system of realistic size quickly becomes bogged down. I know of no use of these tools subsequent to their validation.

This is a practical criticism, but one of undoubted power. The second quote is more theoretical, but equally powerful:

Fountain and Norman (059):
Reisner (1981,1984) uses Formal Grammar as a means of comparing alternative interface designs.... Reisner's Formal Grammar is more obviously Class 2 — its production rule notation for user action languages, and explicit terminology and formal structure are directly parallel to general phrase structured grammars.... All grammars above Class 0 impose restrictions upon the languages which are capable of being specified. This has important bearing upon the field of human-computer interaction, because the manner in which the language is specified is saying something about human cognition. Class 2 grammars allow only one non-terminal symbol to the left of a rule so that (1) we are implicitly assuming that the human cognitive process is strictly serial and monotonic: only one goal or task at a time may be attempted, (2) the ability of a human to solve goals is context-free and history insensitive: the current task is not affected in any way by either previously completed tasks or future unstarted tasks. Only the current task environment is to have any bearing on the goal at hand. It is not clear that either of these conditions are necessarily true of the human cognitive process.

The third criticism is again a rather practical one, in that it comes from direct experience of the problems of developing specifications:

Erich and Williges (060):
Conventional methodologies (for software design) have several drawbacks when viewed from a perspective that considers the end-user interface as just another part of the system design. For example, methodologies that use data as the basis for design are inappropriate for the human factors analyst, who is concerned with functional relationships rather than with the data structures used for implementation.

Another, rather depressing, observation is that while the code that is produced may match the requirements specification, what is the guarantee that the specification itself is correct? Here one encounters a problem that is quite widely recognised within the oftware industry, but to which there is little in the way of a solution. It has taken some time to recognise this as a problem in knowledge elicitation, both from the head of the systems analyst and from the heads of those operators of the erstwhile system that is about to be replaced. Firstly, there is the question of whether the clients actually know what it is that they want. All too often, the protagonists negotiating the requirements specification are either too removed from the problem or do not have the global view that allows them to see it for what it is. Secondly, none of this activity occurs in a vacuum and organisational politics may well take a hand, especially if the introduction of a computer system is likely to result in a shift of the balance of power. The outcome may well be what suits the office politicians, not what is in the best interests of the organisation. Thirdly, while the clients may well be honest and knowledgeable, there is the problem of communication with the systems analyst and the building of understanding within his head. As Downs puts it:

Downs (061):
Systems analysts are the highly paid souls who are supposed to find out what a user wants and then break it down into a sensible systems blueprint for the application builder to follow. Like architects, systems analysts are used to criticisms. Every computer system — like every building — will upset someone, and all bystanders feel they could have done a better job themselves.

Much of the criticism is probably unfair. But there is one accusation that usually holds true. That is that the carved-in-stone methodologies followed by analysts in drawing up blueprints pay too little regard to the human realities of systems development.

Walsh *et al* state:

> *Walsh et al:*
> *The design and management of the software life-cycle represents a different approach to software development. SADMs typically recommend that system development should undergo specific stages from specification through to implementation and maintenance. SADMs make explicit the decisions which are to be made, how to make them and the order in which they are to be made. The development process is organised more strictly with the aim of getting the design right first time. JSD is an example of a widely used SADM. The authors consider JSD to have much in common with other SADMs, but it is not possible to explore this complex issue here.*
>
> *The role for human factors in the process of developing a system using an SADM is often restricted to evaluation and occurs after implementation. We term this the 'too little, too late' problem of integrating human factors. Delayed involvement results in a contribution that may be little more than advice, that is 'too little'. In addition the contribution may be 'too late', since the human factors activity does not constitute a basic part of system specification. Software is delivered to the human factors engineer at a late stage in the development process, and the lateness of evaluation frequently ensures that the advice cannot be acted upon. As a result, attempts to 'put it right' are thwarted by the difficulty and expense of modifications. SADMs, then, as used at present pose a problem of timing for the integration of human factors with system development. An additional problem is that, even if human factors contributions are made early in the development process, software engineers find them difficult to incorporate into the design, because their expression or format is insufficiently structured and incompatible with their own. Human factors contributions to system development need to be expressed in a format that is usable by software engineers.*
>
> *Human factors activities, then, are poorly integrated into current system development practices such as rapid prototyping and SADMs. Typically, the human factors element fails to contribute directly to the specification of the system. Any solution to the problem of integration needs to address the issues of timing and format of the human factors contributions to the system development process.*

Nevertheless, the need for tools is clearly there; one has only to recall one's own experience of recalcitrant interfaces. A cameo of the consequences of not having appropriate methodologies is the following, which applies to an existing system:

> *Erich and Williges (060):*
> *The comma key on the minikeypad is the HELP key for forms. While in the ABC-style editor and Calendar Management, use PF2 for HELP; use 'H' for HELP while in the Desk Calculator; use the 'GOLD' key plus an 'H' key when using the XYZ-style editor....*

The search for tools goes on — see for example the work of Erich and Williges *(060)* in their developments of SUPERMAN and the work of Thimbleby and his coworkers *(062-064)* with their Generative User Engineering Principles (GUEPs). The latter have an interesting approach, which sidesteps the formal specification problems discussed earlier rather neatly. Implicitly, they have started from the premise that, whatever the specification, if sound principles of dialogue design are used the resulting dialogue will be optimal (or nearly so) for the users, even if the application software as a whole does not accomplish the task efficiently. They have started from formal analysis of abstract models of interactive systems and as they have expressed it:

> *Thimbleby (062):*
> *Distinctly generative user-engineering principles meet four criteria: (1) they can be expressed formally, (2) they have a colloquial form, (3) in common with user engineering principles (which can be instantiations of GUEPs), they embody certain ergonomic guidelines and (4) they are constructive rather than descriptive....*
>
> *GUEPs will be most practical as a contribution to design method, rather than as a contribution to catalogues of acceptable interface techniques. To this end we must recognise what characterises GUEPs.*

> *For the user, GUEPs explain in straight-forward language higher-order properties of the user interface which affect its 'feel'. For example, a GUEP may verbalise a perceptual-motor routine, or a group of related routines.... For the designer, the principles constrain the interface to avoid what has been termed 'interaction uncertainty' or 'under-determination' — as the user interface is powerful enough to exhibit any behaviour, the user has less confidence that it will exhibit any particular behaviour.*
>
> *Thus GUEPs constrain the machine and explain the interface — in a manner which was not previously accessible to the user, and once verbalised may be used by the user constructively, probably using an acquired or taught inference procedure.*

GUEPs promise much for dialogue design at the interface and considerable development work is being undertaken. However, their applications are not widely available, nor is a suitable methodology.

In the meantime, until such tools are developed, we must turn to the guidelines put forward by many different authors. Perhaps the most famous of these are by Smith and Mosier (065). These are now widely available and have been used with some success by many designers. However, it is wise to bear in mind some of the caveats posed by one of the authors:

> *Smith (066):*
> *One significant aspect of our software design standards and guidelines is that they are largely based on expert judgement and accumulated practical experience, rather than on experimental data and quantitative performance measures. Until research on user-system interaction catches up with application, which may take a long time, that limitation will remain....*
>
> *Some cautionary comments about the application of guidelines deserve consideration here. Guidelines cannot take the place of experience. An experienced designer, one skilled in the art, might do well without guidelines. An inexperienced designer might do poorly even with guidelines. Few designers will find time to read an entire book of guidelines. If they do, they will find it difficult to digest and remember all of the material.... An expert will know how to trade off the competing demands of different guidelines, in terms of operational requirements.... Guidelines cannot replace task analysis.*

We turn now to a different topic, closely related to the foregoing. There has been a shift in the way that designers conceive of the interface. In the early days, it was the way in which people could communicate with the inner workings of the computer; it was a way to control the manipulation of data almost directly via the machine's internal construction. Since the advent of the Xerox Star, and its much more famous derivative, the Apple Macintosh, there has been a new way to conceptualise the interface. Firstly, there has been the rise of models, viz:

> *Norman (067):*
> *The Design Model is the conceptual model of the system to be built. Ideally, this conceptualisation is based on the user's task, requirements and capabilities. The conceptualisation must also consider the user's background, experience and ... most especially processing resources and short-term memory limits.*
>
> *The user develops a mental model of the system — the User's Model. Note that the User's Model is not formed from the Design Model; it results from the way the user interprets the System Image. Thus, in many ways, the primary task of the designer is to construct an appropriate System Image, realising that everything that the user interacts with helps to form that image: the physical knobs, dials, keyboards and displays, and the documentation, including instruction manuals, help facilities, text input and output, and error messages. The designer should want the User's Model to be compatible with the underlying conceptual model, the Design Model, and this can only happen through interaction with the System Image. These comments place a severe burden on the designer. If one hopes for the user to understand a system, to use it properly, and to enjoy using it, then it is up to the designer to make the System Image explicit, intelligent, consistent, and this goes for everything associated with the system. Remember too that people do not always read documentation, and so the major (perhaps entire) burden is placed on the image that the system projects.*

Coupled with this has been the realisation that it makes more sense to enable the user to devote as much of his or her cognitive resources to dealing with the problem, rather than to have to divert an appreciable amount to driving the computer. This has led to the concept of 'direct manipulation' in this concept, the user works as naturally as possible with what is on the display, and the computer's internal workings are then hidden from view because it is no longer necessary for the user to be aware of them:

> Hutchins et al (068):
> For [the authors], *the notion of Direct Manipulation is not a unitary concept nor even something that can be quantified in itself. It is an orienting notion. 'Directness' is an impression or a feeling about an interface.... At the root of our approach is the assumption that the feeling of directness results from the commitment of fewer cognitive resources. Or put the other way round, the need to commit additional cognitive resources in the use of an interface leads to the feeling of indirectness. As we shall see, some of the production of the feeling of directness is due to adaptation by the user, so that the designer can neither completely control the process, nor take full credit for the feeling of directness that may be experienced by the user.*

Schneiderman has suggested that direct manipulation systems have the following virtues:

> *Schneiderman (069):*
> *1 Novices can learn basic functionality quickly, usually through a demonstration by a more experienced user.*
>
> *2 Experts can work extremely rapidly to carry out a wide range of tasks, even defining new functions and features.*
>
> *3 Knowledgeable intermittent users can retain operational concepts.*
>
> *4 Error messages are rarely needed.*
>
> *5 Users can see immediately if their actions are furthering their goals, and if not, they can simply change the direction of their activity.*
>
> *6 Users have reduced anxiety because the system is comprehensible and because actions are so easily reversed.*

Such an approach offers simple, novel ways for users to carry out their activities. Already, one can point at icons, and drag them round the screen to indicate to the computer what is required, as on the Macintosh; a rather more sophisticated use is where icons represent specific functions, which can be chained together to perform a task by linking their inputs and outputs together with lines.

Such representations are not only much easier and quicker for experts and frequent users to use, they are also far more appealing to intermittent users and novices; the pervasive spread of computers to include the latter in all walks of life demands simplicity and visibility of actions. However, the concept, while appealing and clearly effective, is not always easy to implement and direct manipulation interfaces do not always have the generality of application and use that is sometimes inferred. Problems that have been discovered among applications include:

1 There can be difficulties in handling variables.

2 There can be problems of accuracy and precision.

3 Directness does not always equate to ease of use, nor to speed.

4 Repetitive operations are best handled by scripts or by other symbolic representations.

5 There needs to be separation of the applications software and the interface, with an interface management system (UIMS) of some power to manage the display and communications to the applications software.

6   There are specific needs for hardware; the minimum requirement is for bit-mapped displays, pointing devices, and window support.

7   There can be semantic problems in interpretation — for example if I as a user am able to create an algebraic expression on the screen involving a numerator and denominator (eg the formula for a student's t test), how is the computer to know reliably when a horizontal line is a 'divide' symbol or an underline?

Nevertheless, there can be no question that direct manipulation represents a great advance in interface design. When this is coupled with multiprocess operating systems and sophisticated window management as is to be found on the current engineering workstations, for example (X-windows, Sun News), it becomes possible to introduce a much higher degree of 'naturalness' into HCI. Consider the following:

> *Cypher (070):*
> When we design programs, we think about the sorts of things users will want to do and then we build tools for carrying out those tasks. Implicit in this approach is the belief that there will be a fairly good match between computer programs and user activities. But how well does this assumption hold up in practice?.... One way for a mismatch to occur is for a single activity to call upon more than one program. The activity of 'arranging a meeting', for example, involves two programs: mail and calendar. The ramifications of this simple fact are far-reaching and have a dramatic effect on how a user interacts with a computer system....
>
> A system which is oblivious to the use of several programs for a single activity places all of the burden of program management on the user: in the case of 'arranging a meeting' (an earlier example), I would have had to abort my message when I realised that I did not know when I was free tomorrow. Then, after consulting the calendar program, I would then have had to call the mail program anew and retype the message.... At issue here is the fact that when one engages in an activity, one builds up a context.... Even a momentary interruption will cause this elaborate mental context to collapse. Complex activities on a computer can lead to equally elaborate computer contexts.... With proper design, these elaborate computer contexts can be interrupted without collapse ... by saving the complete state of a program. The Berkeley UNIX 'Stopped jobs' facility is an example of this approach.... It is often said that windows support multiple activities, but in fact it is the underlying 'multiple user processes' that enable multiple activities. Windows are a particularly good representation for the user.

It is possible, then, to achieve a closer match between the computer's activities and the user's tasks, in effect, by 'shuffling' the available windows about and swapping between them, much as one does on a cluttered desk. There are some difficulties still remaining; context is one of them:

> *Reichman (Adar) (071):*
> Current window systems mainly assume that each window (process) is independent of the other. This radically undermines the power and utility of such systems. It is in direct conflict with how users view their interaction. Communication postulates are violated and errors result. In language, for example, we do not randomly start up different topics of conversation. There is a coherence to our communication. Similarly in the window domain, we are not randomly creating twenty unrelated windows and engaging simultaneously in twenty unrelated tasks. Often, in fact new tasks are started because they are required by existing tasks....
>
> The problem is that while the user sees and knows the inter-relations the computer does not.... There are no markers or underlying representations in the computer for window/activity inter-relation. Currently, users do not have the means to indicate to the computer that they will, for example, be leaving for the moment activity 1 to pursue activity 2, and that they'll be going back to activity 1 shortly. Nor can they return to preceding contexts by means of specifying a functional and semantic relation. But it is in these terms that they view the flow of their interaction.

Another problem is that of the 'house of mirrors'; one can fairly rapidly become lost amongst the windows, or even by injudicious resizing of windows, lose a few windows. What seems to be a very necessary step forwards is the provision of contextual information; a means, for example, for the user to tell the computer 'While I am at it ...' to break temporarily to a new task and 'Well, anyway ...' to return to a suspended task. Similarly, there is a need for the computer to be able to tell the user what is going on — what windows are open, what processes are running in the background, and so forth. One example of this approach is the 'Lisp Listener', on the symbolics Lisp machine. Whatever is adopted as a means of reminding people, there are the following requirements:

Miyata and Norman (072):
What should an ideal reminder look like? It should:

1 *Inform the user when conditions are ready for resumption of a suspended or backgrounded activity.*

2 *Remind the user when something has to be done immediately.*

3 *Not distract from the current activity.*

4 *Continuously or periodically list activities that have been suspended or backgrounded.*

5 *Help resumption of an activity by retrieving the exact previous state of the activity and making it available to the user.*

The provision of multiple windows, then, is another step which has yet to be fully assimilated into interface design. It has great potential; as Draper has pointed out, it demands that system designers reconceptualise their approach:

Draper (073):
The terminal is now viewed as a display with a finite size and known contents. Like a disk, the contents can be read and changed; it is not a sink absorbing a one-way traffic, but a piece of memory shared by user and machine. Implementing this requires a different viewpoint of terminals than is usually provided by computer systems. The system must now maintain a program-accessible model of what is displayed at any time, allowing programs to specify changes to it directly.

This provides the opportunity for the user to perform higher-level control actions. One can envisage the freedom for the user to lasso an object in one window and drag it to another to play an active part there. Thus, one could take a continuously running process dealing with the national sales of a line of products, and tap the ongoing, changing data from one window directly to another, perhaps generating production schedules for that set of products. Or one might take information regarding gear-wheels directly from a supplier's catalogue provided from an external database in one window across to a design in another window, to incorporate the gears directly into a three-dimensional model of a new product. The functionality to perform such manipulations is already available in some systems, but we have yet to exploit it fully.

The state of the art, then, is much as Norman stated earlier. We do indeed have real problems to solve. Interfaces will always be of limited generality as regards their functionality and usability, requiring careful consideration of their implementation. In turn, while we may now reasonably describe the requirements for the single user performing single tasks, we have as yet to deal with the multi-user team. We still have to adequately describe the tasks that users perform, not least because of cultural differences between different disciplines, and then to develop tools to implement them. Unquestionably, hardware and software developments are enabling much more natural interfaces to be embodied; windowing and direct manipulation are allowing us to conceive of a much closer rapport between the computer and the user, even if at the expense of compounding the problems for software designers and programmers. While we may have come a long way, we have much further to go.

6: Conclusion

This Section examines future developments and the work of national and international initiatives. The change in the perception of the user and the effects that users are having on interfaces are discussed. The effects of hardware technology advances on interfaces are looked at, together with the move from research laboratories to the office of potentially key developments such as parallel processing and new display technologies. New developments in software and the factors which affect the introduction of these new developments in the office are considered. The importance of human factors in the design process and the aspects which will influence good design are looked at. The main national and international strategies are briefly outlined and the role that standards play in interfaces is studied.

Conclusion

Change in perception of the user

The user and computer as a partnership to accomplish tasks

There is an old remark that says 'To find a human/computer interface, just follow a data path outwards from the central processor until you come to a person'. There is an implicit emphasis here which is now disappearing slowly, but is still all too prevalent in the IT world. It is that the important part of any system is what happens inside the computer and that the user is very much a peripheral adjunct to it. Admittedly, the remark was aimed at such people and was therefore worded appropriately, but the approach is still a common one. However, it is now becoming apparent to most IT suppliers that this view is no longer sufficient, because most large users have learnt their lessons with earlier generations of computer systems and are no longer prepared to accept a computer-centric view of the world. It is now not uncommon to find a view that says that computers and people are a partnership in accomplishing tasks and, as a consequence, it is the allocation of tasks and the quality of the dialogue that is now the important thing — in other words, it is the performance of the whole system, not just the computing parts, that is important.

The non-monotonic, opportunistic user

The resulting concentration on the task has, in turn, led to deeper consideration of the user of the system. The implicit, classical assumption frequently made by designers of earlier generations that the user is a logical automaton who never forgets, never gets tired and who, when things go wrong, will automatically guess correctly what the designer intended, is now nearly a thing of the past. The 'user' is now seen to be any of a range of users, from naive to well-practised expert, and furthermore a user who changes, not necessarily in a smooth manner. It is now accepted that a user may be an expert for certain functions of a system and a novice for others. It is also becoming accepted that even experienced users may make inadvertent slips, such as reverting to the commands of an old, much-used, but now replaced, package and that users may make sudden, abrupt switches in what they do and in what goals they wish to accomplish. This is particularly true in problem solving activities such as design, where the user may be totally opportunistic in his or her use of available information, switching rapidly from one piece to another and working on different parts of the problem in rapid succession and not necessarily in a logical manner. The difficulties that this raises for the development of models of the user are now being appreciated, as are the resultant difficulties of designing an appropriate interface with its necessary user support.

The user team

As an extension of the 'user' described above has come the notion of the user team, where there may be a number of users in sequence at a terminal using a group user number and carrying out different, related (and perhaps interrelated) tasks, perhaps in total ignorance of what has gone on before. The clear need for intelligent process managers, let alone dialogue managers, that this conjures up is an area of future research for interface design.

Effects of hardware technology advances

The move to parallel processing chips

There has in the past few years been a gradual emergence of parallel processing hardware from the laboratories into commercial systems. As with most technological breakthroughs, this promises tremendous changes in the future. The massive increase in processing speed that will result from this will enable far more exotic uses of graphics in dialogue design as standard software features. It will also allow the development of associative memory systems, with their inherent retrieval advantages which, in turn, will simplify the design of interfaces for the search of the massive databases and knowledge bases of the future. As computer systems pervade our lives further, particularly in the hands of government departments, it is likely that it is only the development of such technology that will make social security systems and the like sufficiently flexible to be useful, rather than the realisation of an Orwellian spectre.

Display technology

Flat screen technology
Whatever the technology, the fact of being able to produce thin, high-resolution displays will again release designers to explore new ideas. Layered, colour displays which at present are not much more than laboratory toys give the promise of the illusion of depth in displays, thus allowing designers to exploit three-dimensional effects. It also frees designers to consider collecting panels together to form the equivalent of a desktop or a full-size drawing board, so that users really do have room to spread their tasks out on a human scale and system designers have the scope to consider layout and user support problems more imaginatively and to allocate functions accordingly.

Hologram technology
This too is moving out of the research laboratories. Already, head-up displays are appearing in military equipment and in time they will make an appearance commercially. The technology could revolutionise displays, in that it might, by use of phase-conjugate mirrors and other laser technology, allow users to not only see three-dimensional displays, but to move through them. The possibilities of this seem endless, from space games to more serious simulations, and from database exploration (in the form of libraries, for instance) to system control.

Of course, a prerequisite is the development of the appropriate technologies, such as parallel processing, mentioned earlier, together with great advances in manufacturing technology.

Effects of software technology

AI and blackboard approaches

The promises that AI and its cognate disciplines held out in the early days for intelligent interfaces seem to be still only promises. However, the concepts have profoundly affected the perceptions of system designers and their emergence in the design of software has serious implications for the design of interfaces. An example is the development of truth maintenance systems, which will allow conflicting representations of 'reality' to coexist and grow (as do humans). This raises opportunities both for the predictive control of the interface and for the greater allocation of functions to the computer, with the consequent dialogue requirements for higher-level control by the user.

Size and invasion of IT

Large government systems with massive databases
As mentioned earlier, we are now reaching the stage where computers impinge on our lives in more ways than we imagine. For example, as governments computerise our tax records and other areas of our lives, in the interests of efficiency, accuracy, law enforcement, etc, interface considerations become very important. Firstly, there is the problem of accessing particular data records and exploring the linkages to other data records within massive databases, and the concomitant problem of doing this within acceptable time limits and presenting the information in an understandable manner to the user. These problems are an order of magnitude larger than those we currently address, and it is quite possible that our current approaches in query languages will not be sufficient as a dialogue for the user. Secondly, there are the

consequences of user decisions. Because of the inter-related nature of these databases, it is possible for an error to have extensive ramifications; presenting the consequences of a user decision in a manner that will be understood poses problems both for the designers of applications software and for interface designers.

Decision making within the computer

Sheridan has made several pertinent comments regarding human alienation arising from the introduction of computers into organisations. He has identified 10 examples:

> Sheridan (074):
> 1 Human considers alternatives, makes and implements decision.
>
> 2 Computer offers a set of alternatives which human may ignore in decision making.
>
> 3 Computer offers a restricted set of alternatives, and human decides which to implement.
>
> 4 Computer offers a restricted set of alternatives and suggests one, but human still makes and implements final decision.
>
> 5 Computer offers a restricted set of alternatives and suggests one which it will implement if human approves.
>
> 6 Computer makes decision but gives human option to veto before implementation.
>
> 7 Computer makes and implements decision, but must inform human after the fact.
>
> 8 Computer makes and implements decision, and informs human only if asked to.
>
> 9 Computer makes and implements decision, and informs human only if it feels this is warranted.
>
> 10 Computer makes and implements decision if it feels it should, and informs human only if it feels this is warranted.

We are now beginning to understand some of the implications of these various examples from a systems performance point of view, especially when errors occur. It is under these circumstances where it falls to operators firstly to understand the current status of the system, secondly either to choose a strategy or devise a new one, and thirdly to execute and adjust the chosen strategy. It is clear now that interface design includes not only the interaction between a user and a given operational software module, but also the presentation of system structure and (mal)function. The latter represents a different mode of interaction, with different demands for user support, which must now be included within interface design.

Importance of human factors in the design process

The need to understand the design problem

> Gardner:
> The point being made here is to argue that a true methodology for the human factors design of UCIs has to provide advice on task allocations (as in the task allocation charts), on the logical and physical properties of the interfaces (as in the UCI protocol) and on the management of the design process (as in the human factors plans and QA checklists).

The rise in formal methods in the development of software is obviously a much needed step. Unfortunately, these tend not to consider the user interface in any great detail:

> Downs (061):
> One of the popular topics being studied at the moment is the Government's official Structured Systems Analysis and Design Methodology [SSADM] and how to improve its rather rudimentary way of specifying user requirements. The methods being looked at include the use

of prototyping to check quickly if systems will match user needs, and the use of artificial intelligence and databases to put more power behind the specifications process.

However, fresh insights into handling the human aspects of analysis may come from the field of social science rather than computer science.

SSADM is not alone in receiving this criticism. Most of the methods and methodologies in current use suffer from the same problem, and it is becoming a matter of some urgency that methods appropriate to user interface design be made available. As Gardner says:

Gardner:
Most handbooks exist in a design vacuum — they do not concern themselves with what precedes the detailed design of an interface (for example task analysis and task allocation) or with what might follow the design of an interface (for example the design of user tasks, jobs, work organisations or the problems of user training, system installation and in-use support).

The difficulties are threefold. Firstly, those who provide the problem brief may not understand what the problem really is. Secondly, because organisations are social environments and not logical structures, office politicians may produce particular biases in the presentation of the problem to systems analysts. Thirdly, the systems analysts themselves may not have sufficient background to understand the problems, nor to see the ramifications of their intended solutions — deep logic from the depths of an armchair does not provide a sufficient answer.

Models and design principles

The approach, tried on several occasions, of modelling the user has not been conspicuously successful, despite the valiant attempts that have been made. Perhaps the two most widely known are the 'Keystroke' model and the Goals Operators and Methods (GOMS) model, both produced by Card *et al (017)*. The obvious alternative has also been undertaken, that of producing design guidelines *(065)* or design principles *(075)*. These have certainly had a beneficial effect, if only to educate interface designers as to the problems of interface design. The main problem with all such guidelines is that for them to be of wide applicability they must be general statements of principle. This in turn exposes them to two main criticisms; firstly, they do not cover the full range of required interface designs and, secondly, because of their generality they can be very difficult to apply in a given set of circumstances. A third problem that has been expressed is that one subset of principles will often produce conflicts with another subset; however, such criticisms are endemic to any design guidelines. So far, they offer the best hope for satisfactory initial design solutions.

Prototyping

Norman:
Prototyping calls for the availability of a software environment (usually some form of User Interface Management System (UIMS)) ... that will permit the easy construction and revision of the interface to an application system.... The objective is to demonstrate and evaluate the user interface as a way of making good any deficiencies in the requirements specification or the designed interface. The difficulties arise from the amount of time that can be taken in this process, the amount of effort needed to construct the prototype and the reluctance of users to stop the process of refinement.

This approach to interface design is without doubt an essential step in the production of satisfactory interfaces. Particular benefits claimed for this approach include the opportunity to educate the system designers into the real nature of the problems before the design is frozen, the fact that it allows the initial design solution (arising perhaps from the use of guidelines as discussed above) to be incrementally improved and that it helps to ensure the acceptability of the final design to the users.

Walsh et al:
Rapid prototyping supposes that effective development results from the iterative testing of prototypes which provides feedback for design. Rapid prototyping allows the demonstration of the proposed system to the user and facilitates user suggestions on improvements and

modifications. Prototyping helps solve the problem that users cannot imagine what type of system could better support their work. Rapid prototyping serves to match the design with the user requirements. Human factors may contribute by supplementing feedback, provided directly by users, with behavioural data derived from testing users on the prototype. Finally, human factors methods may be used to evaluate the implementation. However, though a description of users' errors and difficulties may give designers a better analysis of the problem of usability, it does not by itself constitute a solution.

In the absence of any more formal methods, this has become a widely adopted approach within the IT industry.

Usability

While the approaches to design from a human factors point of view remain somewhat haphazard, the evaluation of interfaces is rapidly becoming a formalised methodology. Shackel states:

Shackel:
Usability depends on the following:

1 The design of the tool (the VDT and the computer system) in relation to the users, the tasks and the environments.

2 The success of the user support provided (training, manuals and other job aids such as on-line and off-line 'help' facilities).

Usability metrics and their associated methods have been widely discussed, and a consensus is beginning to form. However, it is not yet clear that this approach is sufficiently well developed to cope with very complex systems. There is little doubt that at the individual interface level, and at the syntactic level, usability approaches work well; the doubt arises at the semantic and strategic levels.

User support

User support has gained much credence in recent years, if only in response to the anguished howls of user organisations. However, much as is the case with the design of the interface itself, the models and principles still await development before they can be exploited usefully and widely. In the meantime it is to the use of guidelines and prototyping, together with inferences from usability trials, that we must look to develop adequate user support. The view is gradually gaining ground that user support is not just a matter of providing the user with information when things have gone wrong, but of carrying out a combination of distance learning and reference support as well. This has the important implication that the information and justifications elicited throughout the design stages are necessary components of user support systems and require as much attention as the interface design itself.

User tailoring of the interface

As complex, modular systems are being designed for general industrial use, it seems that the view is developing that clients should be given the option of tailoring the system they have purchased to their own specific needs. In turn, this demand changes to the interface. A problem is the provision of tools to enable the user to do this, without compromising either the functionality of the system or the usability of the interface, thereby undoing the development work. This again reflects the shortcomings in the models and principles of interface design.

Locus of control/alienation

Sheridan's paper *(074)* is a classic in this field. As a summary of the main alienation problems, he describes seven factors:

Sheridan (074):
1 A first factor is that some people compare themselves with computers and worry about their inferiority and threatened obsolescence.

2 A second alienating factor is the tendency for computer control to make human operators remote from their ultimate task.

3 A third and related aspect of alienation occurs in jobs that have demanded considerable training and skill on the part of humans. The advent of computer control means that skilled machinists, typesetters, laboratory technicians and aircraft pilots are 'promoted' to button pushers and machine tenders.

4 Closely related is a fourth factor akin to our system of formal education and C P Snow's 'two cultures'. This is the greater access to information and power by the technologically literate minority as compared with the technologically illiterate majority.

5 A fifth aspect of alienation is mystification ... it is easy to attribute magical properties to the computer — our pop media encourage us to do so at every turn — but there is great danger in this.

6 This naturally leads to a sixth factor of alienation: higher stakes in decision making. Because computer-controlled systems are growing larger, more complex, more capital intensive, more centralised, and more tightly controlled, the costs of failure are huge though the probabilities of failure may be small.

7 The seventh and final basis for alienation is phylogenesis. That is the threat, real or perceived, that the race of intelligent machines is becoming more powerful than humans.

Failure to consider alienation will cause even well-designed systems to fail.

Need for reform and education of designers

It will have become clear by now that the human factors considerations, far from being *post hoc* polishing and tidying of software, are critical to the specification of the problem and are pervasive throughout the design cycle. As design is undertaken, it becomes increasingly necessary to ensure that the designers are well versed in general human factors knowledge and are able to identify when to call in human factors specialists.

As part of the support for the MoD/DTI HF Guidelines, training and education is seen as integral to ensure that the guidelines are used. Increasingly, design courses are including human factors.

National/international initiatives

The Alvey Programme

The Alvey Programme began in 1982 following a report from British Telecom's John Alvey, who recommended a £500 million programme to promote IT and IT awareness in the UK. The programme was split into four main areas, one of those areas being the Man/Machine Interface (MMI). The eventual Alvey Programme was for £350 million (£200 million from industry and £150 million from the Government). MMI remained one of the four main areas. Unfortunately, this included many aspects of the interface which had little or nothing to do with human factors and the monies to human factors research and development was substantially less than had been originally hoped for. Nevertheless, the Alvey initiative was able to sponsor a number of large and small projects and it also served to 'legitimise' the study of the interface in a most effective manner.

The main output from the programme is still being assessed. The final monies were allocated in 1987 and some of the projects will be running into the 1990s. However, centres of human factors excellence have been set up in London, Loughborough and Scotland and human factors practitioners have been able to provide significant input to a large number of the 'demonstrator' (large, multidisciplinary) projects such as the Design to Product project and the Machine Assisted Speech Translation (MAST) project.

The idea of a second, Alvey II, initiative, has been recently turned down by the Government, who have preferred to follow a more European route and back more fully the ESPRIT II project. However, there will be some £29 million available for more 'blue-sky' research. The effects of this decision on the UK human factors community are not yet obvious. The aim is to encourage a more European outlook in terms of markets, applications and products. It is too early to say whether this will succeed.

European Strategic Programme for Research into Information Technology (ESPRIT)

ESPRIT was a direct European response to the JIPDEC report (the so-called Japanese Fifth Generation Programme). ESPRIT differed from Alvey both in size and in style. Unlike Alvey it did not recognise discrete disciplines but concentrated on different domains. Thus much of the human factors work was carried out in the Office Automation (OA) programme.

ESPRIT II is different again. It is to start in 1988/89 and will concentrate on bringing ideas to market and developing ideas which will increase European competitiveness. Like ESPRIT I, the programme has been divided into several problem areas, with no specific recognition of human factors as a discipline in its own right. The advantages of such an approach is that human factors issues can be seen as all-pervasive and can slot into any part of the programme. The disadvantages are that ESPRIT II makes no specific demands on fundamental HCI work and provides no framework within which to carry out HCI work. The fear is that HCI will once again be neglected by the major European manufacturers in a way which would please the US IT companies.

Microelectronics and Computer Technology Corporation (MCC)

There is no specific IT initiative within the US. The nearest to such a venture is the MCC. The problems with the MCC have been primarily related to US anti-trust laws and the failure of many of the major IT companies to participate. The thrust of the work is very much precompetitive research and there are interesting developments in the technology associated with the design of interfaces, though little has been done in the cognitive and organisational areas. One of the interesting problems associated with US National Programmes is the sheer size of the research arms of corporations such as IBM, Xerox and AT&T. Feigenbaum and McCorduck (076) describe the MCC as 'An optimistic organisation with an optimistic and accomplished leader ... [which] must coordinate among fractious firms who have spent corporate lifetimes in savage competition with each other'.

Standards

One of the main ways in which the design of end-user interfaces is likely to be influenced is through the widespread introduction of standards. This Report has mentioned several (and a list of relevant standards is included in the Bibliography). The production and implementation of standards, especially by large user organisations such as governments, should help ensure that HCI is taken seriously. Issues about how effective these standards can be, and how prescriptive they should be, still need to be addressed. Certainly there is potential to use the DTI/MoD (PE) draft HF Guidelines and the BSI draft standards to good effect. It seems likely that standards will be applied to operational requirements and that customers will insist on interfaces which are usable and useful.

Conclusion

The aim of this Report has been to review the state of the art in the design of end-user interfaces. It has examined the scope of the problem and placed it into a wider context. It has attempted to delineate the problem, to illustrate it and to propose ways in which the design of end-user interfaces can be improved.

The capabilities of the hardware and software might change, as the technology evolves, but the need to consider the user will not. Alphonse Chapanis has stated: 'Computers are machines and machines exist for one purpose and that purpose is to serve people'. Designers would do well to bear this in mind.

Analysis references

001
'Common user access'
IBM
(1987)

002
'Human factors in design' series
ICL
(1986)

003
Gardner A and McKenzie J
'Human factors guidelines for the design of computer-based systems'
Parts 1-6 Issue 1
Ministry of Defence (PE) and Department of Trade and Industry
(1988)

004
Shackel B
'Ergonomics in design for usability'
In 'People and computers: designing for usability'
M D Harrison and A F Monk (eds)
Proc BCS HCI SIG
Cambridge Univ Press
(1986)

005
Thimbleby H
'User interface design: generative user engineering principles'
In 'Fundamentals of human-computer interaction'
A Monk (ed)
Academic Press
(1985)

006
Christie B and Gardiner M M
'Applying cognitive psychology to user-interface design'
John Wiley & Sons Ltd
(1987)

007
Grandjean E
'Fitting the task to the man'
4th ed
Taylor and Francis
(1988)

008
IBM
Private communication

009
Mowshowitz A
'The conquest of the will: information processing in human affairs'
Addison-Wesley
(1976)

010
Hirschheim R A
'Office automation: a social and organizational perspective'
John Wiley & Sons Ltd
(1985)

011
Schneiderman B
'Software psychology: human factors in computer and information systems'
Winthrop
(1980)

012
Carey T
'Dialogue handling with user workstations'

217

In Proc INTERACT '84 Conf
B Shackel (ed)
Elsevier Science Publishers BV
(1985)

013
Smith E E and Collins A
'Applied psychology'
BBN Rep #5499
(Oct 1983)

014
Shackel B (editor)
'Man-computer communication'
State of the Art Rep
vol 2
Infotech International
(1979)

015
Draper S W
'The nature of expertise in UNIX'
In Proc INTERACT '84 Conf
B Shackel (ed)
Elsevier Science Publishers BV
(1985)

016
Brocks R et al
'Software psychology: the need for an interdisciplinary program'
National Science Foundation
82-SP-1011
(1983)

017
Card S K, Moran T P and Newell A
'The psychology of human-computer interaction'
Lawrence Erlbaum Associates
(1983)

018
Miller G A
'The Magic Number 7 ± 2: some limits on our capacity for processing information'
Psychological Review
vol 63 pp 81-87
(1956)

019
Norman D A
'The trouble with UNIX'
Datamation
vol 81 no 27 p 12
(1982)

020
Leavitt H
'Applied organizational change in industry'
In 'Handbook of organizations'
J March (ed)
Rand McNally
(1965)

021
Central Computer and Telecommunication Agency
'Expert systems: some guidelines'
HM Treasury
(1986)

022
Card S K, English W K and Burr B J
'Evaluation of mouse, rate-controlled isometric joystick, step keys and text keys for text selection on a CRT'
Ergonomics
vol 21 pp 601-613
(1978)

023
Karat J, McDonald J E and Anderson M
'A comparison of selection techniques: touch, panel, mouse and keyboard'
In Proc INTERACT '84 Conf
B Shackel (ed)
Elsevier Science Publishers BV
(1985)

024
van Cott H P and Kinkade R G
'Human engineering guide to equipment design'
McGraw-Hill
(1972)

025
Damodaran L, Simpson A and Wilson P
'Designing systems for people'
NCC Publications
(1982)

026
Marshall C J, Christie B and Gardiner M M
'Assessment of trends in the technology and techniques of human-computer interaction'
In 'Applying cognitive psychology to user-interface design'
B Christie and M M Gardiner (eds)
John Wiley & Sons Ltd
(1987)

027
Marshall C J
'More bite for mailbox users'
In 'Man/machine integration'
N Bevan and D Murray (eds)
State of the Art Rep
series 13 no 1
Pergamon Infotech Ltd
(1985)

028
Whitefield A
'Pointing as an input technique for human-computer interactions'
In 'Future of input techniques for man/machine interaction'
Digest No 1983/42
Proc IEE Colloq
(1983)

029
Schneiderman B
'Designing the user interface: strategies for effective human-computer interaction'
Addison-Wesley
(1987)

030
Young R M
'The man inside the machine: users' models of pocket calculators'
Intl J of Man/Machine Studies
vol 15
pp 51-85
(1981)

031
Hammond N and Barnard P
'Dialogue design — characteristics of user knowledge'
In 'Fundamentals of human computer interaction'
A Monk (ed)
Academic Press
(1984)

032
Norman D A
'Some observations on mental models'
In 'Mental models'
D Gentner and A Stevens (eds)
Lawrence Erlbaum Associates
(1982)

033
Hamill B W
'Psychological issues in the design of expert systems'
Proc Human Factors Society 28th Annual Meeting
(Oct 1984)

034
Schneider M L
'Models for the design of static software user assistance'
In 'Directions in human computer interaction'
A Badre and B Schneiderman (eds)
Ablex Publishing
(1982)

035
Minsky M
'Matter, mind and models'
In 'Semantic information processing'
M Minsky (ed)
MIT Press
(1968)

036
'IBM dictionary of computing'
IBM
(1987)

037
Bramer M
'Expert systems: some guidelines'
HMSO
(1986)

038
Cleal D M and Heaton N
'Knowledge-based systems: implications for human-computer interfaces'
Ellis Horwood
(1988)

039
Ramsay A
'Dialogue handling in an IFE'
Rep of the 2nd IFE Workshop
(1984)

040
Wilson P A et al
'The active mailbox: your on-line secretary'
Proc Conf on 'Computer-based message services'
Intl Federation for Information Processing
(1984)

041
Uschold M et al
'An IFE for ecological modelling'
Proc ECAI-84
(1984)
'An expert system for ecological modelling'
Alvey IFE Workshop No 1
(1983)

042
Bose P and Rajinikith M
'Karma — an intelligent assistant to a database system'
Expert System J
(Jan 1986)

043
Bundy A
'IFEs'
Proc BCS Ann Conf '84
(1984)

044
McDonald R K
'Factoring out investigative inferences'
Proc BCS Ann Conf '86
(1986)

045
Clancy W J
'The epistemology of a rule-based system: a framework for explanation'
Artificial Intelligence
vol 20
(1983)

046
Frudes N
'The intimate machine'
Century
(1983)

047
Hollan J D
'Intelligent object-based graphical interfaces'
In 'Human-computer interfaces'
G Salvendy (ed)
p 193
Elsevier Science Publishers BV
(1984)

048
Schaffitzel W and Kersten U
'Introducing CAD systems:
problems and the role of
user-developer communication
in their solution'
Behaviour and Information Technology
vol 4 no 1
pp 49-51
(1985)

049
Rasmussen J and Goodstein L P
'Decision support in supervisory control'
In 'Analysis, design and evaluation of man-machine systems'
G Johannsen, G Mancini and
L Martensson (eds)
Proc 2nd IFAC/IFIP/IFORS/IEA Conf
Varese Italy 10-12 Sep 1986
p 34
(1986)

050
Axe R
'CAD in British industry'
Lecture delivered to the Royal Society of Arts
9.12.87
RSA J
p 256
(1988)

051
McPhater N S
'Bridging the culture gap between engineers and software developers during the joint development of a bespoke CAD system'
Computer-aided Engineering J
vol 2 no 3 pp 84-85 (1984)

052
Packham K
'The way we work'
Network
p 24
(Apr 1988)

053
Sweet P
'The risk business'
Network
p 75
(Apr 1988)

054
Norman D A
'Cognitive engineering principles in the design of human-computer interfaces'
In 'Human-computer interfaces'
G Salvendy (ed)
pp 11
Elsevier Science Publishers BV
(1984)

055
Jacob R S
'Formal specifications in the design of an interface'
Communications of the ACM
vol 26 no 4 pp 209-222
(Apr 1983)

056
Moran T P
'The Command Language Grammar:
a representation for the user interface of interactive systems'
Intl J Man-Machine Studies
vol 15 pp 3-50
(1981)

057
Reisner P
'Formal grammar and human factors design of an interactive graphics system'
IEEE Trans Software Engineering
vol SE-7 pp 229-240
(1981)

058
Roberts T L
'Perspective of a modern user-interface designer'

In 'Human-computer interfaces'
G Salvendy (ed)
p 62
Elsevier Science Publishers BV
(1984)

059
Fountain A J and Norman M A
'Modelling user behaviour with formal grammar'
In 'People and computers: designing the user interface'
P Johnson and S Cook (eds)
pp 3-12
Cambridge Univ Press
(1985)

060
Erich R W and Williges R C
'Human-computer dialogue design'
Vol II of 'Advances in human factors/ ergonomics'
Elsevier Science Publishers BV
(1986)

061
Downs E
'Analysing office politics'
Computing
p 24
(24 Mar 1988)

062
Thimbleby H W
'Generative user-engineering principles for user interface design'
In Proc INTERACT '84 Conf
B Shackel (ed)
pp 102-107
Elsevier Science Publishers BV
(1985)

22063
Dix A and Runciman C
'Abstract models of interactive systems'
In 'People and computers: designing the user interface'
P Johnson and S Cook (eds)
pp 13-22
Cambridge Univ Press
(1985)

064
Harrison M D and Thimbleby H W
'Formalising guidelines for the design of interactive systems'
In 'People and computers: designing the user interface'
P Johnson and S Cook (eds)
pp 161-171
Cambridge Univ Press (1985)

065
Smith S L and Mosier J L
'Design guidelines for user-system interface software'
Tech Rep ESD-TR-84-190
USAF Electronic Systems Division
Hanscom AFB MA
NTIS No AD-A154-907
(1984)

066
Smith S L
'Standards versus guidelines for designing user interface software'
Behaviour and Information Technology
vol 5 no 1
pp 47-61
(1986)

067
Norman D A
'Cognitive engineering'
In 'User-centered design'
D A Norman and S W Draper (eds)
p 47
Lawrence Erlbaum Associates
(1986)

068
Hutchins E L, Hollan J D and Norman D A
'Direct manipulation interfaces'
In 'User-centered design'
D A Norman and S W Draper (eds)
p 93
Lawrence Erlbaum Associates
(1986)

069
Schneiderman B
'The future of interactive systems and the emergence of direct manipulation'
Behaviour and Information Technology
vol 1 pp 237-256
(1982)

070
Cypher A
'The structure of users' activities'
In 'User-centered design'
D A Norman and S W Draper (eds)
p 249
Lawrence Erlbaum Associates
(1986)

071
Reichman (Adar) R
'Communication paradigms for a window system'
In 'User-centered design'

D A Norman and S W Draper (eds)
p 296
Lawrence Erlbaum Associates (1986)

072
Miyata Y and Norman D A
'Multiple activities'
In 'User-centered design'
D A Norman and S W Draper (eds)
p 277
Lawrence Erlbaum Associates (1986)

073
Draper S W
'Display managers'
In 'User-centered design'
D A Norman and S W Draper (eds)
p 349
Lawrence Erlbaum Associates (1986)

074
Sheridan T B
'Computer control and human alienation'
IEEE Technology Review
(Oct 1980)

075
Harrison M D and Thimbleby H W
'Formalising guidelines for the design of interactive systems'
Proc BCS HCI SIG
Cambridge Univ Press
(1985)

076
Feigenbaum E A and McCorduck P
'The Fifth Generation'
Pan Books
(1984)

Bibliography

An annotated bibliography of end-user interface design

N Heaton

M Sinclair

HUSAT Research Centre
University of Technology
Loughborough
Leicestershire
UK

© N Heaton and M Sinclair 1988

N Heaton
Nigel Heaton graduated with an Honours Degree in Ergonomics from the Loughborough University of Technology. His first post was with GEC's Hirst Research Laboratory in the Man-Machine Systems Group where he was involved in several internal human factors projects as well as with ESPRIT and Alvey work. He then joined the Central Computer and Telecommunication Agency (CCTA) where he worked on a number of projects concerned with the introduction of new technology into central administrative Government. He was involved with one of the first digital optical records to be installed in the UK, looking at workstations. Mr Heaton has also worked on speech recognition and studied some of the human factors issues associated with speech. He now works for the Human/Computer Interaction (HCI) Service at the HUSAT Research Centre.

M Sinclair
Murray Sinclair has been an Ergonomist for 20 years and he is currently a lecturer in the Department of Human Sciences, Loughborough University of Technology. Having obtained his Ergonomics Degree he spent two years as an Industrial Engineer with J Lyons and Co before returning to Loughborough University. Latterly he has been engaged in the human factors implications of advanced manufacturing technologies in the mechanical engineering field. Current research areas are centred on advanced manufacturing technology; the design of CAD systems to optimise downstream activities in manufacture, assembly and field services; the problems of human supervision and control in heavily automated manufacturing environments; knowledge elicitation, knowledge structures and the roles of knowledge within organisations; and user/system interface design. Mr Sinclair's special interest lies in understanding, within a system engineering framework, the kinds of knowledge and expertise that provide commercial enterprises with their 'competitive' edge.

An annotated bibliography of end-user interface design

Introduction

The design of end-user interfaces covers a wide range of fields. In theory, any system built for users must have an interface, and the design of that interface ought to assume importance equal to the design of other aspects of the system. Until recently, this has not been the case. Interfaces have been overlooked and their importance has been underrated. A direct consequence of this neglect has been the introduction of systems which have proved to be expensive failures. For example, work carried out under the Department of Trade and Industry's Office Automation Pilot Scheme indicated that some 40 per cent of all projects were outright failures, for reasons which were often directly attributable to poor human factors. The situation is starting to change and this change is reflected both in the production of better systems and in the explosive growth in the literature in the last 20 years. A bibliography on the design of end-user interfaces written in 1968 would have contained few entries and would have concluded that most of the research into the problem still needed to be carried out. Fortunately, 20 years later, most aspects of the problem have been addressed, to a greater or lesser extent. This causes another problem: the size and diversity of the field. The Analysis has highlighted the many areas which contribute to the design of end-user interfaces from cognitive psychology to Artificial Intelligence (AI). The aim of this Bibliography is to provide key references to work undertaken recently (within the last 10 years) in the field of end-user interfaces. It is often difficult to assign texts to particular categories, for example most texts which deal with the design of hardware aspects of a system will at least make passing reference to software and job design aspects of the system. The best way to use this Bibliography is as a guide to the major theme of a text, rather than to assume that a text in any of the sections provides an analysis of that particular subject. The completeness of any bibliography is always hard to assess. The aim is to make this as complete as possible in terms of the areas covered and issues raised. We have aimed to equally reflect the differing camps within the field of end-user interface design in the texts described. However, within any rapidly changing and expanding field, by the time a bibliography is completed, it is already slightly out of date. For this reason, a list of key conference proceedings is included. These should be referred to for the latest work in the field. In general, new ideas and work in progress are reported at the conferences, with more complete work presented in the journals. However, the tendency for conferences to contain one or more invited papers allows key workers to provide summaries and snapshots of their specialised areas and provides the reader with a valuable insight into an institute's or group's state of the art. This bibliography is structured along similar lines to the Analysis. It details work in four main areas, as set out below:

1 *General texts:* here we include work which is concerned with the field as a whole, usually books which attempt to summarise the picture or which describe fundamental ideas or research which have significantly changed our knowledge about end-user interfaces. Readers who wish to gain a more detailed technical insight into the design of end-user interfaces or who wish to investigate where some of the fundamental research has come from, should refer to titles in this section. Also included are books which are more general texts, forming suitable reading for those with an interest in the whole field but not wishing to go into too much detail on any particular aspect of it.

2 *Expert texts:* this section concentrates on texts which are aimed at individuals who already have a good knowledge of the field and wish to investigate a topic in depth. Generally, texts included in this section are not suitable for people with a passing interest.

3 *Guidelines:* this section reflects the many guidelines which have been produced in the field of human factors.

4 *Standards:* this section will reflect the many company, national and international standards which are starting to emerge.

5 *Proceedings:* the final section will outline some of the conferences and proceedings which are available to the designer, allowing him to gain a snapshot of current work and 'hot' research topics.

Abstracts

General texts

100
Alty J and Coombs M (editors)
'Computing skills and the user interface'
Academic Press
(1981)

This book concentrates on key research issues in the design of software and the user interface. It includes papers on such issues as the needs of naive computer users, user involvement and user support.

101
Bennett J, Case D, Sandelin J and Smith M
'Visual display terminals: usability issues and health concerns'
Prentice-Hall Inc
(1984)

This book contains two main sections. The first covers developing and implementing Visual Display Terminal (VDT)-based usability issues and the second the use of VDTs and health concerns. The book includes a paper by Shackel on the concept of usability which continues to develop some of his ideas on this subject. There is also a paper by Card on human limits and the VDT computer interface.

102
Card S K, Moran T P and Newell A
'The psychology of human-computer interaction'
Lawrence Erlbaum Associates
(1983)

This is viewed as one of the seminal books on a mechanistic approach to Human/Computer Interaction (HCI), it contains reference to Goals, Operators and Methods (GOMS) and keystroke-level modelling as well as an extensive bibliography. The book was constructed over a period of time and includes much which is widely quoted (that is mouse versus other input devices). An important and influential book in the field of end-user computing.

103
Chapanis A, Anderson N S and Licklider J C R
'User-computer interaction'
In 'Research needs for human factors' Chapter 5
Committee on Human Factors, Commission on Behavioural and Social Sciences and Education, National Research Council
National Academy Press
(1983)

This chapter concentrates on identifying research needs in human factors, making recommendations in the areas of users, tasks, hardware, software and documentation. The main emphasis is on developing new methodologies to evaluate what is meant by ease of use in HCI terms.

104
Christie B (editor)
'Human factors of information technology in the office'
John Wiley & Sons
(1985)

This book was produced while Christie was working for the Human Factors Group of ITT at Harlow. It contains some collaborative papers with academics and presents a view of human factors from a systems psychology rather than an ergonomics approach. Areas looked at include product trends, product liability and introducing systems into organisations.

105
Feigenbaum E A and McCorduck P
'The Fifth Generation'
Pan Books Ltd
(1984)

Feigenbaum's view of Fifth Generation computing is somewhat distilled for a mass market, though there are some interesting comments on the Japanese and European initiatives. The book tends to present an American view and proposes an American solution. Interestingly, there is no mention of the human factors problems associated with the Fifth Generation.

106
Frude N
'The intimate machine'
Century Publishing Co Ltd
(1983)

An interesting book written for the non-specialist. Its theme is the human tendency to anthropomorphism. Frude sees that this will be extended to computers and will have consequences for the way in which people relate to machines.

107
Gardiner M M and Christie B (editors)
'Applying cognitive psychology to user-interface design'
John Wiley & Sons
(1987)

A collection of papers on user-interface design arising directly from an ESPRIT project. Heavily biased towards psychology and psychological principles it does contain two chapters on applications by Marshall, Nelson and Gardiner; and Marshall, Christie and Gardiner. The book deals with 'deep' psychological issues such as memory, skill and language and is of interest to people who have a specialist knowledge or those who need detail.

108
Grandjean E
'Ergonomics in computerized offices'
Taylor and Francis
(1987)

This book's main areas of concern are with the physiological aspects of the user. The chapters include vision, lighting, the ergonomic design of the VDT workstation and noise. The book also includes chapters on the occupational stress, work satisfaction and job aspects of computerisation as well as detailed recommendations for the design of VDT workstations.

109
Grandjean E
'Fitting the task to the man'
4th ed
Taylor and Francis
(1988)

The importance of this work is indicated by its recent revision and publication as a fourth edition. The subtitle of the book is 'A textbook of occupational ergonomics'. Although it has a physiological bias it offers a comprehensive review of many aspects of task design, particularly in relation to VDTs. A textbook of information on most human physical characteristics which affect performance, emphasising the need for a user-centred approach.

110
Monk A (editor)
'Fundamentals of human-computer interaction'
Academic Press
(1984)

A collection of papers presenting a review of work undertaken into HCI (particularly at York University), looking at the user as a processor of information, the use of behavioural data and the user interface.

111
Norman D A and Draper S W (editors)
'User-centered design'
Lawrence Erlbaum Associates
(1986)

This is an edited collection of chapters by many of the leading thinkers in the field of HCI. The range of topics covered is comprehensive, from strategies, to dialogue design, to window management, to user support, etc and there are many good ideas and thought-provoking concepts. The book is intended to show the current thinking on the design of the interface, and therefore is not directly useful in a given interface design situation. However, it is expected to become one of the seminal texts in the years to come. Chapters 2, 3, 5 and 16 are particularly helpful.

112
Oborne D J
'Computers at work'
John Wiley & Sons
(1985)

The book is subtitled 'A behavioural approach' and is split into the following four areas: social aspects, hardware, software and computer applications at work. The book emphasises the need to consider the complete environment in which the interaction takes place.

113
Otway H J and Peltu M (editors)
'New office technology: human and organizational aspects'
European Communities Directorate-General Information Market and Innovation (Luxembourg)
(1983)

This book aims to provide practical advice for those involved in making decisions about and implementing new office automation systems. It contains contributions from workers in EEC member states who are active in the field of new technology and human issues.

114
Shackel B (editor)
'Man/computer communication'
Infotech International Ltd
(1979)

A State of the Art Report on man/computer interaction covering the main areas (as in 1979). The Invited Papers are from some of the key workers in the field of HCI. However, some of the work is a little dated and most of the contributors have produced more recent work.

115
Schneiderman B
'Designing the user interface: strategies for effective human-computer interaction'
Addison-Wesley
(1987)

This book is divided into four parts: motivations and foundations; interaction styles; considerations and augmentations; assessment and reflection. It covers most of the areas relating to the design of end-user interfaces once some of the basic user and organisational issues have been solved. It also presents understandable, usable (but fairly low-level) rules on how to build better interfaces. Good for an overview of design of specific areas, for example, menu, command languages and direct manipulation.

116
Schneiderman B
'Software psychology'
Winthrop Publishers Inc
(1980)

One of the first books to explicitly address the issues of software psychology, it is now becoming a little dated. However, it does provide an excellent guide to many of the key issues as well as containing a 'Practitioner's summary' and a 'Researcher's agenda' on each topic to provide more practical advice and highlight areas which were still of concern in 1980. The text contains many practical and experimental findings which are directly applicable to the design of end-user interfaces.

117
Sime M E and Coombs M J (editors)
'Designing for human-computer communication'
Academic Press
(1983)

One of a series of books concerned with all aspects of man/computer relationships. This volume concentrates on two main areas: the user interface, with information on issues such as natural language and design of database query languages; the task interface, with papers covering issues such as the design of a medical consultation system and air traffic control systems.

118
Smith H T and Green T R G (editors)
'Human interaction with computers'
Academic Press
(1980)

A collection of papers looking at people in computer systems, applications research and programming research. The contributors to the book come from diverse research backgrounds yet identify many human factors problems which are common to their differing disciplines.

119
Stewart T M F (editor)
'Ergodesign '86'
Behaviour and Information Technology
vol 6 no 3
Taylor and Francis
(1987)

This special edition of Behaviour and Information Technology (BIT) contains selected readings from the International Symposium held at Montreux, 21-24 October 1986. The Symposium draws together ergonomists and designers who share a common interest, namely the evolution of the electronic workplace. The selected papers cover most issues associated with the design of the workplace from corporate strategy and planning issues down to specific details such as software ergonomics for interface design.

120
Thomas J C and Schneider M L (editors)
'Human factors in computer systems'
Ablex Publishing
(1984)

There are nine chapters in the book, all concentrating on slightly different aspects of usability. Most of them report the results of laboratory experimentation; as a consequence the book is likely to be of most use in setting a background to design and informing designers of what psychologists perceive to be the current problems in this area, rather than of direct use.

121
Williams D C and Durch J L
'Human foundations of advanced technology: the guide to the select literature'
The Report Store
(1985)

This is an almost comprehensive list of 737 titles in the literature, but is not annotated. The list covers English language publications, including some translations. The titles are indexed, cross-referenced by keywords, and are complete. There are a few omissions, but it constitutes a good starting point for information gathering.

Texts for experts

122
Björn-Andersen N, Easpon K D E and Robey D
'Managing computer impact'
Ablex Publishing
(1986)

As the title suggests, the book is mainly about implementation of computer systems. However, of the 11 chapters, numbers 3 to 6 deal directly with aspects of the interface and with task design. The remaining chapters, from an interface design point of view, indicate what the consequences of design decisions might be. There are useful case studies in a variety of industries.

123
Boff K R, Kaufman L and Thomas J P
'Handbook of perception and
human performance'
vol 1
'Sensory processes and perception'
John Wiley & Sons
(1986)

This text provides a definitive guide to sensory processes and perception presented by key workers in the field. It covers theory and methods, basic sensory processes and space and motion perception.

124
Boff K R, Kaufman L and Thomas J P
'Handbook of perception and
human performance'
vol 2
'Cognitive processes and performance'
John Wiley & Sons
(1986)

Volume 2 of the handbook deals with cognitive processes and performance in the same comprehensive manner as volume 1 dealt with perception and human performance. The areas covered are: information processing, perceptual organisation and cognition, and human performance. The main point about both volumes is that they are aimed at 'deep' specialists and provide a detail of information which would not be required by the general practitioner.

125
Brooks R et al
'Software psychology: the need for an interdisciplinary program'
Order ref: 86319
Document no PB84-176718
Microinfo Ltd
(1983)

A report from the ITT Advanced Technology Center detailing the need to consider software psychology as a specific discipline (as opposed to software engineering, human factors and ergonomics). It contains a useful bibliography as well as a brief state of the art report on software psychology.

126
Cleal D M and Heaton N O
'Knowledge-based systems: implications for human-computer interfaces'
Ellis Horwood Ltd
Distributed by John Wiley & Sons
(1988)

This book contains information on human factors issues and expert systems. There are chapters on the following topics: input and interaction; natural language; IFEs; explanation and help; knowledge acquisition; case studies and commercial tools. The book provides practical information as well as theoretical detail on some of the underlying principles. There is an interesting summary of commercial tools and case studies which attempts to pull the human factors issues into context.

127
Cohen B G F (editor)
'Human aspects in office automation'
Elsevier Science Publishers BV
(1984)

Only seven of the papers contained in this publication focus specifically on office automation. The main thrust of the book appears to be more towards safety and stress in the modern office. The book is organised into five sections which broadly cover: office environmental health issues; work organisational factors; ergonomic aspects of the workplace; physiological and psychological effects of office work; and strategies for alleviation of worksite stress.

128
Cuff R N
'On casual users'
Intl J Man-Machine Studies
vol 12 pp 163-187
(1980)

The paper looks at the concept of a casual user and constructs a detailed profile of such users. It then uses this profile to construct a list of general requirements for a query system which is aimed principally at casual users as distinct from regular and committed users. The paper's conclusions detail the consequences of infrequent use, the need for a 'natural' feeling system and the limited mathematical and programming skills of casual users.

129
Erich R W and Williges R C (editors)
'Human-computer dialogue design'
Elsevier Science Publishers BV
(1986)

The book is based on a three-year programme of research effort on human/computer dialogue design. It includes chapters on multidisciplinary research in human/computer dialogue design, dialogue management, integrated tools for program construction, user assistance in HCI and research issues.

130
Gaines B R and Shaw M L G
'The art of computer conversation'
Prentice-Hall Intl
(1984)

The book is very conversational, being aimed at a wide audience. It covers briefly user expectations, formal interaction, menus and forms, graphics, and (restricted) natural language. The conclusions are summarised as a series of brief generalisations. It is a useful book to ensure that gross design errors are avoided.

131
Green T R G and Payne S J
'Organization and learnability in computer languages'
Intl J Man-Machine Studies
vol 21 pp 7-18 (1984)

This paper looks at the overall structure or organisation of the computer language and proposes a new principle, that of consistency between language rules. An experiment demonstrates that the organisation of the lexical rules is more important than the match between any one command and its name.

132
Green T R G, Payne S J and van der Veer G C (editors)
'The psychology of computer use'
Academic Press
(1983)

A collection of conference papers covering the psychology of using computer and the psychology of programming. The book is part of the 'Computers and people' series edited by B R Gaines. Papers in this volume include computer-aided problem solving with graphical display of information, problem solving by novice programmers and the evaluation of a programming support environment.

133
Hamill B W
'Psychological issues in the design of expert systems'
Order ref: 86319
Document no: AD-A146081
Microinfo Ltd
(1984)

This report was produced by The John Hopkins University Applied Physics Laboratory and details conceptual issues underlying AI with reference to psychological as well as AI literature. The report emphasises the need to consider issues apart from the purely technical ones.

134
Helander M G, Billingsley P A and Schurick J M
'An evaluation of human factors research on visual displays in the workplace'
In 'Human factors review'
F A Muckler (ed)
pp 55-129
Human Factors Society
(1984)

The authors reviewed a total of 82 studies. In common with many other reviewers, they concluded that many studies suffer from flaws in design, making them of dubious relevance. Their conclusions were basically that organisational and job design factors have at least as much effort on stress and usability as the interface itself. They also reached the conclusion that some European guidelines lack experimental justification.

135
Hopgood F R A et al (editors)
'Methodology of window management'
Springer-Verlag
(1985)

This volume records the output from a workshop on window management held at Rutherford Appleton Laboratories, Didcot. The book reviews different window management systems, looking at issues such as a graphic standards view of screen management and user-interface issues.

136
Linde L
'Man/computer communication:
from artificial intelligence and
behavioral science perspectives'
Document no N82-18942
Microinfo Ltd
(1981)

This report was produced at the Research Institute of National Defense, Stockholm, Sweden. It contains many references which are relevant to the area of HCI, though these are somewhat dated. It refers to models of dialogues, database interactions, cognitive models of computerised tasks and the human factors requirements of interactive computer systems.

137
Majchrzak A et al
'Human aspects of computer-aided design'
Taylor and Francis
(1987)

This book deals with a restricted but important area of interface design. It covers technical aspects of CAD, the human/computer interface and the management of CAD. It gives a good overview of the problems that will be encountered, and of the organisational consequences of introducing CAD into an organisation.

138
Mumford E
'Designing human systems'
Manchester Business School
(1983)

This book describes Mumford's work with Effective Technical and Human Implementation of Computer-based Systems (ETHICS). It describes Mumford's approach to systems design and includes chapters on the following: managing change; participation and systems design; diagnosing needs; designing the system; and ETHICS step-by-step.

139
Newman W M and Sproull R F
'Principles of interactive computer graphics'
2nd ed
McGraw-Hill Inc
(1979)

This book was originally published in 1973 and was extensively revised for the second edition, published in 1979. The perceived importance of the book, and its influence in computer graphics, is evidenced by its frequent reprinting (11 by 1984). Chapter 28 is the most relevant to the design of user interfaces and contains a brief description of the field.

140
Norman D A
'Five papers on human-machine interaction'
AD A116031
Rep no: ONR-8205
Microinfo Ltd
(1982)

This report was produced at the Center for Human Information Processing at the University of California, San Diego. It contains five brief papers which outline the author's view on different aspects of human/machine interaction. Of particular interest is the paper on mental models. The other papers are 'A psychologist views human processing: human errors and other phenomena suggest processing mechanisms'; 'Steps toward a cognitive engineering'; 'The trouble with UNIX'; and 'The trouble with networks'.

141
Pearce B (editor)
'Health hazards of VDTs?'
John Wiley & Sons
(1984)

A collection of papers taking a look at the tricky subject of health and safety at work in relation to the use of VDTs. The book is split into three untitled sections which reflect the contents of three one-day meetings held at Loughborough University in 1981 and 1982. The book covers most of the contentious issues of the time but does not cover RSI which has become a more debated topic since the book was written.

142
Rasmussen J, Duncan K and Leplat J
'New technology and human error'
John Wiley & Sons
(1987)

In this book 16 contributors deal with the causes and nature of human errors in the context of large systems. Chapters 1 to 4 deal with the definitions and taxonomies of errors, and are of greatest relevance to the design of the human/computer interface.

143
Smith E E and Collins A
'Applied cognitive science'
Bolt, Beranek and Newman Rep no 5499
Document no AD-A136780
Microinfo Ltd
(1983)

This report was prepared for the Office of Naval Research, Psychological Sciences Division, by Bolt, Beranek and Newman. It provides an overview of some of the psychological issues in system design and is particularly relevant for work carried out on mental modelling, summarising some of the research undertaken in this area.

144
Winfield I
'Human resources and computing'
William Heinemann Ltd
(1984)

The text deals with an overview of the issues concerned with HCI and is aimed at undergraduates who are studying the topic as a minor part of their studies. Apart from AI and interface issues, the book also considers games and learning, errors and management issues.

Guidelines

145
Bailey R W
'Human performance engineering: a guide for system designers'
Prentice-Hall Inc
(1982)

This textbook presents information about the human as a user, the basic design systems, interface design, facilitator design, the environment, and tests and studies (that is data collection and performance testing). The book is based on Bailey's work at Bell Laboratories and contains many interesting studies (for example the Three Mile Island disaster).

146
Benz C, Grob R and Haubner P
'Designing VDU workplaces'
Verlag TÜV Rheinland GmbH
(1983)

This book contains anthropometric data on the design of VDUs as well as concentrating on the broader systems aspects of job design and the introduction of new technology. There are sections on the following topics: the VDU workplace as a work system; basic ergonomic factors; data and advice on workstation design; data and suggestions on the design of the working environment; hints and examples on job reorganisation; hints and examples on preparing the user; and ergonomic checklists for the design of VDU workplaces.

147
Cakir A, Hart D J and Stewart T F M
'The VDT manual'
John Wiley & Sons
(1980)

This book provides the design facts and figures necessary for the design of a workstation. It covers the finer details of character size and resolution, key shapes and profiles etc, as well as higher level, more diffuse concepts such as job satisfaction, etc. It constitutes an excellent source-book for design, particularly hardware design, though it is a little weak on non-keyboard input devices and was written before the introduction of multiwindow environments.

148
Damodaran L, Simpson A and Wilson P
'Designing systems for people'
National Computing Centre
(1980)

This was one of the first books to tackle the problem of designing systems for people. The six chapters in the book comprise: 'Planning the development'; 'Systems analysis — user aspects'; 'Equipment selection'; 'Systems design — user aspects'; 'workplace design'; and 'User support'. The sociotechnical systems approach adopted by the book is a model for the design of systems for people.

149
Galitz W O
'Handbook of screen format design'
2nd ed
Elsevier Science Publishers BV
(1985)

This book is literally a handbook of screen format

design. It takes the reader through the problems people have with existing dialogues and attempts to outline the qualities of future dialogues. It contains sections on system considerations, considerations in screen design, data entry screens, enquiry screens, multipurpose screens, question and answer screens, menu screens, colour in screen design, graphics, source documents and screen design stops.

150
Gardner A and McKenzie J
'Human factors guidelines for the design of computer-based systems'
Parts 1-6 Issue 1
Ministry of Defence (PE) and Department of Trade and Industry
Available through HUSAT Research Centre
(1988)

A comprehensive approach to inputting human factors into the design cycle. Produced to go alongside other, existing methodologies which do not include human factors, these documents provide a complete methodology applicable to all stages of the design process. The books have been produced in collaboration with the DTI and the MoD and may have a significant impact on human factors and large computer-based projects over the next few years.

151
Parrish R N et al
'Design guidelines and criteria
for user/operator transactions
with battlefield automated systems'
US Army Research Institute for Behavioral and Social Sciences
(1983)

The guidelines are concerned with the provision of human factors advice for the design and use of user/operator transactions. They are split into eight major sections: control methods; display techniques; data entry and handling; message composition aids; data retrieval assistance; symbology and terminology; error handling; and user/operator configurations.

152
Salvendy G (editor)
'Handbook of human factors'
John Wiley & Sons
(1987)

This book is a massive tome on all aspects of human factors. It is set in a small type-face, too close together and is still over 1800 pages long. It contains contributions from many human factors experts, with a bias towards US workers. The 12 main sections are: the human factors function; human factors fundamentals; functional analysis; job and organisation design; equipment and workplace design; environmental design; design for health and safety; design of selection and training systems; performance modelling; system evaluation; human factors in the design and use of computing systems; and selected applications of human factors in computer systems.

153
Smith S L and Mosier J N
'Design guidelines for user-system interface software'
Project no 522A
Rep nos MTR-9420 and ESD-TR-84-190
The MITRE Corporation
(1984)

Design guidelines provide a comprehensive guide to the design of user interfaces. The report comprises the six areas of data entry, data display, sequence control, user guidance, data transmission and data protection. It is one of the most comprehensive sets of guidelines yet produced and provides a level of detail which is available in few other places. Its size might limit its use to specialists (being 460 pages long), but the guidelines present information on most of the low-level problems associated with the design of interfaces.

Standards

154
'Draft British Standard recommendations for ergonomics requirements for design and use of Visual Display Terminals (VDTs) in offices'
British Standards Institution (BSI)
(1987)

These draft standards on VDTs are likely to become accepted in the near future. The standards are split into five sections, the first, Part 1, is an introduction; this is followed by task requirements, visual display requirements, keyboard requirements and VDT workstation design.

155
'Ergonomic principles of office automation'
Ericsson Information Systems AB
(1983)

This book was based on a study by ErgoLab of work in human factors and contains six chapters covering the visual display unit, keyboard design, workstation design, the software interface, health and safety aspects, and organisational aspects. The book presents an excellent overview in the form of reviews of literature and standards.

156
'Visual display units'
Health and Safety Executive
(1983)

The document should be viewed in the context of five years of union recommendations and the emotive issues that have been raised. The document omits any explicit statement on the alleged teratogenic effects of VDUs — probably the most emotive allegation that has been made about VDU work. There is little which could be described as restrictive compared to the West German DIN norm.

157
'Common user access'
IBM
(1987)

This book presents IBM's definition of the user interface across three major systems — System/370, System/3X and the personal computer. This document provides a valuable insight into how a major computing corporation views some of the key issues associated with the design of end-user interfaces. The document contains detailed information about specific aspects of three systems and how they should be designed, down to detailed information on the location of information on the screen.

158
'Dialogue design standards'
Technical rep no R50213/01
'Human factors in design' series
ICL
(1986)

This report provides standards covering the style, format and content of screens that a user will see and respond to. The six sections in the report include the user interface, general screen design, forms design, menu design, and navigation instructions and functions.

159
'Introduction to dialogue display'
Technical rep no R50212/01
'Human factors in design' series
ICL
(1986)

This report provides advice suitable for non-ICL as well as ICL systems. It contains seven chapters covering the preparation for dialogue design, developing a dialogue structure, dialogue types, common problems and how to overcome them, graphics in dialogue design, and successful dialogue design. The book is one in a series on human factors issues of computing and demonstrates the importance assigned to the problem by a major UK manufacturer.

160
'Use of colour'
Technical rep no R50214/01
'Human factors in design' series
ICL
(1986)

This report details key issues associated with the design of screens and colour. It provides guidelines and standards for using colour on screens that the user will see and respond to. There are four sections including sections on how to use colour, when to use colour and a standard scheme for colour use.

161
MoD Defence Standard 00-25
'Human factors for designers of equipment'
Ministry of Defence
(Multidated)

Defence Standard 00-25 is evolving rapidly into a multidocument standard covering many aspects of human factors. It is constantly updated so it it always necessary to ensure that the latest update is being seen. The 12 parts are: introduction; body size; body strength and stamina; design of the workspace; the physical environment: stresses and hazards; vision and lighting; visual displays; auditory information; voice communication; controls; design for maintainability; and systems.

162
Pheasant S
'Ergonomics — standards and guidelines for designers'
British Standards Institution
(1987)

This book draws together a wide range of information on British, European and international standards as well as other standard texts. It contains sections on people, the environment, information and products, and spaces. While not oriented towards HCI the book does contain much useful information on the design of systems in general as well as having a specific section on HCI.

163
Rubinstein R and Horsh H
'The human factor'
Digital Engineering Corporation
(1984)

This book is DEC's summary of human factors and the importance of adopting a user-centred approach. It provides an overview of many key issues and is important in explaining some of the work undertaken at DEC, as well as encapsulating a measure of their perception of human factors.

Proceedings

164
Edmonds E (editor)
'Special issue on constructing user interfaces'
Intl J Man-Machine Studies
vol 16 no 3 (1982)

This special issue concentrates on the work of a particular research group. There is a discussion of a set of software tools for dialogue design (SYNICS), and a paper giving references to other published work on design guidelines. Other papers discuss applications.

165
Ann Proc Ergonomics Society
Taylor and Francis (Since 1984)

The annual proceedings of the Ergonomics Society are particularly notable for the keynote addresses which often present excellent state of the art summaries by recognised experts; for example, in 1987 Boyce ('Lighting and human performance') and Reason ('The cognitive bases of predictable human error'), and in 1988 Corlett ('Where have we come from and where are we going?'), Drury ('The human as optimizer') and Salvendy ('Megatrends in ergonomics and their implications for human-computer interaction and expert systems').

166
Proc INTERACT '84 and '87
Elsevier Science Publishers BV
(1984 and 1987)

Proceedings from the last two INTERACT conferences (sponsored by the International Federation of Information Processing) contain much of the recent work in HCI and the design of end-user interfaces. Papers are presented by most of the people active in the field over the last 10 years. References to specific papers are contained within the body of the Analysis. The conference is organised every three years, INTERACT 3 is due in 1990.

167
Proc BCS Conf of the Human/Computer Interaction (HCI) Specialist Interest Group (SIG)
Cambridge Univ Press
(1985, 1986 and 1987)

The proceedings of the BCS HCI SIG's annual conferences contain reports from most of the key HCI workers within the UK. The conference papers tend to date rather quickly, though the invited papers maintain their relevance for longer. Papers from the 1986 conference by Shackel ('Ergonomics in design of usability') and Long ('People and computers: designing for usability') are particularly relevant to the theme of this Report. The overall conference title for 1986 was 'People and computers: designing for usability' and the proceedings contain the papers most relevant to designing end-user interfaces.

168
Megaw E D and Lloyd E
'Ergonomics abstracts special issue: human/computer interaction'
Ergonomics Abstracts
vol 16 no 1
(1984)

Over 1000 references are listed, with abstracts, classified in a three-level, hierarchical index, with full cross-referencing. A very useful starting place for information searches.

169
Salvendy G (editor)
Proc 1st US-Japan Conf on HCI
'Human-computer interaction'
Elsevier Science Publishers BV
(1984)

This joint conference is held yearly. The first proceedings are especially interesting as they highlight some of the human factors work which the Japanese are undertaking. The conference covers a broad range of topics under the following eight main headings: conceptual and theoretical issues in human/computer interaction; taxonomies, standardisation and evaluation of HCI; software design and use; AI, expert systems and decision supports; ergonomics and visual issues in the design and use of VDTs; stress, health and psychological issues in computerised work; applications of HCI; and speech.

170
Salvendy G
'Cognitive engineering in the design of human-computer interaction and expert systems'
In 'Advances in human factors/ergonomics' series
G Salvendy (ed)
vol 10b
Elsevier Science Publishers BV (1987)

68 papers from the second international conference on HCI are reported. As befits the title, a very wide range of issues is explored in the papers. A number of distinguished authors have contributed papers, and there are several papers reporting from a basis of experience, as opposed to experiment. There are many lessons and good ideas to be found here.

Reference sources

In the list of bibliographic references above journal titles are abbreviated as little as possible. The full title is given below together with the address from which the publication is available. Book publishers and other sources are also included in the list.

Ablex Publishing Corporation
Norwood
NJ 07648
US

Academic Press Inc (London) Ltd
24-28 Oval Road
London
NW1 7DX
UK

Addison-Wesley Publishing Co Inc
Jacob Way
Reading
MA 01867
US

British Standards Institution
Linford Wood
Milton Keynes
Buckinghamshire
MK14 6LE
UK

Cambridge University Press
The Pitt Building
Trumpington Street
Cambridge
CB2 1RP
UK

Century Publishing Co Ltd
76 Old Compton Street
London
W1V 5PA
UK

Digital Engineering Corporation
Digital Press
30 North Avenue
Burlington
MA 01803 US

Ellis Horwood Ltd
Market Cross House
Cooper Street
Chichester
West Sussex
PO19 1EB
UK

Elsevier Science Publishers BV
PO Box 1991
1000 BZ Amsterdam
The Netherlands

Ergonomics Abstracts
(*See* Taylor and Francis)

Ericsson Information Systems AB
S-161 83 Bromma
Sweden

Lawrence Erlbaum Associates
365 Broadway
Hillsdale
NJ 07642
US

European Communities Directorate-General
Information Market and Innovation
(Luxembourg)
5 Dryden Street
London
WC2E 9NW
UK

Health and Safety Executive
1 Chepstow Place
London
W2 4TF
UK

William Heinemann Ltd
10 Upper Grosvenor Street
London
W1X 9PA
UK

Human Factors Society
John Hopkins University Press
Baltimore
MD 21218
US

HUSAT Research Centre
The Elms
Elms Grove
Loughborough
Leicestershire
LE11 1RG
UK

IBM Corporation
Entry Systems Information Development
Dept 18Q 3666
PO Box 1328
Bocca Raton
Florida
US

Infotech International Ltd
(See Pergamon Infotech Ltd)

ICL Literature and Software Operations
60 Portman Road
Reading
Berkshire
RG12 4SN
UK

International Journal of Man-Machine Studies
Academic Press
Berkeley Square
London
W1X 6BA
UK

ITT Advanced Technology Center
Shelton
CT 06484
US

John Hopkins University
John Hopkins Road
Laurel
MD 20707
US

Manchester Business School
Booth Street West
Manchester
MI5 6PB
UK

McGraw-Hill Inc
1221 Avenue of the Americas
New York
NY 10020 US

Microinfo Ltd
PO Box 3
Alton
Hampshire
GU34 2PG UK

Ministry of Defence
Standards Section
Admiralty Arch
London
UK

The Mitre Corporation
Bedford
MA 01730
US

National Academy Press
Washington DC
US

National Computing Centre Ltd
Oxford Road
Manchester
M1 7ED
UK

Pan Books Ltd
Cavaye Place
London
SW10 9PG
UK

Pergamon Infotech Ltd
Berkshire House
Queen Street
Maidenhead
Berkshire
SL6 1NF
UK

Prentice-Hall Inc
Englewood Cliffs
NJ 07632 US

and

Prentice-Hall International
66 Wood Lane End
Hemel Hempstead
Hertfordshire
HP2 4RG UK

The Report Store
Client Services
910 Massachussetts Street
Suite 503
Lawrence
KA 66044 US

Rutherford Appleton Laboratories
Informatics Division
Chilton
Didcot
Oxon
OX11 0QX UK

Bibliography: reference sources

Springer-Verlag
37A Church Road
Wimbledon
London
SW19 5DQ
UK

Taylor and Francis Ltd
4 John Street
London
WC1N 2ET
UK

and

Taylor and Francis Inc
242 Cherry Street
Philadelphia
PA 19106-1906
US

Verlag TÜV Rheinland GmbH
Cologne
W Germany

John Wiley & Sons Ltd
Baffins Lane
Chichester
Sussex
PO19 1UD
UK

Winthrop Publishers Inc
17 Dunster Street
Cambridge
MA 02138
US

University of California
San Diego
La Jolla
CA 92093
US

US Army Research Institute for Behavioral
and Social Sciences
5001 Eisenhower Avenue
Alexandria
VA 22333 US

Index

Subject and contributor index

Accent	82
Acceptability	22
Access	34
ACM Computer Human Interaction (CHI)	108
Adaptive systems	175
AI (*see* Artificial Intelligence)	
Alienation	213
Alvey Programme	153,214
Apple Macintosh	91
Application domain	20
Application issue	93
Applications	23
Artificial Intelligence (AI)	59,181,190,210
AT&T Communications	83
Autoguide	66
BBC TV	61
Bellacore consortium	71
Benefits	14
Bespoke interfaces	176
BIT (*see* Block Image Transfer)	
Blackboard approaches	210
Blitter chips	64
Block Image Transfer (BIT)	64
British Standards Institution (BSI)	54,71,72,155
British Telecom	214
BSI (*see* British Standards Institution)	
CAD (*see* Computer-aided Design)	
Calculating values	8f
Cambridge Z88	69
Case study in expert system interfaces	3ff
Cathode Ray Tube (CRT)	65,71,170
CD-ROM (*see* Compact Disk Read Only Memory)	
Character recognition	59
Checkland	33
Cleal D M	3ff,181, 182
Cognitive capabilities	160
Command language	174,200
Communication with the user	121ff

Compact Disk Read Only Memory (CD-ROM)	70,126
Compaq 386	69
Computer	
engineering	46
input	53
mediation	31
Computer-aided Design (CAD)	23,64,102,198
Concept keyboards	56
Control	78
Controlled Requirements Expression (CORE)	47
CORE (*see* Controlled Requirements Expression)	
CRT (*see* Cathode Ray Tube)	
Cursor keys	56
Data input	59
Databases	210
Decision making	211
Department of Health and Social Security (DHSS)	109
Department of Trade and Industry (DTI)	39,72,75,154,164
Design	
end-user interfaces	97ff
methodologies	37ff
principles	89,212
problems	22f
Desktop Publishing (DTP)	64
Developments in user interfaces	85ff
DHSS (*see* Department of Health and Social Security)	
Dialogue design	173
Digitised speech	65
Digitising tables	59
Direct manipulation	174
Display technology	210
Displays	64,128
Dowell J	17ff
DTI (*see* Department of Trade and Industry)	
DTP (*see* Desktop Publishing)	
Dvorak	55
Eason K D	25ff,152,159,162
ECO	183
Electroluminescent displays	65
Electronic Paper Project	61
ELIZA	188
End-user interfaces	85ff,97ff,99,149ff,159
Engineering human/computer interactions	22f
Epistemological enquiry	20
Ergodesign	54
ETHICS	33
Expert system interfaces	3ff, 190
Eye movement	64
Failure, of IT systems	154
FAX	71
Feedback	
information	125
to writers	129
Flat screens	65,210
Form filling	175
FORTRAN	183
Function	34

Functional specification	32
Functionality	22
Future	15,92,207ff
Gardner A	37ff,153,211, 212
Gateways	34
General interfaces	176
Generative User Engineering Principles (GUEP)	202
Generic Representation Forms (GRF)	23
GEOMOD	23
Gesture	63
Government systems	210
Grammar	81
Graphics tablets	59
GRF (*see* Generic Representation Forms)	
GUEP (*see* Generative User Engineering Principles)	
Guidelines	89
in interface design	73ff
Hard copy	67
Hardware	
interface	99
problems	155
technology	210
HCI (*see* Human/Computer Interaction)	
HCIE (*see* Human/Computer Interaction Engineering)	
Hewlett-Packard	83
HF Guidelines	49
Hologram technology	210
Human and machine functions	29
Human/Computer Interaction (HCI)	51,89,156
Human/Computer Interaction Engineering (HCIE)	17ff,19,23,153
Human/computer systems	20f
Human factors	39,108,152,211
engineering	46
integration	111,115
management	41
plans	41
practitioners	40
HUSAT Research Centre	25,37ff,51,73,97ff,109
Husky Hawk	69
HyperCard	93,94
HyperTalk	93
HyperText	93
IAO	54
IBM	83,84,108,153,154
IBM AT	54
IBM PC	69
IFEs (*see* Intelligent Front End processors)	
Image capture	62
Impact of systems	29,32
Inference	15
Information needs	123
Initiatives	207ff,214
Integrated Services Digital Network (ISDN)	71
Integration	69
Intelligent Front End processors (IFEs)	179,182,183ff
Intelligent Spreadsheet Utility Environment (ISSUE)	3ff,8,14,15
Interaction	88

Interface	
design	73ff,101,107,167ff,179ff
features	90
Interfaces	16
problems with	5,149ff
International Standards Organisation	155
I/O technology	172
ISDN (*see* Integrated Services Digital Network)	
ISSUE (*see* Intelligent Spreadsheet Utility Environment)	
Issues	175
IT systems	87
in social systems context	28
Jackson System Development (JSD)	113,114,115,118
Joysticks	59
JSD (*see* Jackson System Development)	
Keyboards	53
Keystroke	212
Klockenburg	54
Knowledge	6
accessibility	11f
acquisition	14,189f
elicitation	6,16
interfaces	5f
representation	15,16
structure	16
Kurzweil	59
Language type	81
choices	127
Large screens	64
Laser disks	70
LCD (*see* Liquid Crystal Display)	
LED (*see* Light-emitting Diode)	
Light-emitting Diode (LED)	65
Lightpens	57
Linguistic model	49
Liquid Crystal Displays (LCDs)	65,71
Logical UCIs	44
Long J B	17ff
Loughborough	25
Macintosh	83
Magnetic Ink Character Recognition (MICR)	61
Maguire M	51ff
Man/Machine Interaction (MMI)	153
Mark recognition	61
McKenzie J	73ff, 169,171,175,177
Menu selection	174
Messages	34
Methodology	39
Methodology issue	93
Mice	58
MICR (*see* Magnetic Ink Character Recognition)	
Ministry of Defence (MOD)	39,72,75,120
MMI (*see* Man/Machine Interaction)	
Models	212
Multiplicity of actors	16
MYCIN	14

National Electronics Council Report	108
National Physical Laboratory	61
Natural Language Front Ends (NLFEs)	179,182,187
Network Extensible Window System (NeWS)	94
NeWS (*see* Network Extensible Window System)	
NLFEs (*see* Natural Language Front Ends)	
Norman M A	85ff,151,152,181.182,200
Numeric pads	55
Office Document Architecture Standard	94
Office equipment	71
Olympic Message System	109
OMS (*see* Optical Mark Sensing)	
Open Systems Interconnection (OSI)	47
Open Systems Task Analysis (OSTA)	33
Optical character recognition	59
Optical Mark Sensing (OMS)	61
Optical storage	70
OSI (*see* Open Systems Interconnection)	
OSTA (*see* Open Systems Task Analysis)	
PA Consulting Group	3
Parallel processing chips	210
PAS/WP (*see* Personal Assistant Secretary and Word Processor)	
PCD Maltron	55
Performance	21f
Personal Assistant Secretary and Word Processor (PAS/WP)	21
Personal computers	69
Plasma displays	65
Plotters	69
Pointing devices	56
Portability	69
Portable computers	69
Printers	67
PROLOG	6,14
Prototyping	89f
Psion Organiser	69
Psychological factors	157ff
Quality Assurance (QA)	41,75
QWERTY keyboard	84
Reference information	124
Representation	5f
Representative Strain Injuries (RSI)	54
Roller balls	58
Royal Armaments Research and Development Establishment	120
RSI (*see* Representative Strain Injuries)	
Rules	186
SADMs (*see* Structured Analysis and Design Methods)	
Security systems	34
Shackel B	97ff,153,154,159,195,213
Sharp	69
Social factors	157ff
Sociotechnical systems	25ff
Soft function keys	55
Software	
interface	99
problems	155

technology	210
Spreadsheet	8
SSADM (*see* Structured Systems Analysis and Design Methodology)	
Standard Telephone and Radio	54
Standard UCIs	83
Standardisation	14
STARTS	39
Stephen Hobday	55
Storage	69
Strategy	186
Structured Analysis and Design Methods (SADMs)	113,114,115
Structured Systems Analysis and Design Methodology (SSADM)	47,200,212
STR-keyboard	54
SUPERMAN	202
Synthesised speech	65
System	
aspects	193ff
facilities, access to	31f
life-cycle	41
operation	16
Systems analysis	32
Tandy	69
Task	
allocation charts	44
analysis	115,117
Tasks model	117
Terminology	153
Tomorrow's World	61
Toshiba 3200	69
Touch screens	57
Training	14
Transport and Road Research Laboratories (TRRL)	66
TRRL (*see* Transport and Road Research Laboratories (TRRL))	
Tutorial information	123
UCIs (*see* User Computer Interfaces)	
UID (*see* User Interface Design)	
UIMS (*see* User Interface Management System)	
Uncertain knowledge	15
University College London	17
Usability	22,213
context	103
evaluation	105ff
User action modality	80
User/Computer Interfaces (UCIs)	37ff,44,153
design solutions	76
devices	82
dynamics	77
imagery	81
protocol	47,49,76,77
User effector	80
User guidance	78
User interface constraints	118
User Interface Design (UID)	88,91
User interface engineering	89
User Interface Management System (UIMS)	89,91,118
User interface specification	118
User sensory modality	80
User support	117,213

User/System Interaction (USI)	213
User tailoring	90,213
User team	209
Users	154f,160,209ff
in sociotechnical systems	25ff,162
USI (*see* User/System Interaction)	
VDTs (*see* Visual Display Terminals)	
Visual design options	127
Visual Display Terminals (VDTs)	83,104
Vocabulary	82
Voice input	62
Voice output	65
Walsh P *et al*	111ff,202,212
What You See Is What You Get (WYSIWYG)	84,161
WIMP (*see* Windows, Icons, Mice and Pull-down menus)	
Windows, Icons, Mice and Pull-down menus (WIMP)	87
Work	20
Workspace	100
WORM	70
Wright P	121ff,177
Writers Workbench	127,185
WYSIWYG (*see* What You See Is What You Get)	
Xerox Documenter	91
Xerox Star	91
Zenith	69